D0765578

Blind Tom,
the Black Pianist-Composer
(1849–1908)

Continually Enslaved

Geneva Handy Southall

The Scarecrow Press, Inc.
Lanham, Maryland, and London
1999

SCARECROW PRESS, INC.

Published in the United States of America
by Scarecrow Press, Inc.
4720 Boston Way, Lanham, Maryland 20706
http://www.scarecrowpress.com

4 Pleydell Gardens, Folkestone
Kent CT20 2DN, England

British Library Cataloguing in Publication Information Available

ISBN 0-8108-3594-0 (cloth : alk. paper)

This book has been catalogued by the Library of Congress as part of a set.
It may be referenced by the following catalog card number: 79–54227.

The paper used in this publication meets the minimum requirements of
American National Standard for Information Sciences—Permanence of
Paper for Printed Library Materials, ANSI/NISO Z39.48–1992.
Manufactured in the United States of America.

In Memoriam to Clarence Stoddard Carter (1938–1996), the publisher-editor of my first two books, who had plans to publish this third volume until his untimely death.

His support in this project for over twenty years will be forever remembered and appreciated.

My infinite affection for and deep admiration of an extraordinary individual, whose kindness, integrity, and strength were unmatched. I cherish our times as an author-publishing team.

Contents

Blind Tom (1859)

Blind Tom (1880s)

Blind Tom (1898)

Preface

I FIRST BECAME AWARE of Blind Tom in 1964, when a fellow doctoral student at the University of Iowa brought a copy of Harold Schonberg's *The Great Pianists*, in which Blind Tom was mentioned, to Professor John Simm's Piano Literature class.

My initial reaction to Tom was understandably negative since Schonberg had described him as "a curious and pathetic Negro slave born a mental defective" who "because of a successful promotional myth was exhibited as a musical prodigy."[1] He further added that Blind Tom "could not do anything except play a few tunes he knew, and after his 1866 English Tour dropped from the scene to be heard of no more." Because Schonberg considered his book to be a discussion of keyboard specialists whose playing had made a mark on their own generation and who, in many cases, had helped shape the playing and the keyboard philosophy of the generation that followed, I inwardly questioned Schonberg's inclusion of Blind Tom while he excluded the acknowledged Black prodigy-composer-pianist Phillipa Duke Schuyler.[2]

Schonberg's claim of "having sifted through an enormous amount of material, discarding that which was obviously false or unreliable," meant that he had engaged himself sufficiently in the scholarship necessary to describe the activities of Blind Tom with accuracy (although I did raise questions to my classmates about the omission of footnotes and a bibliography in the book). For this reason, my own sense of self worth as a Black student in an all-White class demanded that I disassociate myself from the so-called "circus freak" Tom and try to counteract what I took as a personal affront to Black musicians and Black people by informing the class about Hazel Harrison, the internationally acclaimed Black concert pianist who performed several piano concertos with the Berlin (Germany) Philharmonic Orchestra in 1904.[3] After studying with the famed pianist, Ferruccio Busoni, in Germany, she became a noted artist-teacher at Tuskegee Institute (1931-1934), Howard University (1934-1955), and Alabama A & M University (1958-1964), while continuing to perform throughout this country and Europe.

It was in the spring of 1967, while presenting a paper on "John Field's Seven Piano Concertos" at Florida State University,

Gainesville, for the Gulf States Chapter meeting of the American Musicological Society, that I again heard about Blind Tom. Dr. Frederick Crane, a friend of mine from the University of Iowa years, then head of L.S.U.'s (Louisiana State University, Baton Rouge) musicology department, shared what he had read about this "unique and inexplicable musical phenomenon" known as Blind Tom when he unexpectedly discovered James Monroe Trotter's *Music and Some Highly Musical People* gathering dust on the shelves of the L.S.U. Library. Not only did Dr. Crane express surprise that Trotter's book, published only thirteen years after Emancipation, had been written by a Black historian (at a time when no book on American music history had yet been published), but that it contained biographical sketches of Black composer-performers in the classical tradition who were active in the South and North from 1820 to 1870, one of whom was Blind Tom.[4] Trotter's book subsequently became my major source for a post-doctoral paper entitled "The Contributions of Black Classical Musicians Prior to the Civil War" which I presented in summer 1969 at the University of Iowa's Afro-American Studies Institute, thereby forcing me once again to confront this "Blind Tom."

Though these three encounters left me with more questions than answers, I did not engage in any serious investigation concerning Blind Tom until the fall of 1969 when, while planning a faculty lecture-recital at Grambling College on the "Contributions of Black Musicians to Keyboard Literature from 1850 to 1950," I started a search for Blind Tom's "Rainstorm" since I wanted to include it on the program. Aware that Blind Tom had been a slave in the state of Georgia, I made inquiries at the University of Georgia at Athens, concerning their archival holdings on Blind Tom. A letter from a Mrs. Susan B. Tate, Assistant Librarian, Special Collections, made known to me that they did have several of Blind Tom's compositions on microfilm, numerous articles about him, and a copy of the biographical monograph published in 1868 by Tom's managers for promotional purposes. After obtaining these materials through interlibrary loan, I discovered that several of the compositions were written and published after the 1880s and that several of the articles discussed performances by him after 1900. It then became apparent to me that Harold Schonberg, contrary to his statements, had not done the scholarly research necessary to describe Tom's musical career with accuracy. Blind Tom had not only made another successful European tour after 1866, but several articles revealed that he had continued to give highly acclaimed concerts throughout the United States and in parts of Canada until a few years before his death in 1908. As the result of my own analytical keyboard expertise and audience enthusiasm for Tom's compositions, these pieces not only offered a microcosm of the pianist and theoretical practices of the romantic era in which he lived, but they also gave some indication of Tom's keyboard development over several decades.

With these revelations, I began what has been an off-and-on twenty-five-year research project concerning the life and career of Blind Tom (interruptions due to teaching obligations at the University of Minnesota). I was determined to give him the scholarly treatment that I felt he deserved so that his place in history as a serious pianist-composer could be secured, rather than continuing what had been an "unexplainable musical curiosity" treatment. By 1975 I had accumulated enough materials to submit an article titled "Blind Tom: A Misrepresented and Neglected Composer" to the *Black Perspective in Music* (May, 1975) beginning what I perceived as my quest to "Right the historical wrong."

After sifting through nineteenth-century newspapers, music journals, travel accounts, memoirs and other legal sources, most accounts of Blind Tom could be described as a "literary medley of misinformation." I discovered that his life clearly divided into three chronological divisions, which led to the decision to publish my research in a three-volume series. Book I, *Blind Tom: The Post-Civil War Enslavement of a Black Musical Genius* (1979), placed emphasis on Blind Tom, the musician, from his birth through the Civil War, with a section devoted to his legal re-enslavement by the former slavemaster's family. Book II, *The Continuing Enslavement of Blind Tom, the Black Pianist-Composer (1865-1887)*, published in 1983, follows Tom's concert tours chronologically from city to city until the celebrated court trial which brought to an end his neo-chattel relationship with his former slavemaster, when the former daughter-in-law gained custody. Valuable information about the format of his programs, his repertory, his technique and skill as an pianist and improviser as well as reaction of audiences to him are placed within the context of Anglo- and Afro-American concert life of the period. Besides correcting many misconceptions about his musical education, readers are introduced to prominent concert artists and cultural leaders active in Black and White America in the late nineteenth century. A tape of seven of Blind Tom's compositions (performed by me) was made available to readers to provide them with an aural indication of Tom's virtuosity and expression at the keyboard.

This third book will be devoted to the continuation of the exploitation of Blind Tom by his new guardian-manager. Some of the research will focus on his career in vaudeville and his relationship to other musical personalities of the time. In addition, legal aspects will be offered and the controversies that continued about Blind Tom following his death in 1908. As in the first two books, efforts will continue to: 1) correct some of the inaccuracies written about Blind Tom, his family, and those persons involved in the economic aspects of his musical career, 2) acknowledge his contributions to piano literature of the mid-nineteenth century, and 3) show how the contemporary announcements and reviews and other writings of his day reflect the socio-political events taking place during those times.

These books hopefully have provided the reader with a better understanding of the impact of legal exploitation of black Americans following the Emancipation Proclamation. More importantly, it is hoped that they served to "debunk and demythologize" the accomplishments of one of America's most important musical personalities.

Notes

1. Harold C. Schonberg. *The Great Pianists* (New York: Simon & Schuster, 1963), pp. 189-90.

2. The daughter of black journalist George Schuyler and Josephine Cogdell, a Texas heiress and granddaughter of slave owners, Phillipa was able to read and write before her 3rd birthday and a composer by five. On June, 19, 1940, the late Mayor LaGuardia declared "Phillipa Duke Schuyler Day" at the New York World's Fair, where she performed two recitals (besides works by Bach, Schumann and Ibert), including several of her own compositions, which then numbered over 50, though she was only eight years of age. Her "Manhattan Nocturne" for a 100-piece orchestra was written during her twelfth year, resulting in her becoming the youngest member elected to the National Association of Composers and Arrangers. Her debut as a composer-pianist came when she performed the Saint-Saëns G Minor Concerto at the age of fifteen with the New York Philharmonic. This was followed by their playing her orchestra piece, titled "Rumpelstiltskin." Her death in a U.S. Army helicopter on May 9,

1967, occurred as she was helping evacuate several Vietnamese orphans from a Catholic school in Danang, South Vietnam. At the time she was a correspondent for the *New Hampshire Manchester Union Leader*. Her fame as a composer-pianist was international. She performed in over 75 countries (while in her twenties) before royalty and commoners alike. The premiere of her Piano Concerto came in 1965 when she appeared with the Cairo Symphony.

For the most detailed source on this pianist, see: Kathryn Talalay. *Composition in Black and White: The Life of Phillipa Schuyler* (New York: Oxford University Press, 1995).

3. Hazel Harrison, born in Laporte, Indiana (May 12, 1883), revealed musical talent at an early age and studied piano with local teachers Victor Heinz and Richard Pillow. Through their contacts she was invited in 1904 to play at the Royal Theater in Berlin, Germany where she studied with famed pianist Ferruccio Busoni, gave recitals, and appeared with the Berlin Philharmonic. In 1919 she made her Chicago debut at Kimball Hall, and May 1922, her New York debut at Aeolian Hall. She returned for study with Busoni in 1926, and after resettling in the United States, studied with Percy Grainger. She appeared with leading symphony orchestras during her career and gave lecture-recitals.

    For the most information concerning her illustrious career, see: Jean C. Cazort and Constance Tibbs Hobson. *Born to Play: The Life and Career of Hazel Harrison.* (Westport, Connecticut: Greenwood Press, 1983).

4. James Monroe Trotter. *Music and Some Highly Musical People* (Boston: Lee and Shepard, 1878), pp. 144-159.

Acknowledgments

SO MANY PEOPLE have encouraged and assisted me in carrying out this project that it is impossible to mention them all by name. Some obligations, however, stand out above all others. I am especially indebted, for example, to the following librarians who, in my opinion, went far beyond the call of professional duty in procuring information and materials: Hazel Jones, Grambling College, Susan B. Tate, Special Collections, University of Georgia, David F. Covert, Columbus College Library, Columbus, Ga., Dena Epstein, University of Chicago, Robert A. Barron and Ana K. Lee, Fauquier Historical Society, Patricia Turner, University of Minnesota, Richard S. Brownlee, Director and Leona S. Morris, Research Assistant, State Historical Society of Missouri, and the staffs of Newberry Library, Chicago, Library of Congress and Moorland-Spingarn Special Collection, Howard University, Washington, D.C. My debt to the entire staff of the University of Minnesota's Interlibrary Loan Division can never be paid since it was they, more than any others, who for many years became involved in doing the invaluable interlibrary loan search for those vitally needed and all-too-often hard-to-find mid-nineteenth century newspapers. Robert (Bob) Barron, Warrenton, Virginia, Robert Hodge, Fredericksburg, Virginia, William A. Donnelly, Buffalo, New York, and Jesse C. McCarroll, New York City Community College, all served as individual researchers who located valuable materials, which many times became the needed key for unlocking a mystery about Tom's musical movements during a particular period of time.

I am also indebted to such distinguished musical-scholar friends as Dr. Eileen Southern, Harvard University Professor Emeritus and editor-publisher of *Black Perspective in Music* (Spring, 1975) for publishing my first important article on Blind Tom in her journal. Dr. Samuel Floyd, Director, Center for Black Music Research, Columbia College, Chicago, for endorsing my first book by doing the Introduction and including it with a positive description in his *Black Music Biography* (Kraus Publication, 1987). Arthur LaBrew, independent musicologist of Detroit, Michigan, helped by sharing some research on Tom discovered while preparing his book *Elizabeth T. Greenfield: The Black Swan* (1969).

To the internationally renowned composer, Dr. T. J. Anderson, Fletcher Professor of Music Emeritus, Tufts University, who not only endorsed my research efforts by writing the foreword to my second book but gave his much-needed compositional ear to the critiquing of the companion tape, I owe a special thanks. In addition were the ever helpful suggestions by C. Edward Thomas, Director of the Afro-American Music Opportunities Association, Minneapolis, who doubled as the piano coach and producer for the companion tape. To my sister, D. Antoinette Handy Miller, former Head, National Endowment for the Arts Music Division, Washington, D.C., I can only give a sisterly hug for being so caught up emotionally in my efforts that, while doing her own research on *Black Women in American Bands and Orchestras* (Scarecrow Press, 1981), kept an eye open for any materials on Blind Tom, producing some of my most treasured leads. Similarly, Warren C. Swindell, Director, Center for Afro-American Studies, Indiana State University, sent several newsclips on Blind Tom which he found while doing research on "John Williams (Blind Boone)."

To Bettye C. Thomas, Director of Historical Development, National Council of Negro Women, Howard G. Turner and Hubert D. Bennett, Supreme Court of Virginia, Richmond, and W. Carleton L. Brown, Director, National Archives and Records Center, Washington, D.C., I owe a special debt of gratitude since without their personal involvement, I may not have been successful in locating those most important legal documents. Special thanks to Peter Johnson, Librarian, Princeton University and John Wirth, a Minneapolis-based freelance writer-editor for providing the needed critical commentary during the earliest stages of the manuscript. I am particularly indebted to the University of Minnesota library staff members Barbara Steimasik and Don Kelsey for their crucial roles in editing and preparing the manuscript of Books I and II for publication. They not only caught the many typos and misspellings, but offered numerous substantive stylistic suggestions which have been incorporated and have improved the presentation of my findings. My analytical insights about reconstruction politics were greatly sharpened through conversations with my brother-in-law, Dr. Calvin Miller, Professor Emeritus, Political Science Department, Virginia State College. Also gratitude to Austin McLean, Creator, Special Collections, University of Minnesota, for obtaining photographic materials for inclusion in the book.

Acknowledgments

Especially important to any author is to find positive commentary about their research in newpapers, among them being: Paul Dienhart, *University of Minnesota Report* (January, 1980), Charissa Marie Eason, *Minnesota Daily* (January 17, 1980), Lisa Renee Taylor, *Columbus College (GA) Saber* (November 14, 1984), Richard Hyatt, staff writer, *Columbus (GA) Enquirer* (November 19, 1984), Mikki Morrisette, *Minnesota Alumni Bulletin* (April, 1984), editor of the *Iowa Alumni Bulletin* (March, 1988) and Pauline Walle, life-style special writer, *Rochester, MN Post-Bulletin* (February 12, 1991). Book Reviews by William Kearns, *Sonneck Society Newsletter* (Spring, 1985), Josephine Wright, College of Wooster, *American Music* (Spring, 1987) and Eileen Southern, *Black Perspective in Music* (Spring, 1985) brought evidence that my research focus was appreciated.

As in all things, my family has remained a source of inspiration and emotional support in a project that has exceeded 25 years. And, as might be expected, secretarial help is always vital for any writer, making Antoinette Ziegler and Mary A. Chisley, Afro-American Studies Dept., University of Minnesota, central participants in the project. Above all, I express my appreciation to Dr. Dominique-René de Lerma, for his long-time support of my musicological-performing efforts and most of all, for his writing of the foreword to my third publication. Further acknowledgment is the validation of my research focus from the community of scholars which includes the provision of a six-month paid leave during summer and fall 1977 from the University of Minnesota's Liberal Arts College and the Graduate School's Research Grant during summer 1982. Thanks above all to the Carter family for encouraging me to continue bringing to completion something their loved one (my publisher) would have wanted despite his untimely death. To Art Sidner, thanks for typesetting the manuscript for publication.

While many people named and unnamed have influenced and assisted me, any errors or deficiencies that appear are my sole responsibility.

Introduction

GENEVA HANDY SOUTHALL had demonstrated her virtuosic skill in music research before her trilogy on Blind Tom, certainly starting with her work on John Field. With this volume, she brings to a long-awaited conclusion the decades-old original research she has conducted on one of the most misunderstood and misrepresented figures in American music. It has been both an exciting and distressing journey, but one we needed to make.

How could American society accept the unmistakable genius of Blind Tom at a time when others of his race were subjected to lynching on a daily basis? How can a racist explain a gift, so very rarely encountered anywhere, from one whose genealogy was said to include apes, rather than humans? It had to be witchcraft or voodoo, or else this phenomenon was an *idiot savant*—or just a plain idiot.

His uncanny ear had a parallel with Mozart. Perhaps young Wolferl really was exploited in his youth by his father, but he was nonetheless being guided and educated toward a self-sufficient career by a well meaning adult, one which did not inhibit his creative powers in the process. While Dr. Southall makes a valid case for the quality of Blind Tom's musical contacts, it still remains evident these were more exploitative than educational in intent. We do see an influence of Chopin's nocturnes in Blind Tom's own works (in *Rêve charmant,* for example, which Dr. Southall has recorded) and we find an ambition in form, harmony, and expression that is rarely encountered in American music of the nineteenth century, but what might have evolved had the composer-pianist been treated in his younger days as a student, rather than a side show? What did he gather from the major figures of his time: Brahms, Liszt, Wagner, Verdi? What might have happened had he been enrolled at the Leipzig Conservatory, if no American institution would have accepted him? That such was not considered, of course, is a reflection on American culture and sociology of the period. This factor, to which legal matters were so often added, causes Dr. Southall to move outside of purely musical matters more than once, suggesting a methodology no less valid for any musical biography. The case against interdisciplinary studies will find no justification here, nor in *any* study of Black music. Dr. Southall's students and colleagues at Grambling College and the University of Minnesota doubtless were reminded of this quite often!

Of course Blind Tom was eccentric. This was expected of artists in his day (and not rarely encountered at other times). But to what extent was this encouraged by prejudice, blindness, social isolation, and his coaching? Unlike the instances of others, this seems not to have been an affectation. It was possibly an absence of discipline (which is a nuance of education).

His repertoire largely reflected popular culture and its evaluation by his management. We have repeated instances of Black artists attempting to break socially imposed stereotypes with varying degrees of success: Scott Joplin as an opera composer, Duke Ellington working in opera and extended instrumental forms, James P. Johnson eyeing the piano concerto. When we examine the repertoire of Marian Anderson, rarely are amorous opera arias encountered—sacred music was thought more suitable. With Leontyne Price and her contemporaries, we began to see Italian opera enriched by the blues and spiritual orientations, and then Miss Price added anything else she wished to her repertoire.

A century ago, audiences clamored to hear Blind Tom perform one of his original imitation pieces (a rainstorm or sewing machine, for example). Had Jessye Norman been one of his contemporaries, we might wade through an evening of Sambo and Bones, hoping the finale would feature her in our all-time favorite, Ernest Hogan's "All coons look alike to me." Such was the shameful waste of talent Americans made of Blind Tom, with parallels in the cases of those who lived in this period, each of whom Dr. Southall appropriately bids enter within her chronology.

Reading through this important volume will evoke pain, grief, and outrage. In that respect we find a ready parallel to Sam Dennison's *Scandalize My Name* (Garland Publishing, 1982). But these stories must be told. The message is not only music or biography, it is not even only American history. Sentient readers will know how far the implications can reach.

It is then a tribute to a lady who is not hesitant, in her Southern-bred gentility, to be both feisty and funky, to provoke and soothe, to offer new insights to the ordinary and uncommon, to be innovative while respecting valid traditions, to push for radical improvements within established channels.

Dominique-René de Lerma
Conservatory of Music
Lawrence University
Appleton, Wisconsin

MOTHER DEAR MOTHER
I STILL THINK OF THEE

BLIND TOM
POPULAR CONCERTS
ENGLAND, IRELAND, SCOTLAND & FRANCE
(1866-1867)

Chapter 1

Early Years through 1889

THOMAS GREENE WIGGINS (popularly known as Blind Tom) was born of slave parentage May 25, 1849, on the Wiley Edward Jones Plantation in Harris County, Georgia.[1] Blind from birth, he was "thrown-in" as a bargain when Colonel James Neil Bethune, a highly respected Columbus, Georgia, lawyer and newspaper editor purchased his parents, Charity and Mingo Wiggins, and two of his brothers at a slave auction in fall 1850.[2] From infancy Tom manifested an extraordinary fondness for the musical sounds he heard in the Big House and had shown exceptional retentive skills. According to most accounts, Tom demonstrated his aptitude for music before his fourth birthday, having slipped unnoticed to the piano and picked out several tunes he had heard played by the Bethune daughters, all of whom were accomplished musicians.[3] After that revelation Tom became something of a "household pet" with all members of the family joining in the "educational game" of teaching him to associate words with objects. Mary Bethune became his piano teacher. Because she had studied with Professor George W. Chase, the highly respected New York-trained pianist-composer-conductor, one can assume that Tom received a solid theoretical and technical musical foundation.[4]

Soon after, his love of music and music-making led him to write original songs and imitate sounds of nature and other musical instruments on the piano. His progress was such that, by the time of his sixth birthday, he had become a "prized possession," with the Bethune children proudly exhibiting him to their neighbors.[5]

Following his first public concert at Columbus' Temperance Hall on October 7, 1857, Tom was taken to Atlanta, Macon, and

Athens, where the editor of Athens *Southern Watchman* described his performance at the University of Georgia as the "most remarkable ever witnessed in Athens, one that would put to blush many a professor of music."[6]

On May 22, 1858, the *Columbus Daily Sun* reported the death of Colonel Bethune's wife. According to the obituary account, she had died of "pulmonary disease, her suffering severe and protracted." She was described as the "amicable and universally beloved wife of Colonel Bethune, who in death had left an afflicted husband and interesting family." Mrs. Bethune, a Marylander of Welsh descent, at the time of her wedding on July 25, 1832, was employed as Co-Superintendent (with a Mrs. Griggs) of the Columbus Female Academy. According to Katherine Mahan, she was listed as "a music teacher with the Muscogee Female Academy in 1844."[7] Following her death, Mary Bethune assumed the maternal responsibilities for her younger siblings. Since it was announced in the June 24, 1858, *Columbus Daily Sun* that Colonel Bethune would be present at the Court of the Chattahoochee Circuit and the Supreme Court Hearing at Macon, Georgia, that day, it is evident that his jurisdictional responsibilities left him little time for outward grief.

Shortly thereafter, Tom became a hired-out slave musician to Perry Oliver, a Savannah tobacco planter, under a three-year contractual agreement with Colonel Bethune, who was paid $15,000 for the right to exhibit Tom in other parts of the country.[8] After several concerts in Savannah, Perry Oliver began to exhibit Tom in other southern and pro-slavery states as the "Musical Prodigy of the Age: a Plantation Negro Boy." By 1861 Tom's reputation was such that he appeared in a private concert held at Willard Hall in Washington, D.C., in honor of the first visiting Japanese delegation to this country. In addition, his Baltimore concerts of July 1860 had so impressed the famous piano manufacturer, William Knabe, that he gave the ten-year-old slave an elaborately carved rosewood grand piano with a silver plate bearing the inscription "a tribute to Genius." He was also a published composer by this time, his *Oliver Galop* and *Virginia Polka* having been published by the prestigious Oliver Ditson publishing firm in 1860.

With the outbreak of the Civil War Perry Oliver cancelled Tom's non-southern engagements and returned to Georgia where he began to make use of Tom's talents for the financial benefit of the

Confederacy. By October 1862 Tom was back with the Bethunes who continued to use his talents for the pro-slavery cause. Since the May 10, 1864, *Columbus Daily Sun* announced that Blind Tom had "given $5,000 from his recently completed three month tour to benevolent causes," it is evident that Tom's concert schedule was both profitable and exhaustive. Among the works performed on those programs was his own programmatic piece, titled "Battle of Manassas," written after he heard one of Colonel Bethune's sons (then a member of the Second Georgia Regiment) describe that famous Confederate victory. Inasmuch as a report in the December 17, 1861, *Atlanta Southern Confederacy* noted Tom's playing of "Dixie" with one hand, "Yankee Doodle" with the other while singing "The Girl I Left Behind Me" at the same time, it is apparent that Tom had been exposed to music and discussions connected with the Civil War from its outset.

Determined to continue his monetary control over Tom's talents in case of a Confederate defeat, Colonel Bethune "persuaded" Tom's parents to sign a five-year indenture agreement giving him legal guardianship of Tom.

> Georgia, Muscogee County—Indenture made the 30th day of May, 1864, between Mingo Bethune and Charity, his wife, on the one part and James N. Bethune of the other part, binding their son "Blind Tom," now sixteen years of age, the said J. N. B. to provide and furnish to the said Charity and Mingo a good home and subsistence and $500 a year so long as he shall retain possession and control the service of said Tom and to pay him $20 per month and two per cent of the net proceeds of his services. Endorsed and approved until further order.
>
> J. E. Bryant
> General Superintendentary Freedom Bureau, Ga.[9]

He left for Florida with Tom to join his daughters who had already gone there to be with relatives following the capture of Atlanta in September 1864.[10] Although Colonel Bethune returned to Columbus shortly after the war, he left soon after with his two sons to exhibit Tom in the north after President Andrew Johnson removed the federal blockade of southern states. It was after his third concert in New Albany, Indiana (July 16, 1865), that Tabbs Gross, a Black man from Cincinnati, brought legal action against Colonel Bethune, claiming that he, and not Bethune, was Tom's guardian—such based on a bill-of-sale agreement made between himself and Bethune in Macon, Georgia. When Colonel Bethune and his sons hurriedly left New Albany to avoid the legal action, Tabbs Gross followed them to Cincinnati (where Tom was scheduled for a one-week engagement) and filed a "Writ of Habeas Corpus" suit against the Bethunes. As was revealed in my first book of the *Blind Tom* series (Minneapolis: Challenge Productions, Inc., 1979), this historic "guardianship trial," which was held before Judge Woodruff of the Hamilton County Probate Court, had both political and racial overtones, and ended with the judge's decision to allow Bethune, an ex-slave owner, to keep Tom in a "neo-chattel" relationship. Inasmuch as the guardianship agreement permitted the Bethunes to receive ninety percent of Tom's earnings with nothing to guarantee that they would not expropriate the ten percent promised to Tom and his parents, the trial offered one more example of how ex-slave owners were able to re-enslave their slaves, the Emancipation Proclamation notwithstanding.

In the July 25th, 1865, *Cincinnati Enquirer,* the editor, speaking to the humane aspects of the decision, asked:

> why is Tom compelled to support Bethune and
> his two able-bodied sons who, fresh from the ranks
> of treason, are making the tour of the North with
> abundant leisure and purses well filled by the tal-
> ents of what they would have us believe, an idiot?
> Why don't they go to work?

Similar sentiments were expressed by a reporter in the *New York Times* of July 31, 1865, in an article titled "Blind Tom, or a Rebel General Turned Showman." After giving readers a brief overview of the case, which included the judge's decision in favor of the ex-slavemaster, the political attitude of the reporter toward Southerners became apparent:

> General Bethune is an old white-headed man and
> wealthy. He belongs to the Southern aristocracy

that formerly exhausted itself in ridiculing the
Yankee for driving sharp bargains. He believed in
southern rights and wrongs, and sent his sons into
the army to maintain the former and redress the
latter. Of course, he wouldn't be under any obli-
gation to the Yankees, but in the way of a business transaction it will be all right to let them see
and hear the prodigy for so much Yankee currency
per head. Self-interest is the impelling motive. He
don't like the Yankee a bit better today than he
did at the bitterest stage of the war, nor is the
respect he had for the Negro as a slave one par-
ticle increased. The evidence in the case showed
that Tom's brothers and sisters were not as well
treated as he was, because "there was no money
in them." Self-interest decidedly. Two of the
General's sons, who were officers in Lee's army
and paroled, accompany him to help in the show
business. Valiant, high-toned officers are they!
What a nice party it is!—the venerable Southern
planter, the leader in his neighborhood in all moral
reforms, and his two sons—paroled officers of
Lee's army—traveling the country with two old
Negroes and their idiotic child, in order to make
money, claiming the benefit of the Emancipation
Proclamation at the expense of the laws of the
State for whose sovereignty they fought for four
weary years. Principle is lost sight of by these men,
if they ever had any, and self-interest alone con-
trols them. The lesson taught by this example is,
that the Southern people, as soon as they per-
ceive their own material interests clearly, will re-
sist the government no longer, and will throw
themselves under the protection of the Federal
Constitution, laws and proclamations.

Though Tom was only sixteen at the time of the trial, his repertory included many of the most technically and musically demanding works of Bach, Chopin, Liszt, Beethoven, Thalbert, and
other European masters (*See* p. 43). Like other pianists of that

time, he demonstrated his improvisational and theoretical skills by performing variations and fantasias on operatic airs and popular ballads of the day. Other astonishing feats included his alleged ability to perform difficult selections almost flawlessly after one hearing, sing and recite poetry and prose in several languages, duplicate phonetically lengthy orations by noted statesmen, and reproduce sounds of nature, machines, and musical instruments on the piano. Being possessed of a rich baritone voice, Tom also included original and sentimental songs by such English songwriters as Henry Russell and Henry Bishop in his concerts.

The trial was obviously beneficial to the Bethunes. Not only did they retain custody of their talented slave, thus ensuring their own post-Civil War financial stability, but because of the pre-trial publicity they reaped a larger monetary gain during the Cincinnati performances. For example the July 20 *Cincinnati Commercial* had reassured readers that "Tom's concerts would take place notwithstanding the suit for his guardianship" then pending in the Probate Court. Since this had been "agreed to by the Counsels for both Parties" it is further evident that Tom's physical welfare was a secondary factor for both the plaintiff and defense. From Cincinnati, Tom was taken to several other cities in Ohio, and then made his eastern debut at Philadelphia's Concert Hall on September 12th. Despite the fact that Professor W. P. Howard, an Atlanta music teacher, was accompanying the Bethunes as Tom's music tutor for what was then an exorbitant salary of $200 a month plus travel expenses, Tom was still being promoted as a "natural untaught" pianist. Obviously the Bethunes had decided to retain the characterization of Tom as an "idiot" whose "incomprehensible creative and retentive powers" were the result of some "unexplained satanic gifts" as a promotional gimmick.

In Philadelphia Tom's owner-managers would be facing their greatest promotional challenge with regard to Tom's musical ability, since Philadelphia was then considered America's foremost cultural center. Much of Philadelphia's recognition as a world music center had started with the establishment of the Musical Fund Society in 1820 for the "relief of the distressed musicians and their families, and the cultivation of taste and the performing of the musical Arts."[11] The Society maintained an orchestra and chorus, had a well-established opera series and promoted concerts by local and internationally acclaimed artists in its Musical

Fund Hall, which was built in 1824. This two-story building, which could seat 1,800 persons, is considered America's first concert hall. Concerts were given for the members every other week and public musical entertainment was performed at least twice during the winter season.[12]

With the construction in 1855 of the Academy of Music, Philadelphia's prestige as a leading cultural center was enhanced. Not only did the Academy's auditorium accommodate 3,000 paying customers, but its excellent acoustics made it the marvel of the musical world.[13] American premieres of such operatic productions as *La Traviata*, *Aida*, *Faust*, and *Lohengrin* were staged there, and for several years, Philadelphians boasted that their city contained "the only allowable temple of Italian opera."[14] Besides being the country's major musical center, dramatic presentations, political meetings, balls, and other amusements were held at the Academy. Considering that many cultural events were held at the Academy throughout the Civil War, managers of the Blind Tom concerts would have to convince the continuously exposed, highly sophisticated Philadelphia musical community that their attendance at a Blind Tom concert would have musical worth.

Added to these aspects, Tom was being presented in a city that was then regarded as the cultural and intellectual capital of Black America, the city where several Black musicians had already achieved international acclaim. It was, after all, Frank Johnson, a Black Philadelphian, who had in December 1838, introduced thousands of Philadelphians to the Parisian-style Promenade Concerts.[15] These concerts, which were advertised as "Musical Soirees," took place after Frank Johnson had returned with his famous all-Black band and orchestra from a successful tour in England, followed by an extended concert tour in several northern and eastern cities in the United States. According to Robert Gerson, Johnson's all-Black band had, from its inception in 1815 as the Washington Guards Company, Three Band, "outshone all other musical groups in Philadelphia."[16] Besides being the conductor-founder of the then leading military band, and the chief supplier of dance music for the most fashionable and political personages on the eastern seaboard, Frank Johnson had also built an enviable reputation as a violinist, hornist, and trumpeter. According to Scharff and Westcott, he was reputed in his time to be "one of the best performers on the bugle and French horn in the United States."[17] Since, as Gerson notes, he had, in 1821, presented to Mrs. Ann Rush piano arrangements for eighty-seven of his compositions, one can presume that Frank Johnson was also proficient on the keyboard.[18]

With such a history, it is not unexpected that a positive reaction from Philadelphians regarding Tom's musical ability would become a crucial factor in any future promotional activities in the North by those managing Tom. For this reason, having failed to attract the professional musicians to Tom's first appearance at Concert Hall, the Bethunes held an invitational concert for a group of Philadelphia's most esteemed musicians and scientists, after which they issued the following signed statement:

> Philadelphia, Sept. 16, 1865
>
> DEAR SIR,—The undersigned desire to express to you their thanks for the opportunity afforded them of hearing and seeing the wonderful performances of your *protege,* the blind boy pianist, Tom. They find it impossible to account for these immense results upon any hypothesis growing out of the known laws of art and science.
>
> In the numerous tests to which Tom was subjected in our presence, or by us, he invariably came off triumphant. Whether in deciding the pitch or component parts of chords the most difficult and dissonant; whether in repeating with correctness and precision any pieces, written or impromptu, played to him for the first and only time; whether in his improvisations, or performances of compositions by Thalberg, Gottschalk, Verdi and others: in fact, under every form of musical examination,—and the experiments are too numerous to mention or enumerate, he showed a power and capacity ranking him among the most wonderful phenomena recorded in musical history.
>
> Accept, dear sir, the regards of your humble servants.

B. C. CROSS,	J. H. REDNOR,
JAMES M. BECK,	CARL ROESE,
G. BLANDNER,	C. BLANCGAUR,
J. A. STERN,	J. A. GETZA,

And several others.[19]

After this, Tom's concerts began to attract other than the curious in such large numbers that Tom's one-week engagement was extended to four weeks. According to a report in the September 27th *Public Ledger* "many professors of music of great eminence were ready, after listening to him, to declare that they would never touch the piano again." Though it was known by those in attendance that W. P. Howard, the Atlanta music teacher, was serving as Tom's musical tutor during those engagements, the reporter for the *Public Ledger* still provided his readers with those biographical promotional statements that reinforced the commonly held "natural untaught, unexplainable" characterizations regarding Tom's talent.

After a second four-week concert engagement at New York's Irving Hall (April, 1866), Tom was taken to Europe where he was continuously subjected to rigorous tests by noted musicians like Ignaz Moscheles and Charles Halle—whose testimonial letters were published by the Bethunes in a pamphlet, *The Marvelous Musical Prodigy Blind Tom*. By 1868 the Bethunes moved to Warrenton, Virginia, where they bought a farm, which they named "Elway." It was here that Tom was brought every summer following his concert season. He continued to tour yearly throughout the country and Canada with John G. Bethune serving as his manager. On July 25, 1870, John Bethune had himself appointed Tom's legal guardian in a Virginia Probate Court, thereby negating the 1865 Indentureship Agreement. By now the Bethunes were realizing $50,000 yearly from Tom's concerts. They began to schedule concerts in the South and returned to Columbus, Georgia's, Springer Opera House on February 10, 1879.

For nine years, Tom lived in New York, since his manager had married a Mrs. Eliza Stutzback, owner of the boardinghouse where they stayed. In the summers Tom studied with Professor Joseph Poznanski, who also wrote down many of Tom's compositions. When John G. Bethune was killed (February 16, 1884) trying to board a train, General Bethune had himself legally appointed Tom's guardian and continued the concert tours. According to the March 23rd *New York Times,* the will presented for probate in the Surrogate's office the previous day revealed that the late John G. Bethune had left "all his property to his father, General James Neil Bethune, with provisions that his estate should succeed to his four sisters," and that he "purposely refrained from giving anything to one Eliza Bethune, whose true name was declared Eliza Stutzbach." Expressing his already-stated doubts regarding the legality of their marriage, John Bethune had stated that:

> she (Eliza Bethune) is cut off from any legacy in the Will by reason of her gross misconduct since the alleged marriage, and particularly in divorce suits that had been before the New York Common Pleas Courts—believing that she never had any genuine regard for me, but was rather a heartless adventuress who sought to absorb my estate, the fruits of my savings during a bachelorhood of 50 years.

The charge of her "marrying for money" is debatable considering that Mrs. Bethune owned the boardinghouse where the deceased had lived with Blind Tom for several summers. A three-year court battle between him and Eliza Bethune (who had divorced John Bethune before the accident) for Tom ended July 31, 1887, when the court granted custody to the widow. The custody battle began on July 9, 1885, when Tom's mother, Charity Wiggins, filed a petition in the United States Circuit Court, Alexandria, Virginia, for the return of her son. A. J. Lerche, Eliza Bethune's lawyer, was among those requesting permission of the Hon. R. W. Hughes to practice as attorneys and counsellors in his court, and it is obvious that Mrs. Eliza Bethune was using this action as a method of revenge. There is little doubt that John G. Bethune's widow was aware of the "technical legalities" used by the Bethune family to retain custodial rights over Blind Tom, and that Tom's mother was without the necessary funds to hire a lawyer to challenge those decisions. According to the July 10th *Baltimore Sun,* the "writ of Habeas Corpus" was served upon General Bethune in Warrenton the previous evening by Marshal Scott and Deputy

Marshall O'Neal, who accompanied the General and Tom by train to the Alexandria Court House the next morning, where a crowd was assembled. Because the lawyers for both sides were unprepared at that time to begin their arguments, the hearing was postponed until the next day.

After listening to arguments from both parties regarding which court had jurisdiction in the case, the judge filed the following handwritten decision with the court:

Court opened Pursuant to Adjournment
Present
Hon. Ro. W. Hughes, Judge
Ex-parti—Charity Wiggins
on petition for Habeas Corpus

This Cause came on to be heard
Friday, July 10, 1885

On this 10th day of July 1885, on the petition of said Charity Wiggins. The proof thereon, and the return and the amended return of Jas. N. Bethune and the exhibits therewith filed, and on the affidavit of Charity Wiggins in response to the said returns. On consideration whereof, and the proofs addressed on the hearing, and on the argument of counsel, the Court doth order for reasons stated in writing, that the said writ be discharged, and the said Thomas Wiggins otherwise called Thomas Bethune, and known publicly as Blind Tom, be remanded to the legal custody and control of his committee James N. Bethune, and that the petition of the said Charity Wiggins be dismissed for want of jurisdiction in this court from which order of dismissal the said Charity Wiggins in open court appeared, and the said appeal is allowed of the court.

Ro. W. Hughes
Judge

According to the press release concerning the trial, the judge's decision against the argument that the Alexandria, Virginia, Court had no jurisdiction over the case was based on the facts that: 1) General Bethune had become a resident of Warrenton, Virginia, in 1870, and 2) Tom, being then in possession under a contract, also became a resident.

On October 8, 1885, the *New York Times* issued the following report on the Charity Wiggins vs. James N. Bethune hearing as it has been transmitted to them from their corespondent in Richmond the previous day.

"Blind Tom's Mother Anxious"

> *Richmond, Va. Oct. 7*—In the U.S. court today, Judges Bond and Hughes presiding, a decision was rendered in the case of Blind Tom, the colored pianist. This is a suit in the name of Blind Tom, through his mother Charity Wiggins against James N. Bethune, for many years Tom's guardian, requiring an account of the earnings of Tom and their proper investment for the benefit of himself and hers and that Bethune be required to surrender the possession of claimant, and pay into court the money to defray the expense of the suits. The motion was overruled without prejudice to plaintiff's right to renew the same. It was further ordered that the injustices heretofore granted restraining the defendant (Bethune) from removing the plaintiff beyond the limits of the state be continued in full force unless permission of one of the Judges of the Court be first obtained.

On October 2nd, the Wiggins *vs.* Bethune Equity and Jurisdiction Case was argued in the Circuit Court. Its importance was such that reference to the arguments and decisions were used in two later "next Friend guardian cases" (See Voss *vs.* Neineber, July 22, 1895, and Toledo Tractions *vs.* Camero, April 25, 1905). Such was based on the following settlement submitted to the *Federal Reporter:*

Wiggins, (otherwise known as "Blind Tom") by his Next
Friend, etc. v. Bethune
(Circuit Court, E.D. Virginia, October 2, 1886)

I. *Courts—Federal Jurisdiction—Citizenship—
Suit By next Friend*

In a suit brought by the next friend of one who
is *non compos mentis,* federal jurisdiction cannot be based on the citizenship of the next friend,
as he is only a nominal party. Hughes, J., dissent-
ing, in case of the next friend is the real plaintiff.

II. *Same—Residence of Lunatic—Committee.*

If a committee of one changes his residence
from the state where he was appointed, and where
the *non compos* also resided to another state, and
takes the latter with him, the latter becomes a
resident of the state to which they remove, and
retains such residence after the committee's death,
notwithstanding he is afterwards taken away to
his original state, and elsewhere, and another committee is appointed for him in such original state;
and in a suit in the latter state, brought by him
against said last-mentioned committee, a citizen
of that state, the citizenship of the parties is such
as to give jurisdiction to a federal court.

In Equity. Bill for an accounting. Plea of want
of jurisdiction. Charity Wiggins, who sues as next
friend of Thomas Wiggins, (Blind Tom) is a citizen
of New York; James N. Bethune, the defendant of
Virginia.

A. J. Lerche and L. R. Page, for complainant.
S. Ferguson Beach, for defendant.

Bond, J. This is a bill filed by the complainant
for an account, to which a plea of want of jurisdiction has been interposed. The facts, as they
appear from the affidavits filed by the parties, and
as they have been stated at bar by the respective
counsel, are these: John G. Bethune, who at the

13

time was a citizen of Virginia, having Blind Tom in his keeping, was on the twenty-firth day of July, 1870, by a probate court of this state, appointed Tom's committee, he being found *non compos mentis*. As such committee, Bethune took Tom from place to place, through the various states of the Union, giving musical entertainments, so that he was seldom in Virginia. Finally, John G. Bethune changed his place of residence from Virginia to the city of New York, taking Blind Tom with him, and became a resident of that state, where he died on the ___ day of February, 1884 [*sic*]. Blind Tom was continued on his travels under care of a brother of John G. Bethune, his former committee. While Tom was thus journeying in the state of North Carolina, James N. Bethune had himself appointed by a county court in Virginia as Tom's committee. Charity Wiggins, who sues as next friend, is the mother of Blind Tom, and is a citizen of New York. This being the fact, she could not sue (being a merely nominal party), unless her son is a citizen of New York also. He is the real party in interest, and the jurisdiction of the court depends upon the fact whether or not Blind Tom, at the last appointment of a committee for him, was still a resident of New York, where he had been a resident with John G. Bethune, his committee, up to and at the time of his death. There can be no doubt, we think, that the residence of his committee was the residence of Tom. He, *non compos,* had no ability to change it, and the fact that he was borne away by one who had no legal control over him to another state, away from his mother in New York, who was his natural guardian, cannot be held to change his residence. The fact that he was temporarily in Virginia, under the control of one who merely had physical domination of him, did not make him a resident of the state, and the appointment of a committee for him there, while he was absent in

North Carolina, added nothing to the effort to change his domicile. The bill is framed under the view that both Charity Wiggins and her son Tom, are citizens of New York, while the defendant is a citizen of Virginia, and we think the jurisdictional facts sufficiently appear. The plea is therefore overruled.

Hughes, J. I concur on the ground that the controversy in this case is really between the mother of Blind Tom, a resident of New York, suing as next friend, and a resident of Virginia, claiming to be Tom's committee. Blind Tom, though nominally a party, is really the subject of the controversy, and is not party to the suit in such manner as, even if he were a citizen of Virginia, should defeat the jurisdiction of the court, where the substantial controversy is between citizens of different states. In many cases, the *prochain ami* is merely a nominal party plaintiff; but in others, of which the present is an example, the real plaintiff is the *prochain ami.* Where this is the case, to treat the incompetent party to the record as the real plaintiff would be to allow a technicality to obstruct the course of justice. Technicalities were devised for the promotion of justice between suitors. So long as they serve that end, they should be respected; but when they operate to defeat justice, they should be discouraged by the courts.

For these reasons, whatever may be true on the doubtful point, where was Blind Tom's residence? I am of the opinion that this court had jurisdiction to entertain the suit.

The Bethunes were understandably elated by the decision. Tom's 1886-87 concert season began two days later at Baltimore's Music Academy (October 4-9). According to the October 5th *Baltimore American,* the "large and appreciative audience" was evidence that Tom had lost "none of his popularity, with a number of musical people in the audience loud in their praise of his skills."

Included on the program was his "Cascade" and fantasy from the opera "Lurline," which the reporter described as having been "given perfectly." Since a "large proportion of young people were present," the *Baltimore Morning Herald* reporter felt that there were "many in the audience hearing Blind Tom for the first time." On October 8th, the *Baltimore Sun* reported that the proceeds from Tom's matinee concert the previous day ($34.50) were given to Mr. George H. Dalrymple of the Mayor's office for the Charleston, South Carolina, Relief Fund. The reporter expressed regret that the announcement of the benefit was not made in time to draw a large audience. It would, after all, have been billed as one of the many fund-raising activities being held throughout the nation for Charleston following the "Great Earthquake" on August 31, 1886.

On October 12th, the *Baltimore American* reported that "Blind Tom's mother applied in vain to the New York Supreme Court the previous day to have her son's mental condition inquired into by a committee, and his estate cared for." Inasmuch as Eliza Bethune (his mother's corroborating witness) asserted that Tom (whom she claimed to have cared for for seven years) was "idiotic and incapable of managing himself and his affairs," it is obvious that she was continuing with her efforts to get Blind Tom away from the former in-laws. Despite her arguments, Judge Donahue of the court denied the application on the grounds that "proceedings should be instituted in the state where the committee was first appointed." In the suit already pending in Alexandria, Virginia, General Bethune had been ordered to "make a report of the money received from Tom's concert tours to the court." In its report, the *New York Times* said that:

> Mrs. Wiggins' suit against Bethune for an account-
> ing is based on the theory that he has practically
> kept Tom in slavery and her purpose in having
> her son adjudged a lunatic in this state was evi-
> dently to be put in a position to dispute the cus-
> tody of the sable musician, pending the determi-
> nation of the suit.

Charity Wiggins did not deny that she and Tom's father (the late Mingo Wiggins) had agreed "with Bethune that he should have

Tom for five years, at the end of which he would attain his majority." Her concern was that "without their consent and without giving them notice they had Tom adjudged to be a lunatic, with the General's son appointed as the committee of his person, then put him on exhibition as a pianist." Her suit was therefore against General Bethune for the "services of her son and an accounting of the profits of the exhibitions since 1865." It is interesting that the *Fredericksburg (VA) Free Press,* when reporting on the petition, described Tom's mother as "that old lady that had twelve children, the oldest 60 years old, and the youngest 26, all born in slavery, therefore not born in lawful wedlock." According to the October 12, 1886, *Tribune,* Tom's mother testified that General James N. Bethune had taken Tom away from her three weeks after Emancipation because "there was money in him." She again repeated her charge that, "following the five-year agreement Bethune refused to give Tom up."

Next to testify was Professor Joseph Poznanski, who told the Commissioner that he had been Tom's music teacher for nine summers. Despite this, he expressed the opinion that Tom was "deficient of all senses, except that of music, and that which brings the consciousness of dinner time." Characterizing Tom as an "inordinate eater," Professor Poznanski said he would play on a piano and Blind Tom would "caper around the room meanwhile, then after he finished Tom would seat himself at another piano and reproduce the sounds he heard." Admitting that Tom had a "prodigious memory," Professor Poznanski said it was he "who would sometimes write down the music that Tom composed." His statement that "Tom would get up from the piano, pull his hair, shake his head, grunt, dance around, and act as if crazy" had obviously not been lost on the jury.

1887 possibly was the most traumatic year in the life of General James N. Bethune. His "neo-servitude ownership" of Blind Tom legally came to an end. On January 11th, Judge Bond of the U.S. Circuit Court of Appeals submitted the following decision in the Wiggins vs. Bethune Equity Petition:

> Thomas Wiggins, by his next friend
>
> vs.
>
> James N. Bethune-
>
> Upon motion of the plaintiff it is ordered by the Court, that the defendant do within ten days from this date pay into the First National Bank of Alexandria, to the credit of this Court, in this Cause, all money which he holds or may have come into his possession while acting as Committee of the plaintiff, since March 1884.
>
> Hugh L. Bond
>
> *Cir. Judge*
>
> Ordered that the Court stand adjourned until to-morrow morning at 11 o'clock

On that same day, Tom was performing at the Steubenville, Ohio, opera house to a "well-pleased and fair-sized audience."

On July 31, 1887, the *New York Times* reported that Judge Bond passed an order the previous day in Baltimore which "took Blind Tom out of General Bethune's custody." It was reported that:

> James N. Bethune, who has kept Blind Tom in his possession since the days of slavery, should deliver him to the United States marshal on August 16 at Alexandria, Va., and that the marshal shall deliver him safely into the hands of Eliza Bethune, who was appointed Tom's Committee by the Supreme Court of New York, and also that General Bethune pay over $7,000 to the order of Court for the credit of Blind Tom as his earnings.

In addition, the article noted that "another suit is pending against General Bethune for $100,000" (the amount said to be due from Tom's earnings since 1865). Obviously, Eliza Bethune had used Tom's mother as her "trump card" to obtain ownership of Tom. Her appointment as "Tom's Committee" was based on a request by Charity Wiggins. The *Times* reporter described the General as a "remarkably well-preserved old man, with long white hair and beard who refused a fan offered him as well as a glass of water," preferring instead for his "comfort to puff away on an old-time pipe as if the thermometer were in the forties instead of the nineties." A similar dispatch appeared in the *Tribune* as well as in many of the newspapers throughout the country, making it evident that the Blind Tom litigations attracted more than local interest. While most accounts considered the victory one for Mrs. Bethune, the Black *New York Freeman* and the *St. Paul Western Appeal* considered Tom's mother to have been the "winner" in the case.

According to the August 1st *Alexandria Gazette,* General Bethune "objected to the proceedings," saying that "it is all a mistake about Tom being an idiot and I will look into the New York proceedings." Although the request for $10,000 (as the amount alleged to have been earned by General Bethune since March 1884 from exhibiting Tom) was overruled by the judge in favor of a lesser amount, the major victory had come from the fact that he ratified an agreement entered into that spring by the two counsels ordering General Bethune to give Tom over to his deceased son's former wife. That was the most important aspect of the litigation.

According to the August 18, 1887, *New York Times,* when Tom arrived in New York, he was taken "directly to his old-time quarters at 7 St. Mark's Place where Mrs. Bethune lived, and where he had lived for seven years with the late John G. Bethune until the latter's death in 1884." It was further noted that, though Tom was then "about 39 and very fat, he lost none of his mimicry and as a result of an oculist's treatment to his eyes, he had been able to see enough to distinguish the larger objects about him." In addition, the reporter wrote that "though Tom had been before the public since he was five years old, he was being returned to his mother with nothing but his wardrobe and a silver flute." Moreover, he contended, that despite the "court ordering General Bethune to pay Tom's new guardian $7,000, the amount earned by exhibiting Tom during the past three years, there seemed to be little prospect of her getting it, since Marshall Scott of Alexandria, Virginia, found it necessary to levy a large amount of General Bethune's personal property to satisfy a judgement for lawyers' fees." However, the reporter was of the opinion that, with Mrs. Eliza Bethune, "Tom would now be able to benefit from earnings beyond his expense."

It was not evident that Blind Tom experienced any "relocation traumas," since he performed in New York's Association Hall September 26 to 30th. Since the press advertised those concerts as his "first since his freedom under new managers," it is apparent that many viewed Tom's "neo-servitude" status as having been only a continuation of that former guardianship relationship with his former slaveowner.

The Blind Tom "insanity case" was being discussed among members of the Black community during this period. This is evident from a lengthy article in the February 5, 1887, *Washington Bee* titled:

BLIND TOM

NOT SO DUMB AS HIS MANAGER

MAKES OUT

During the trial it was revealed that the Bethunes had cleared $3,000 monthly exhibiting Tom and he also studied for 15 years with Joseph Poznanski. He also studied two piano concertos with a Mme. Amelia A. Tutein (a student of Liszt) during his Philadelphia concerts in 1886.[20] When describing his playing, she said it was:

> expressive and for the most part very accurate. He never seemed to forget and could play such pieces as the 'Sonata Pathetique' (which he studied in Germany) with surprising skill. His technical exercises were limited to a very few simple things that General Bethune's daughter had taught him. His playing was by no means a mirroring of the playing of others. He put in his own expression and exhibited much individuality. His octaves were very fine and clear and his great physical strength and elasticity made his playing forceful.

Especially noteworthy was Mme. Tutein's contention that Tom played "well and even better than many white contemporary pianists who made great pretensions and who took years to learn what Tom could learn in a few hours." For her, the most unbelievable feat had been when after she taught him the solo part of the Beethoven "Third Piano Concerto," he "turned his back to the keyboard and played the entire Concerto standing in that position," meaning that "his right hand played the left hand part and his left hand played the right hand part."

It is interesting that, despite her own assertions about Tom's exceptional musicianship and unbelievable learning ability, Mme. Tutein said that Tom remained, in her opinion, "only a few degrees from the animal." Though she conceded that Tom's "ability to play many compositions by name at command indicated another form of intelligence with which he should be credited," she maintained that it was a "kind of intelligence like that of putting a new record on a talking machine." Unfortunately, Mme. Tutein's "stereotypic mind-set" regarding Blind Tom caused her to contradict the realities of her own musical evaluations.

Blind Tom, at the start of his mid-life years, had finally been "legally freed" from his former slaveowners to begin a new phase of his life. At age thirty-eight the pianist-instrumentalist-vocalist-composer would use his performing and creative talents for the benefit of a new group of Whites—with, ironically, the major profiteer being the former daughter-in-law of his former slave owner. When Mrs. Eliza Bethune became Tom's new committee she initiated two major fund-producing changes in the Blind Tom Exhibitions: allowing him to perform on Sundays, and allowing him to appear with other performers, the first one advertised in the November 10, 1887 *New York Age* as follows:

THE GRANDEST YET!
A DOUBLE TREAT,
TWO CONCERTS IN ONE
By whom?
SELIKA
and
BLIND TOM
Under the auspices of
Bethel A.M.E. Church
These two inimitable musical
phenomena will appear
on the same date and hour at
Steinway Hall, Wednesday
November 23, 1887, at 8 P.M.

> Read: Take notice, as this is the first time in his-
> tory of the city that two of the worlds' leading
> musical wonders have appeared at the same date,
> place and hour, we invite all admirers of music,
> sweet music, to be sure to attend, as such an event
> may never occur again in our day.
>
> General Admission 50 cents
> Reserved Seats 75 cents

According to the reviewer in the November 26 *New York Age*,
"from the opening of the door at Steinway Hall, there was a crush
for seats." Because "the galleries and floors soon crowded, the
ushers allowed a rush for stage-seats, notwithstanding the presence of Tom at the piano." Inasmuch as that historic concert was
being offered as one of Bethel's "Centennial of African Methodism"
features, many noted persons were in attendance, among whom
was the Hon. C.J.J.Taylor, U.S. Minister to Liberia. There was also
evidence of an integrated audience since the reporter noted that
Dr. Derrick (probably the minister) mounted the "much-abused
stage to extend his thanks to the good people present of both races."
That Tom's physically demanding traveling schedule was retained
under his "new committee" is evident from further appearances
at Boston's new theatre, November 24-26, followed by an appearance at Boston's Music Hall with Mme. Selika and several White
artists on the Austin Popular Sunday Sacred Concerts November
27th. He returned to Brooklyn's Williamsburgh Knickerbocker Hall,
November 28-30th where, according to *The Clipper*, he played to
a "very moderate business only." In his Boston concert "people
were turned away before the concert began for the seats were all
sold out and there was standing room only left." The reviewer felt
that the crowd had been attracted by "two large-size magnets:
Blind Tom, the 'phenomenal, natural born pianist' and Mme. Selika,
the 'Creole Patti.' "[21]

In the January 1, 1888, *Boston Globe*, Tom was advertised as
"Heading an array of 60 colored celebrities" in Austin's Popular
Series at Boston's Music Hall. Among those performing were sev-
eral musicians from the Haverly and Callender Colored Minstrel
Troupe, a full military band of 40 uniformed performers and a 20
member drum corps; in addition were vocal selections by

Sissieretta Jones, the Providence Rhode Island soprano who would soon become the most publicized Black prima donna of her time,[22] and Frederick Elliot Lewis, the Boston-based cellist, who had gained recognition as one of two Black string players in the 1876 World Peace Jubilee in that city under the famous Patrick Gilmore.[23] George Warren Shapres, a cornet virtuoso, doubled as soloist and band conductor. A review of the concert in the January 2 *Globe* noted that "the artists were greeted by a larger audience than expected, considering the condition of the weather." Following statements concerning the favorable response to Sissieretta Jones' selections, the reviewer wrote that: "the principal attraction of the evening, however was the appearance of Blind Tom, his name for years a household word throughout New England. He was encored again and again playing many of the familiar pieces which have won him a name of wide repute on both sides of the water."

The response to Tom's performance had undoubtedly created a desire by Bostonians for more appearances since he was booked for a one-week concert series at Horticulture Hall beginning Monday, January 9th. The series was advertised in the *Globe* with Tom's picture under the heading "There is but one Blind Tom! There will never be another!" Especially interesting is the reference to Tom in the advertisement as "the greatest of all musical Prodigies (not excepting Josef Hoffman or any of the recent phenomenal discoveries) since the then eleven-year-old Polish pianist performed in Boston Music Hall, January 4-6 to enthusiastic crowds.[24]

Notwithstanding the excitement over Hoffman's concert, which continued for three extra nights at Windsor Theatre, or the fact that it was the opera season at the Boston Theatre, among which was the first English version of Wagner's *Tannhäuser*, Tom's concerts at Horticulture Hall were still drawing large audiences. After his final appearance in Boston on January 14, Tom appeared at Lynn Massachusetts' Music Hall, followed by other concerts throughout that state, concluding with a performance in Westfield, Massachusetts, on January 30th where it was reported he "drew a good audience."[25]

When writing about Tom for the September 1908 *Human Life* magazine, J. Frank Davis shared several non-musical-related incidents that occurred during that Boston Tour. Among them was Tom's physical attack on the young guide who had been sent by the theatre manager to bring him from the theatrical boarding-house to Horticulture Hall for his concert. When trying to help Tom avoid the crowds that filled the sidewalks, the guide accidentally pushed Tom into a fence. The then 240 pound pianist responded with a powerful blow to the guide's chest, sending him "reeling" while Tom began to cry as an inconsolable child "Mrs. Bethune! Mrs. Bethune! Mr. Davis was trying to take Tom to a lawyer." Only after much reassurance by Mrs. Bethune and a Mr. Gibson (then serving as Tom's lecturer-master of ceremony on stage) that the guide was only taking him to a piano did Tom finally fulfill the engagement. Another more revealing incident was the occasion of Mr. Gibson's taking him to have his shoes shined on way to an engagement. While sitting in the chair and hearing the Black bootblack recount to another Black bootblack a quarrel in which he was told to "go on yo niggah," Tom immediately interrupted and asked the bootblack "Are you a nigger?" to which the bootblack replied in the affirmative, causing Tom to climb down immediately from a chair with only one shoe shined and say "Tom ain't goin' to have his shoes blacked by no nigger." Obviously, Tom's negative reaction to non-Whites reveal that Tom had probably heard racist stereotypes about his people throughout his life, thereby creating an inaccurate understanding about his own identity.

On March 27th Tom gave a two-hour private concert for Josef Hoffman aboard the North German Lloyd Steamer as one of several friends and admirers of the then ailing prodigy before his departure to Berlin and an extensive rest before engaging in musical studies. Besides a beautiful basket of flowers, Tom also brought copies of his own compositions, which reportedly Josef Hoffman performed the following morning before his departure.[26] The decision to remove the prodigy from the stage by his parents had stemmed in part from the numerous complaints from concerned citizens to Elbridge T. Gerry, President of the Society for the Prevention of Cruelty to Children, about what they termed the "exploitation" of the boy.

The day after Hoffman's departure Blind Tom appeared at Philadelphia's Academy of Music for the benefit of Zoar Methodist Episcopal Church with the advertisement noting his "ability to sing in German, French and English."[27] On April 18th, the *Brooklyn Daily Eagle* reported that Tom would be performing for the benefit of "a Colored church." The following day, the *Trenton (NJ) Daily True American* advertised his concert at Taylor's Opera House where he would "do imitations of Josef Hoffman." Reporting on that concert the reviewer felt that his "fingers had lost none of their old cunning" and unlike in previous years Tom "acts the dual role of master of ceremony and performer, using the exact language of the old gentleman who used to do it and speaks of himself in the third person."[28]

For the next several weeks Mrs. Bethune was involved in numerous Court Hearings concerning Blind Tom before the New York Supreme Court as his deponent. In a May 29th notarized deposition she asserted that Charity Wiggins (Tom's mother) had, on April 27th:

> left deponent's residence, No. 7 St. Marks Place unknown to deponent and without any previous intimation to deponent of her intention so to do, or of any dissatisfaction other than frequent demands for money from deponent. That deponent had at various times given her, the said Charity Wiggins, various sums aggregating the sum of one-hundred dollars besides providing her with proper wearing apparel and board, and had provided her with the front parlor of said house as sleeping apartments, the said idiot occupying at the same time the back parlor of said house.[29]

Mrs. Bethune maintained that, on the same day, Mr. Betts, an attorney from the New York State Supreme Court, had requested she pay monies to a John Dempsey—the papers served during a Blind Tom concert at Lakewood, New Jersey's, Baptist Church on February 27th.

According to Mrs. Bethune's statement, when appointed Tom's Committee by the Eastern District of Virginia Court, an order "to give a bond with securities in the sum of twenty-five thousand dollars" was given which she filed on March 3rd, 1887. This, despite the receipt of "no moneys or prospect of said idiot excepting old wearing apparel of the nominal value of $10.00." In addition, she alleged to have "supported and clothed Tom's mother and furnished the legal fees toward relieving Tom from persons who refused to allow him any parts of proceeds from his concerts." She testified that she had hired John Dempsey as advance agent for Blind Tom (September 26, 1887) although he had never held such a position. Finding him unable to adequately fulfill his responsibilities, they argued and she subsequently discharged him; Dempsey brought a suit against her for salary and expenses although no itemized account was made with the request. This reality notwithstanding, she decided to rehire him, but again had to discharge him, refusing to pay the $523.38 request, referring the matter to Albrecht Lerche, her attorney. Because of these proceedings, Mrs. Bethune said "she was unable to give any concerts since said day causing the said idiot (meaning Tom) to be unemployed." Still further, another court claim for $5,000 had been made against her by Attorney Holland for his previous legal services in the successful 1887 Charity Wiggins vs. General James N. Bethune suit.

On April 30th, Mrs. Bethune supplied the court with an inventory accounting, alleging that Tom's "musical exhibitions from September 26, 1887 to April 24, 1888, netted only $1,076.69"; she also stated that "a claim against the estate of John G. Bethune and James N. Bethune was then in the state of Kentucky for services of Tom not collected and value of which cannot be positively stated."[30] Re-emphasizing that she had received "no property of any kind with said Thomas Wiggins (Blind Tom) excepting certain wearing apparel then upon his person and which was of little value and much worn," causing her, as such Committee, with a view to create an estate for Tom. She again reiterated her refusal to pay various claims against Tom's estate since, in her opinion, some had no foundation or were greatly exaggerated. Despite what she described as "many early interferences against her" she maintained that "as Tom's Committee, she succeeded beyond her first expectations and much beyond the success of the persons heretofore serving as Tom's Custodians."

A second petition was filed by John Dempsey on May 21st for requested monies with a Special Hearing held the following day at the County Court House, city of New York in Judge Abraham R. Lawrence's Chambers. After arguments by attorneys for both parties, the judge "ordered and determined that said application is denied with ten dollar costs be paid by said petitioner to said Committee."[31]

Such victory was brief since, on May 27th, a petition on behalf of Tom's mother was brought before the New York Supreme
Court. After identifying Charity Wiggins as Tom's "only next of
kin" and offering a summarized account of how Mrs. Bethune became his legal Committee, the Petitioner reminded the Court that
in that position she was ordered to "render a just and true account every year of all money and other property received by her
in exhibiting Tom," something the Petitioner alleged had not been
done.[32] She alleged that Mrs. Bethune's inventory account of May
15th "was not either in manner or form the account she had been
directed to render" since it did not "contain a just and true statement of all the money and other property received by her and of
the application thereof." Among the objections cited were: 1) that
the place and time of Tom's exhibitions were omitted as well as
any details about expenses used in conjunction with same, 2) none
of the claims against the Bethunes in the states of Virginia and
Kentucky were listed, 3) names of creditors and nature of those
claims were missing, 4) inventory statement was not supported
by documentation, and 5) she failed to use Tom's musical abilities
to his best advantage, thereby losing, in the Petitioners opinion,
the sum of about $10,000 for the Estate, which she should be
charged instead of the $1,076.69 as represented by her. Still fur-
ther, Tom's mother's attorney charged Mrs. Bethune with being
"guilty of acts in the administration of her Trust which were preju-
dicial to the well being and personal comfort of Tom." For these
reasons, Tom's mother through legal representation wanted Elise
Bethune to "either resign or be removed for inability to obtain
other securities," feeling that "unless the said Estate is protected
herein said Committee will escape all liability for her said Acts
and Neglect." Also was a request that the Court should have a
hearing for all creditors against the Estate to further determine if
Mrs. Bethune was a proper and suitable person to continue as
Tom's Committee. Because Tom's mother was still illiterate, a statement with her signature (X) was attached to the Petition, making
known to the Court that she had "heard read the Petition, knew
the Contents, and agreed with them." On June 1st, 1889, the *Indianapolis Freeman* noted that: "Blind Tom is now traveling in the
West, playing to fair sized houses. Blind Tom is a success of the
past. Mrs. Bethune has made comparatively little money off of
him in two seasons and he has made less," some evidence that the
Petitioner's charge was not without merit.

On July 18th following a special Supreme Court Hearing, Justice George P. Andrews rendered a decision that denied "without costs" Tom's mother's petition for a reargument in her son's behalf. However, those allegations concerning Mrs. Bethune's managerial limitations were probably valid since a concert in New York's Bethel Church on July 2nd drew "a very slim but appreciative audience."[33] On that concert he performed a piece by Josef Hoffman which the youthful prodigy had improvised for him in a private concert while both were in Boston. He also reproduced a piece titled "Echoes of Niagara" played for him by Gussie L. Davis, the Black songwriter, who was then performing on the Bergen Star Concerts.[34]

That same week an article concerning Tom's so-called "retirement" appeared in the July 7th *American Musician*. Describing him as a "petted child with a Grand piano for a toy," the writer told readers that Tom was "suffering from some nervous complaint that renders a repetition of his stage performances impossible." He described Tom's living quarters as "a marble-stooped dwelling" in St. Mark's Place, east of the Bowery, where people hurrying to and fro in the streets stop often and listen to the strains coming from Tom's playing in the back parlor." He described him as a "stalwart African who will start up from his seat and rush out upon the porch and pace up and down like an imprisoned animal, beating his chest and moaning piteously."

Despite his alleged nervous condition, Tom was heard imitating "Nearer My God To Thee," that he heard on the Grace Church chimes nearby. Besides his musical reaction to the sounds of birds and nature, the writer told how he reacted angrily to a servant girl's off-key singing in a nearby house, telling her to "shut up," adding "you ought to be ashamed of yourself to make such a frightful noise." According to the writer there were several trained vocalists and pianists in the house nearby whose music Tom would hear and repeat. When not seen for a few days on the porch, neighbors were so concerned that one of them played a piccolo to get him out of the house. Since Tom was continuously involved in such musical antics and spent hours in practice, the writer considered him to be living like "some petted child in a play house and despite his affliction cannot but be intensely happy."

Soon after, Tom gave a three-hour recital at St. Mark's residence for several priests who were especially desirous of seeing how he would be affected by older style church music, something they hoped could be introduced on his tours being scheduled for the following month.[35] Among the numbers performed for him by a Professor Breuer, organist of the Most Holy Redeemer Church, was a Lutheran chorale and the Catholic "Dies Irae," both of which he immediately repeated. Obviously Tom had a positive reaction to these sounds since on September 6th he was advertised in Roundout, New York, as doing a "sacred concert." Victoria Earle, who was in attendance, questioned having Tom perform sonatas and fantasias of Mozart and other similar works with jubilees and camp songs, asking "is there not a selfish disregard for the responsibility of honorably guarding Blind Tom's well-earned fame on the part of those controlling him?"[36]

On October 1st the *Newark (NJ) Evening News* announced that Tom's concerts at Library Hall were to be entirely new, leaving little doubt that more sacred works were beginning to be included among his repertoire. Still further, was a concert in Albany, New York, on October 11th before a "large audience of the leading colored people of the city and many musicians" in Jermaien Hall to benefit the Hamilton Street AME Church. Although the reporter was delighted with Tom's "execution and powers of imitation," he said "noisy ushers, and giddy young people succeeded in robbing the entertainment of much of its pleasure."[38] Among other New York concerts listed in the press were those in Malleawan (October 10th); Saratoga (October 13th); Troy (October 14th);[36] Fort Edwards (December 1st); Glen Falls (December 3rd); Oneida (December 11th) and Syracuse (December 29th).[39] According to *The Clipper*, all were before large audiences.

In the meantime, a decision on attorney Daniel Holland's request for a substitute attorney to replace Mrs. Eliza Bethune's deceased attorney (George H. Forster) was made by Justice Abraham R. Lawrence at a special session of the New York Supreme Court on November 20th.[40] According to attorney Holland's petition, his effort to locate Mrs. Bethune for "recovery of professional legal services rendered by him in regards to the Blind Tom Estate were being thwarted by his inability to locate her through a legal representative following Atty. Forster's death that summer." He had learned from the person looking after Mrs. Bethune's St. Mark's Place of residence that she had gone out of the city "to give concerts with said idiot" and thus was "unable to state when Mrs. Bethune would return." This assertion seems unfounded since

Tom's concerts were continuously being reported in the New York press. This is evident from a report in the November 9, 1889, *Freeman* that: Bethel church was overtaxed by patronage at Blind Tom's concert. Many could not gain admittance. According to the reviewer, "Tom was at his best, the audience had a rare treat and it was a financial success."

Mrs. Bethune was also getting some monetary rewards from Tom's creative talents given the 1888 copyright dates on three works published by the Oliver Ditson Music Company, namely: his *Columbus March, Blind Tom's Mazurka* and *When This Cruel War Is Over*. This latter work, an Introduction and set of Variations on a waltz-like theme in 4/4 time, offers some evidence of his continuing nostalgia with his past "owners."

According to the January 5th, 1889 *Clipper*, Tom performed two concerts at Rochester, New York's New Opera House on New Year's Day. In a January 13th concert in the same city the reporter wrote that: "Tom has grown decidedly corpulent and is more dignified than in the past, made few introductory remarks, and throughout the concert gave a running description of his past life and of his old habits."[41] The review of his Sunday, January 27th concert in the *Buffalo Morning Express* noted that "despite the bad weather, the large audience that greeted Blind Tom had doubtless been compensated for venturing out to hear him." In that same month, a four-year-old blind boy named Oscar Moore was being exhibited at New York's Astor House as "the most remarkable boy since Blind Tom." A native of Waco, Texas, under the management of a H.P. Gammel of Austin, Texas, the child was interviewed by many reporters who had been given a book of nearly one thousand questions on many geographical and mathematical subjects from which to test him.[42] Though not a musical wonder like Blind Tom, the comparative interest between the four-year-old and the then forty-year-old pianist shows that the blind pianist's non-musical memorization of facts was still considered a unique inexplicable phenomena for one characterized as an idiot.

On March 2nd, following another State Supreme Court Hearing before Justice Andrews concerning the Blind Tom Estate, Attorney Jerome Buck was appointed the referee "to hear and determine all matters contained in Daniel P. Holland's Petition, and report whereby he finds that said Holland petitioner is entitled to be paid the sum of three thousand dollars for his said services."[43]

As a response to this, Mrs. Bethune's attorney (Albrecht J. Lerche) retained attorney Leman B. Treadwell to "conduct the matter for Eliza Bethune as Committee of said Idiot."[44] With others taking responsibility for her legal affairs, Mrs. Bethune was able to schedule Tom's concerts outside New York State. On March 16th, *The Cleveland Plain Dealer* announced Tom's concert at their Star Theatre, saying "it is many years since he played here and the present generation of Clevelanders know little of him from personal experience."

Blind Tom remained in the state of Ohio for several weeks. *The Toledo Ohio Commercial* of April 22nd reported that his "mimicry was very laughable and kept the audience in a hilarious humor." According to the *Toronto (Canada) Mail* of April 27th he was "greeted with much enthusiasm by a large audience at Association Hall, having been absent about ten years from the city." Besides his presentation of Beethoven's "Concerto in C Minor" and Liszt's transcription of Mendelssohn's "Wedding March," much merriment was caused when someone gave him the name "Nordheimer" to spell, causing Blind Tom to "momentarily show a ruffled dignity, then gravely and reproachfully say that he must be given legitimate words."

Inasmuch as Tom performed at the Johnstown, Pennsylvania, Opera House on May 14th he fortunately missed becoming a possible flood victim in the famous Johnstown Flood of May 31, 1888. This disastrous flood, which resulted from the collapse of the Commauge Reservoir, caused the loss of thousands of lives and heavy property losses. For several weeks following, there were many press releases to reassure readers that Blind Tom had not perished in the flood. Still further, a June 29th *New York Dramatic World* reporter from Findley, Ohio, noted that "E.O. Marvin, advance agent of Blind Tom, who was reported to have been lost in the Johnstown disaster, has been heard from and is said to be safe." Following his Johnstown concert, Tom gave two farewell concerts at Pittsburgh's Bijou Theatre on May 30th to "liberal patronage,"[45] and closed the musical season at the Tarentum in Pittsburgh, Pennsylvania, on May 31st (day of the flood) before "the most refined audience that ever assembled in the house."[46] Throughout the summer the musical world was involved in doing benefit concerts for the flood victims, including the Fisk Jubilee Singers who sent $300.00 from their concert tour in India.[47]

Although Tom seems to have had no scheduled concerts during the month of June, he remained in the news. For example, when Edwin G. Rivers published an article for the June 15, 1889, *Harrisburg (PA) Telegraph* titled "Some Georgia Wonders: A State Where Freaks Thrive and Strange Things Flourish," he included Blind Tom. By July, Tom was performing in Michigan. Before his concerts at Detroit's Miners Hall (July 21st and 24th), a representative from *The Detroit Free Press* visited Madison House where Tom was staying and reported the following having taken place:

> When a representative of *The Free Press* rapped at the door of room No. 7, Madison House, it was opened by a fat, sleek Negro with a round, bullet head and a most unprepossessing countenance. It was also evident that he was blind and was guided by the instinct of hearing alone.
>
> "Here is someone to see you, Tom" said the manager. "I d-d-don't want to s-s-s-see anybody," was the ungracious reply, and Blind Tom shut the door in the face of the advancing party.
>
> But soon he returned and asked the visitor into his little room. Then he forgot everything but the present. Picking up a comb with but few teeth in it Tom said:
>
> "S-s-s-s-see, my comb is all broken."
>
> "That is not yours, Tom. Where did you leave yours?"
>
> "At Kittanning, Pa.," answered Tom like a parrot.
>
> Blind Tom, the greatest musical phenomenon of this or any other age, is little more than an idiot in his intellectual powers. Fat, sleek and shiny, like a pet animal he stood in the center of his room and caught flies. It is seldom that he will play for visitors, but some old associations moved him and

he allowed himself to be led into the parlor and seated at the piano.

Then a change came over him. He threw back his head, rolled up his sightless eyes, struck the chords on the instrument and softly, like a wave of melody, a strange, sweet song floated out from the thick, uncultivated lips. Blind Tom was singing his favorite piece.

"Them Golden Slippers I want to Wear." He followed this with "Oh, Where is My Boy To-night." His voice has lost none of its sweet tone.

"Tom, would you like to get married?" asked a visitor.

"No-o-o-o-o," Tom stammers terribly, "s-s-s-he might b-b-b-b-eat me, and then the p-p-p-apers would be down on me."

It seems ironic that this reporter, who described Tom as "an idiot in everything but music and repetition," would question him about adult-related matters of a personal nature. He further characterized Tom as having "faculties of a 3-year old child" only, with no idea of the value of money, and can only appreciate sweetmeats and good things to eat. Still further was the statement that Tom "cannot be taught to eat at the table, or even dress himself." Despite these many negative descriptions about Tom, the reporter said that "Tom is a wonderful pianist whose audience was not as large as the merits of the performer deserved" adding that "the programme was a very interesting one and much enjoyed."

On September 21st, the *Huntsville (AL) Gazette*, a Black newspaper, reported that Blind Tom was giving concerts in the far west, while Flora Batson, the then leading soprano of the Bergen Star Concert company was "doing the Pacific slope." According to the *Clipper* when he appeared in Duluth, Minnesota, on August 28th, the people of that city did not think it was the original Tom, thus accounting for a small audience.[48] Only after a report in the *Duluth Daily Tribune* (August 29th) reassured the many music lovers of that city that it was Tom, and described the concert to be a "rare treat," furthering admonishing those "not at the concert to not miss an opportunity to hear his second and final concert that night," did he command a large and enthusiastic audience. Following that concert, the reporter wrote about the varied programme, feeling that the original "March," which was conceived by Tom after he heard the famous Theodore Thomas orchestra perform one of Chopin's marches, was the best number of the evening.

When announcing his September 2nd and 3rd concerts in the *St. Paul Pioneer Press* at First Methodist Church, the reporter said "some may come and some may go but Blind Tom goes on forever." This was followed the next night by a concert in Stillwater, Minnesota, at another Methodist church. On September 13th and 14th, Tom performed at Dyer Hall where it was advertised that "he has not been in Minneapolis for several years, and has been adding to his reputation in the meantime."[49] According to the reviewer:

> The program was long, consisting of more than 20 numbers most of all which were encored . . . the audience was highly entertained, and the imitations were really capital. In the performances of his "Battle of Mannasas," he explained the action of the piece as it progressed, in a resonant voice more often heard in the direction of the movements of the many quadrilles of a dance hall. In Liszt's paraphrase of the Rigoletto quartet, "The Last Hope," and a movement from a Beethoven concerto he displayed considerable native feeling and good execution.

Given what the reviewer viewed as "an artistic rendition of the classical portion of the programme," he expressed an opinion that "more such numbers and less horse play would strengthen his programs." He also challenged the characterization of Tom as an "idiot" and at the "same time as a prodigy" since, in his capacity as a stage performer "he does not show the former trait, and its co-existence with the other function is something of wonderful if true." That he had such large crowds at his concert is further tribute to his reputation given this being the time of the all-important State Fair in Minneapolis and performances of the Keene Theatre company in "The Twelve Temptations" at the Grand Opera House.

Continuing his mid-Western tour, the *Clipper* announced Tom's concert in Elgin, Illinois, October 7th, where he drew a "crowded house and gave an excellent entertainment" followed by performances at Chicago's Madison Street Theatre, October 13-16th, which included four evenings and three matinee concerts. After performing in several other Illinois cities, Tom returned to Chicago on October 28th to perform at the Bethel A.M.E. Church; advertised as the "most renowned Colored pianist living," the reporter for the October 26th *St. Paul (Minnesota) Appeal* credited Bethel's progressive minister, G.W. Gaines for being fortunate in securing him. In an effort to keep finding a "Blind Tom-type successor" a *Cincinnati Enquirer* reporter wrote about a little three-year-old musical wonder visiting their city who was alleged to play over sixty different popular tunes on the piano, promising to be rival of the famous Blind Tom.[50]

During Tom's Illinois concert tour, the many court hearings in regards to the Blind Tom Estate being levied against Mrs. Bethune continued before the referee, with the thirty-fifth hearing taking place on November 7th.[51] Ironically attorney Daniel P. Holland, whose court petition of November 1888 had been responsible for the court-appointed substitute referee to replace Mrs. Bethune's deceased attorney, George H. Forster, had a fatal heart attack on November 27, 1889. An obituary account about his death in the November 28th *New York Times* revealed that the deceased attorney was an Irish immigrant who served for twenty years as a criminal lawyer and state senator in Florida before serving as a Confederate army colonel. After practicing law in Washington after the Civil War, he moved to New York in 1879 where he continued in that profession. Inasmuch as attorney Holland had an obvious antebellum loyalty to the southern cause, it seems an irony that he was the co-attorney who successfully argued the case that took Blind Tom from his former slave owner's jurisdiction in favor of a northerner.

After serving as "Blind Tom's Committee" for two years, Mrs. Bethune seemed now to be regaining some of the money-making momentum from the previous years as she began to schedule exhibitions by him in other parts of the country. Also, more of Tom's compositions were being printed, another money-making profit. His "Imitation of the Sewing Machine," which he dedicated to the wife of his piano teacher (Mrs. Joseph Poznanski), was jointly published by the William A. Pond Company of New York and Chicago Music Company, Chicago.[52] In this programmatic piece, Tom produces an atmosphere of restless agitation requiring a fleet-fingered technique, following the twelve bar introduction, in which he employs a lively, moto perpetuo figure over a sustained solemn choral theme. The contrasting middle section is reminiscent of Mendelssohn's "Spinning Song."

Tom's first two years as the legal ward of Mrs. Bethune coincided with the final years of the 1880s, a time of shifting political change. Benjamin Harrison was inaugurated as the 23rd president of the United States, March 4, 1889, and though with his election the Republican Party remained in control, its narrow majorities in the House of Representatives were such as to allow the opposition party to engage in obstructive tactics. Blacks were so concerned about the possible negative results on them that a delegation of Black Americans had called on the then President-Elect Harrison on January 23rd to urge that "Colored Republicans in the South be given equal recognition with White men belonging to the Party."[53]

Several important American musical events marked the ending of that decade, among which was the November 10, 1888, American debut of Fritz Kreisler, the 13-year-old Viennese violinist, and Hans von Bulow's first of his Beethoven cycle of piano recitals on April 1, 1889, at the New York Broadway Theatre. The American-born pianist-composer Edward MacDowell had returned from his twelve-year sojourn as a teacher-composer in Germany to perform in the world premiere of his "Second Piano Concerto" with the New York Philharmonic Society on March 1889, a success repeated soon after in Boston. In that same month the Metropolitan Opera staged the first complete American performance of Wagner's four-opera cycle "Der Ring des Nibelungen," and Theodore Thomas conducted the first American performance of Tchaikovsky's "Fifth Symphony" at Chickering Hall.

Blacks were also engaged in several musical landmarks during that time. For example, Sissieretta Jones (later known as "Black

Patti"), following her first New York appearance on April 5, 1886 as part of the Bergen Star Concert at Steinway Hall, launched her own career at New York's Wallack Theatre in a private concert; in this concert, representatives from the major metropolitan press were invited, among whom was Mr. Reisen, who recommended her to Henry Abbey, who took her for a West Indian tour with the Tennessee Jubilee Singers. They departed August 2, 1888, and returned January 1889.[54] According to press accounts concerning the tour:

> They opened at the Royal Theatre to an overflow house, which included J.C. Johnson, the Governor. They gave sixty performances in Jamaica and then traveled through the neighboring islands, playing to packed houses. After that they crossed the Isthmus of Panama, stopping at Aspinwall, where they played a week at the celebrated Sara Bernhardt Theatre. They played Panama for two weeks and Mme. Jones was a tremendous success. Nightly the stage was covered with floral tributes presented by the ladies; she also received seven solid gold medals during the tour.[55]

In their May 18, 1888, issue, the *Indianapolis Freeman* reported that: "Madame Jones, prima donna soprano and Louis Brown, baritone, have signed contracts for a short tour of the South." The December 21, 1889, *New York Age* announced that she was "negotiating for a trip to the West Indies and South America, if the terms were agreed on." It was also during this year that Joseph Douglass (grandson of Frederick Douglass), who would later become the first Black violinist to make transcontinental tours, entered the Boston Conservatory.[56]

Continuing their successful concert careers were singers Flora Batson Bergen, Nellie Brown Mitchell and Madam Selika. In addition, the Hyer Sister Company was touring with their musical "Out of Bondage" and their own uniformed band and orchestra.[57] Theodore Drury, the concert baritone, attracted attention when his Drury Colored Opera Company made its debut in Brooklyn, October 10, 1889, presenting operatic scenes, one act from *Il Trovatore* at the Bridge Street Church on December 26th.[58]

Although more press coverage was given to the many Black Minstrel groups, the Astor Place Company of Colored Tragedians opened in 1888 at New York's Cosmopolitan Theatre for a production of "Hamlet" and "Othello." Walter Craig, the legendary violinist who had organized his celebrated orchestra in 1872, began to sponsor chamber music concerts with his Schumann Quintet. According to the November 16, 1889, *New York Age,* the first of these was given at Adelphi Hall "before a brilliant and appreciative audience" adding that:

> The ides of cultivating the popular taste to the proper appreciation of the classic works of the old masters as rendered by competent artists is far from new; but the experiment made by the committee consisting of Messrs. L.A. Gray, H.L. Hopewell, J.W. Dias and W.F. Craig is novel to the constituency it addresses. That the Quintet is capable of efficient and conscientious work was self-evident and they will rank with the best exponents on the American musical stage. . . .

Jubilee groups were still touring the country with much financial and musical success and Blind Boone, who married Eugenia Lange, his childhood companion and sister of his manager in October 1889, was still being advertised as the only musical rival of Blind Tom.[59] Although Blind Boone's concert company featured him in a "challenge format" similar to that of Blind Tom, and several other aspects unique to the Blind Tom exhibitions, the fact that Boone's concert company included other musicians in a variety of mediums left Mrs. Bethune still able to advertise Blind Tom, as "the one and only incomparable" pianist.

Notes

1. Louise C. Barfield. *History of Harris County, Georgia 1827-1961* (Columbus, Georgia: Columbus Office Supply, 1961), p. 443; The *Marvelous Musical Prodigy, Blind Tom* (Baltimore: The Sun Book and Job Printers, 1868), p. 3. In an unsigned article titled "American Slave Beethoven," *Negro* (June, 1945) p. 2, Tom's mother is also reported as having been owned by a farmer, Wiley Jones, at the time of Tom's birth.

2. Inez L. Hunt. *The Story of Blind Tom* (Denver, Colorado: School District No. 11, 1972), p. 4, based on daily records, pictures and anecdotes supplied by Norbonne Robinson, a grandson of General Bethune. According to most sources, Charity Wiggins had been the mother of twenty children which makes it presumable that her other children had either died or had already been sold.

3. *Blind Tom: the Great Negro Pianist* (New York: French and Wheat, 1867).

4. See: *Columbus Enquirer,* June 28, 1858.

5. Southall, Geneva H. *Blind Tom: The Post-Civil War Enslavement of a Black Musical Genius* (Minneapolis: Challenge Productions, Inc., 1979), p.9.

6. *Southern Watchman,* January 28, 1858.

7. Mahan, Katherine. *Showboats To Soft Shoes: A Century Of Music Development In Columbus, Georgia, 1828-1928.* (Columbus, GA.: Columbus Office Supply, 1969), p. 23.

8. *New Albany, Indiana Daily Ledger,* July 27, 1865. Such data was revealed in the Guardianship Trial of Blind Tom.

9. *Cincinnati Daily Commercial,* June 20, 1865.

10. Southall, Geneva H. *Blind Tom . . .* , pp. 40 and 43.

11. J. Thomas Scharf and Thompson Westcott. *History of Philadelphia, 1608-1884, Vol. II* (Philadelphia: L. H. Everts & Co., 1884), p. 1089. See also: Louis C. Medeira's *Annals of Music in Philadelphia and History of the Musical Fund Society,* ed. Philip H. Goepp (Philadelphia: J. B. Lippincott Co., 1896) as a major source for information about the society. It is a compilation of pertinent facts concerning members, musical directors and many of the programs and performers of the society, and written by one of its members from the 1843-44 season to its demise in 1858 who one time served as its secretary.

12. Dale A. Olsen. "Public Concerts in Early America," *Music Educators Journal* (May, 1979), p. 59. According to Olsen, the Musical Fund Hall was erected at a cost of $27,000 with sixty rooms in the lower level, a music library, and suite of dressing rooms.

13. Designed by Napolean la Brun and Gustav Runge, who, as architects, placed a dry well under the main floor to balance the dome on the roof which allegedly contributes to the sound. Also, during the construction, the Academy was allowed to stand roofless for one year to be seasoned.

14. Scarf & Westcott, p. 1084.

15. See: Eileen Southern. "Frank Johnson of Philadelphia and his Promenade Concerts," *Black Perspective in Music* (Spring, 1977), p. 3-29.

16. Gerson, p. 84. Frank Johnson's *Collection of Cottilians* was published by Georg Willig of Philadelphia in 1818.

17. Scarf & Westcott, p. 1092.

18. Gerson, p. 85. According to Gerson, the manuscript of these arrange-
    ments are among the Rush Collection at the Ridgeway Libray in Phila-
    delphia.

19. Odell. *Annals,* Vol. 13, pp. 576 and 595.

20. Mme. Anna Amelia Tutien "The Phenomena of Blind Tom," *Etude*
    (February, 1918), pp. 91-92.

21. *Boston Globe* (November 28, 1887); quoted in *Cleveland Gazette*
    (December 3, 1887).

22. For a more detailed discussion of the career of Sissieretta Jones,
    commonly known as "Black Patti," see: W. E. Daughtry. *Sissieretta
    Jones: A Study of the Negro's Contributions to 19th Century Ameri-
    can Theatrical Life* (Ph.D., Syracuse University, 1968) and Henry T.
    Sampson. *Blacks in Blackface* (Metuchen, New Jersey: Scarecrow
    Press, 1980), pp. 383-388.

23. See: "Frederick Elliot Lewis" James Monroe Trotter. *Music and Some
    Highly Musical People* (Boston: 1878), pp. 180-191.

24. *Boston Daily Globe* (January 7, 1888).

25. Abraham Chasins. *Speaking of Pianists* (New York: Alfred A. Knopf,
    1958), p. 16. According to Roland Gellat, *The Fabulous Phonograph:
    1877-1977* (New York: Collier-Macmillan, 1977), p. 38, Josef Hoffman
    visited the Edison laboratory to inspect the phonograph and make
    the first recording by any recognized artist.

26. *New York Times* (March 28, 1888).

27. *Philadelphia Public Ledger* (March 29, 1888).

28. *Trenton Daily True American* (April 20, 1888).

29. New York Supreme Court "In the Matter of Thomas Wiggins"—
    Thomas F. Byrne, Atty. for the Committee, George H. Forster, Esq. of
    Counsel, filed July 19, 1888.

30. "In the matter of Thomas Wiggins" New York Supreme Court, Inven-
    tory account May 15, 1888.

31. Petition filed, July 21, 1888, of special hearing with John McCrone,
    attorney for Dempsey and George H. Forster for Mrs. Eliza Bethune.

32. "In the Matter of Thomas Wiggins, commonly called Blind Tom"
    Supreme Court, New York County, May 27, 1888.

33. *New York Age* (July 7, 1888).

34. One of the most prolific songwriters of his time and the first Black
    songwriter to reap financial rewards on his music, Gussie Davis pub-
    lished over 300 songs. Besides songs he also wrote musical shows
    and an opera, titled "King Herod." He played with the Bergen Star
    Concerts and also toured with his own Davis Operatic and Planta-
    tion Minstrels during the 1880s. For a compilation of his composi-
    tions and contemporary reviews see: "In Retrospect: Gussie Lord

Davis (1863-1899) Tin Pan Alley Tunesmith" *Black Perspective in Music* (Fall, 1978), pp. 189-230.

35. *American Musician* (August 11, 1888). Among the visitors were a Father Stanislaw, Abbot of St. Meinrads in Indiana, Atty. A. J. Lerche and a Mr. Anthony Spillers, one of Tom's sureties.

36. *New York Age* (September 29, 1888).

37. *Albany Journal* (October 12, 1888).

38. *New York Clipper* (October 12, 1888).

39. *Ibid.* (December 15, 1888).

40. "In the Matter of Thomas Wiggins, commonly called Blind Tom, an idiot" Order and Affidavit directing substitute service, November 28, 1888. A court proceeding with the New York Supreme Court to collect monies owed him had been on or about February 17, 1888 when attorney Forster answered the petition and agreed to have the matter come before a referee.

41. *Cleveland Gazette* (January 19, 1889).

42. *New Orleans Weekly Pelican* (January 19, 1889).

43. See: New York Supreme Court "An Order in the Matter of Thomas Wiggins," noted January 8, 1891, law case filing.

44. Supreme Court (Queen County) in "Louise B. Lynch, Plaintiff, against Albrecht J. Lerche, defendant, January 31, 1893," refers to this as part of historical background for that hearing.

45. *New York Clipper* (June 8, 1889).

46. *Ibid.* (June 15, 1889).

47. *Indianapolis Freeman* (August 31, 1888) on July 14th Edward E. Cooper began publishing this paper as the first Black illustrated news journal.

48. *New York Clipper* (September 14, 1889).

49. *Minneapolis Tribune* (September 13, 1889).

50. *Cincinnati Enquirer* (October 20, 1889).

51. See: "Case of John A. Dempsey against Elise Bethune," New York Supreme Court: General term, 1893.

52. Copies available in the University of Georgia, Athens Special Collections, and at the Library of Congress. Since Oliver Ditson died on December 21, 1888, it was that new publishers of Tom's music were being sought.

53. *Indianapolis Freeman* (February 2, 1889). Those in the delegation were: Bishop W. G. Gaines of Georgia, Bishop B. T. Tanner of Philadelphia and Rev. D. A. Hannah of Washington.

54. W. E. Daughtry, *Sissieretta Jones* (Ph.D. thesis, Syracuse University, 1968), pp. 19-20.

55. Henry T. Sampson. *Blacks in Blackface* (Metuchen, New Jersey: Scarecrow Press, 1980), pp. 384-385.

56. *Huntsville Gazette* (October 7, 1889); *Detroit Plain Dealer* (September 27, 1889).

57. *New York Clipper* (June 20, 1889).

58. *New York Age* (December 21, 1889)

59. Darch, Robert R. "Blind Boone: A Sensational Missourian Forgotten," *Missouri Historical Society Bulletin* (April, 1961), p. 249.

BLIND TOM'S CONCERTS.

PROGRAMME.

Classical Selections.

1. Sonata "Pathétique"...............................*Beethoven*
2.   "   "Pastorale," Opus 28....................   "
3.   "   "Moonlight," 27........................   "
4. Andante...*Mendelssohn*
5. Fugue in A minor....................................*Bach*
6.   "   in G minor...........................   "
7. "Songs without Words".......................*Mendelssohn*
8. "Wedding March".............................   "
9. Concerto in G minor..........................   "
10. Gavotte in G minor................................*Bach*
11. "Funeral March" ....*Chopin*
12. "Moses in Egypt"................................*Rossini*

Piano-Forte Solos.

13. "Trovatore," Chorus, Duet, and Anvil Chorus.........*Verdi*
14. "Lucrezia Borgia," Drinking Song (Fantasia)......*Donizetti*
15. "Lucia di Lammermoor"..........................   "
16. "Cinderella," Non Piu Meste.......................*Rossini*
17. "Sonnambula," Caprice...........................*Bellini*
18. "Norma," Varieties.................................   "
19. "Faust," Tenor Solo, Old Men's Song, and Soldiers'
      Chorus......................................*Gounod*
20. "Le Prophète".................................*Meyerbeer*
21. "Linda"..
22. "Dinora"..................................*Meyerbeer*
23. "Bords du Rhine"...............................
24. "La Montagnarde".............................
25. "Shells of the Ocean".............................
26. "La Fille du Régiment"..........................*Donizetti*

Fantasias and Caprices.

27. Fantasia, " Home, Sweet Home "......................*Thalberg*
28.   "   " Last Rose of Summer "...................   "

29. Fantasia, " Lily Dale," for left hand.................*Thalberg*
30.   "   " Ever of Thee," &c.........................   "
31.   "   " Carnival de Venise ".....................   "
32. Reverie. " Last Hope ".............................*Gottschalk*
33. La Fontaine......................................
34. " Whispering Winds ".............................
35. " Caprice ".....................................*Liszt*
36. Fantasia, " Old Hundredth Psalm "....................
37. " Auld Lang Syne," and " Listen to the Mocking-
       Bird" (Piano-Forte Imitations of the Bird)......*Hoffman*

Marches.

38. March, " Delta Kappa Epsilon "......................*Pease*
39. " Grand March de Concert ".........................*Wallace*
40. " Gen. Ripley's March "..............................
41. " Amazon March "....................................
42. " Masonic Grand March " ....

Imitations.

43. Imitations of the Music-Box.
44.   "   "   Dutch Woman and Hand-Organ.
45.   "   "   Harp.
46.   "   "   Scotch Bagpipes.
47.   "   "   Scotch Fiddler.
48.   "   "   Church Organ.
49.   "   "   Guitar.
50.   "   "   Banjo.
51.   "   "   Douglas's Speech.
52.   "   "   Uncle Charlie.
53. Produces three melodies at the same time.

Descriptive Music.

54. " Cascade "...
55. The Rain Storm................................*Blind Tom*
56. The Battle of Manassas........................... "

Songs.

57. " Rocked in the Cradle of the Deep "..............
58. " Mother, dear Mother, I still think of Thee ".....
59. " The Old Sexton ".................................
60. " The Ivy Green ".................................
61. " Then you'll remember Me "......................

62. " Scenes that are Brightest "....................
63. " When the Swallows homeward fly ".............
64. " Oh! whisper what Thou feelest "...............
65. " My Pretty Jane "...............................
66. " Castles in the Air "...........................
67. " Mary of Argyle "...............................
68. " A Home by the Sea "...........................
69. Byron's " Farewell to Tom Moore "..............

Parlor Selections.

70. Waltz in A flat.....................................*Chopin*
71. Waltz in E flat..................................... "
72. Waltz in D flat..................................... "
73. Tarantelle in A flat.....................*Stephen Heller*
74. " Josephine Mazurka "............................*Heller*
75. " Polonaise ".....................................*Weber*
76. Nuit Blanche............................*Stephen Heller*
77. Spring Dawn Mazurka..................*William Mason*
78. " Monastery Bells "...............................
79. " California Polka "...............................*Herz*
80. " Alboni Waltzes ".............................*Schiff*
81. " L'Esplanade "................................*Hoffman*
82. Anen Polka.......................................

Programme for the evening to be selected from the preceding.

Chapter Two

(1890–1892)

ON JANUARY 11, 1890, Blind Tom performed at the Grand Opera House in Decatur, Illinois, where it was reported he "drew the largest matinee of the season with a small house at night."[1] According to the January 30th *Rock Island Argus,* a concert by Tom in West Brighton the previous evening was a "grand success." It was described as "one of the finest ever given on the North Shore," as "his imitation of various instruments and of a military encounter carried the audience by storm." For his January 31st concert at Harper Theatre, a *Rock Island (Illinois) Banner* reporter wrote: "Some may come and some may go but Blind Tom plays on forever." At that concert a Miss Eva Haas played a difficult selection which was "reproduced by Tom perfectly," and when he performed his own composition the "audience went wild with enthusiasm and delight." Earlier that day he played Gottschalk's "Last Hope" in a private concert for the young ladies at the Rock Island Convent.[2]

Following a month of concerts in Illinois, Tom was taken to Iowa where the *Davenport Democrat* reported that his afternoon and evening concerts on February 1st had delighted both audiences. According to the February 8th *Freeman,* in that concert he appeared before a "large and fashionable audience." On February 26th the *St. Louis (MO) Republican* announced that Blind Tom would begin a one-week concert series that night at Music Hall. When reviewing that performance, the reporter noted that "despite bitter weather, a large audience was present to hear him." On April 5th Tom performed in Detroit, Michigan where he only attracted a "meagre audience."[3] Mrs. Eliza Bethune continued to travel with Tom as he remained in the mid-West, giving concerts in Ohio during the months of May and June. His fall concert tour began in Indiana with *The Clipper* noting that his concerts at Kokomo (September 15th) and Frankfort (September 28th) were to "good audiences" but were less attended than his October 3rd concert in Lafayette, though there was a "good audience" in Evansville on October 18th.[4] Undoubtedly those losses in smaller towns were financially offset by the four concerts in Indianapolis (October 5-8) where, according to the October 6, 1890, *Indianapolis Journal,* Tom's first concert at the English Opera House was given to an "audience much larger than would ordinarily be attracted in as bad a display of weather as there was at the time." While the reporter noted "less antics" by Tom than in his previous concerts to that city, he felt the most comical part was his having adapted the dual role of performer and lecturer since, as lecturer, Tom would describe his own peculiarities, always speaking of himself in the third person. Continuing to describe Tom, the person, the reporter said: "off stage he is simple as a child. He has never been shaved, but always cuts off his beard with scissors. When he has them in his hands he has to be watched, as he makes slashes upon his hair that are not improving to his appearance." The October 18th *Indianapolis Freeman* reported that Tom had "paid a visit to his fellow unfortunates at the Institution for the Blind while there."

Though traveling with Tom, Mrs. Bethune was not removed from her continuing legal problems. On May 22nd the court had appointed Irene Ackerman as Executrix of the late attorney Daniel Holland's Estate, thereby making it possible for her to revive and continue the complaint of the late attorney against Mrs. Bethune for monies still owed. Despite the effort by attorney L.B. Treadwell to the New York County Supreme Court on November 27, 1889, for a dismissal of the charges based on "exception to the findings of fact,"[5] Judge George P. Andrews, following a court hearing on January 9th, ruled against Mrs. Bethune. She was ordered to pay Irene Ackerman or her attorney, John McCrone, the sum of $3,304.75 out of the Blind Tom Estate for previously requested monies owed the deceased and expenses of the proceeding.[6]

Blind Tom's 1890 concerts had taken place in what was to became a landmark year in the country's racial and sectional issues since Mississippi, at its Constitutional Convention that August, began to incorporate disfranchisement provisions in their State Constitution. By imposing a literacy test, and giving White registration officials wide discretionary powers in determining one's ability to read or understand a section of the Constitution (thus allowing loopholes through which White illiterates could pass) and requiring a poll tax which very few, if any Blacks could afford, the states' White supremacists had found a way to legally circumvent the 15th Amendment. Soon after several other southern states would imitate in varied ways disenfranchisement provisions.[7] Aware of the post-Reconstruction resurgence of Negrophobia and following up on T. Thomas Fortune's plan for organizing local and state leagues to address the growing discriminatory problems against Blacks, the National Afro-American League was formally organized on January 25, 1890, in Chicago with 140 delegates from 23 states in attendance; Joseph C. Price, then president of the all-Black Livingston College in Salisbury, North Carolina, was elected president.[8]

Unfortunately the two Republican legislative efforts which would have benefitted Blacks were both defeated. One, by Senator Henry Blair of New Hampshire, would have provided non-discriminatory federal support to public education, and the other, by Representative Henry Cabot Lodge of Massachusetts, would have required federal supervision of all national elections, thereby protecting Blacks from southern efforts to deprive them of their vote. While both bills had passed the House of Representatives with small majorities, they were defeated in the Senate.[9]

Some Whites could probably rationalize their growing need to legally subordinate Blacks by pointing to the negative images of them being reflected in popular culture at that time. Considering that many Black entertainers were part of the "coon song craze" of the 1890s, it is unfortunate that they themselves were aiding in reinforcing the perpetuation of the Black caricature.[10] As Robert Toll, the noted minstrelsy historian, said:

> these syncopated rhythmic lyrics besides continuing the minstrel stereotyping of Blacks as watermelon and chicken-eating mindless fools, emphasized grotesque physical caricatures of big-lipped, pop-eyed black people and added the menacing image of razor-toting violent black men.

Undoubtedly such images offered a subliminal message of Blacks as being intellectually subordinate and potentially dangerous, thus needing control.[11]

To offset the minstrelsy format, Sam T. Jack, a White burlesque theatre owner and manager, produced THE CREOLE SHOW. It opened at New York's London Theatre in September, 1890, making use of popular songs and typical jokes within a non-plantation urban setting, a female announcer and a chorus of sixteen beautiful Black women.[12] Road shows such as "In Old Kentucky," first staged in St. Paul Minnesota in 1892, were one of several shows perpetuating plantation stereotypes during this period. Besides scenes of boys boxing, cock-fighting, and shooting dice, there was an elderly blackfaced Uncle Tom-type character providing banjo accompaniment. Even Blind Boone began to incorporate "plantation songs" in his concert repertory and his two "Concert Caprices" of 1893 were subtitled "Melodies de nègres," reflecting his greater use of Black expressions in both title and rhythmic elements.

Since Mrs. Bethune kept Tom in a non-Black environment, it was not unexpected that his repertory consisted primarily of the virtuoso romanticized style of European composers. It did not, however, mean that the Black community failed to express concerns about what was felt by many to be his retained "neo-servitude exploitative" situation. For example, following their knowledge of Judge Andrew's ruling against Mrs. Bethune, the Black *Cleveland Gazette* published a lengthy article in their paper titled "The Sad Ending" followed by a question subtitle "Of Blind Tom's Eventful Career, Where Is His Money?"[13] Continuing, the reporter said:

> Poor "Blind Tom", the musical genius is drivelling away the remaining months of an eventful life at a private retreat in St. Mark's place. He has been for some time an idiot, and now consumption has set its iron grasp upon his once stout frame and his days are numbered. "Blind Tom" earned in his day something like a half million dollars. Today, he is comparatively a pauper and the wonder is what has become of the fortune he made as he was always in charge of a guardian and never allowed to spend it.

Judge Andrews of the Supreme Court confirmed a report of referee Jerome Buck allowing the estate of Daniel P. Holland $3,000 for services rendered and necessaries furnished the mad musician during the lifetime of Holland. Mrs. Elise Bethune, the Committee, having charge of Tom, vigorously opposed the confirmation of the report. The judge observed that it was sadly apparent that there would be nothing left for the maintenance of the unfortunate pianist after all claims were paid.

Following details concerning the 1887 Court Case which allowed Mrs. Bethune to become Tom's Committee, the writer discussed Tom's physical condition saying:

> Mrs. Bethune had to fight with Mrs. Wiggins and other people for the control of Tom. Soon, however, he broke down in health, became dangerously insane and was placed under restraint. All last summer Tom had delighted audiences in the house adjacent to his retreat at St. Mark's place. He played incessantly upon the piano, guitar and other melodious instruments. He can play no more.

> The wonder is what has become of the money which Bethune was obliged, by mandate of the Court, to deposit for "Tom's maintenance." It was supposed to be twenty-five per cent of the net proceeds of the entertainment's given. That would give him at least $125,000 in his own right. There is none. It is authoritatively stated less than $5,000 in the exchequer. The $3,000 Judgment will make an awful gush in the fund.

The Black *St. Paul (Minnesota) Appeal* in its February 7, 1891, issue also published that article calling Tom's reported insanity a "sad ending of the eventful career of the Great Pianist."

Notwithstanding these publications about Tom's physical incapacities, Blind Tom was then performing in the state of Kansas. The January 21, 1891, *Topeka Daily Capital* announced Tom's engagement at their Opera House on January 26th with the advertisement saying: "Poor Tom shall lead thee-Shakespeare," and its January 25th issue announcing a concert by him at the State Normal School the following Wednesday evening.

In March 1891 Mrs. Bethune took Tom on his first southern tour since becoming his manager. Following appearances in Opelousas and New Iberia, Louisiana, he performed a one-week engagement at New Orleans' St. Charles Theatre. Of his opening night on March 15th, the *Times Picayune* said: "The house did not hold the regular Sunday night crowds, by any means, but considering the threatening weather and the general preference for light drama, the audience was large."[14] His March 21st concert in Baton Rouge was, according to the *Baton Rouge Advertiser*, sponsored by the YMCA of that city. Going next to the state of Mississippi, *The Clipper* announced performances in Natchez (March 23-24); Jackson (March 25-27); Brookhaven (March 28); Hazlehurst (March 31st); Yazoo City (April 6); Greenwood (April 7); Winona (April 8); Oxford (April 11); and Holly Springs (April 12). The Philip Werleins Music Company in New Orleans had shipped a piano for his Winona, Mississippi, concert and according to the April 17th *Winona Times* "many persons from adjoining towns had been present." Such seemed to be a frequent occurrence in that state since the April 2, 1891, *Hazlehurst Capital Signal* mentioned that their town was "honored by a visit from a large delegation from Crystal Springs who had come to attend the Blind Tom concert, arriving around 1 p.m. and spent the evening inspecting the many beauties and attractions of the town and visiting friends." The names of eight ladies, their chaperones and fifteen males were printed. His Brookhaven, Mississippi, concert, under the auspices of their Chess Club, was described as being "a striking illustration of the wonderful way in which God specifically endows certain of his creatures."[15] In Natchez, the parents were informed that their children, through an arrangement with the management, could get excused by their principal for a matinee being held especially for them.

Going next to the state of Tennessee, Tom appeared at the Memphis Theatre (April 14-16) with a reminder that this was his first visit to their city after an absence of nine years. Soon after he performed at the Montgomery, Alabama, Opera House. On May 4th, the *Birmingham Age Herald* advertised Tom's coming as "marking an event in musical history in every town." Returning to Tennessee that summer he opened to a "packed house" at the

Vendome in Nashville on July 20th. The reviewer for the *Nash-ville American* had undoubtedly attended Tom's concerts there during the 1880s since he titled his lengthy article "Same Blind Tom of Yore," adding as a sub-heading "A Little More Obese than Formerly But None the Less Full of Sweet Melodies and Peculiarities."[16] About the performance he wrote:

> A fine audience both in quality and quantity, filled the Vendome last night to hear Blind Tom. The seats were all taken and several hundred people were glad to find standing room. All the upper tier or boxes were full and there were only two empty on the lower tier.

> The audience enjoyed the performance of the blind musician, and the entertainment was a success, as testified by the applause that followed each number. It was the same Blind Tom of former years, fat, black, good-natured and full of melody, with a perfect memory and wonderful powers as an imitator. Tom is little changed in twenty years, save that he is a little more fleshy and that it seems strange to see him on the stage without his former Master and manager Col. Bethune. There was something of deep pathos in the scene the poor blind Negro presented on the stage last night. No one accompanied him before the curtain. He has been previously familiarized with the surroundings and walked about the stage and spoke in words and accents about "Blind Tom" just as his old manager did. He explained what "Tom" was going to do each time and then proceeded to do it.

> He exhibited the same childish delight in his performances as of yore, and his humorous antics amused the audience as much as the rendition of the programme, which he announced throughout.

The reviewer considered Tom's failure to know that he is a Negro a "peculiarity." Continuing with some non-stage activities, the reviewer revealed that:

> Blind Tom spent the entire day yesterday in his room at the Bailey House. From the moment he opened his eyes in the morning until he left the hotel for the theatre he entertained himself in a peculiar way he has of talking aloud when alone. He rarely sat down, and presumably by way of satisfying an instinct for bodily exercise he occasionally danced about the room, poising his bulky body first upon one foot and then upon the other, and now and then bending over the foot board of his bed end putting his great big head hard and rapidly against the mattress.

He then revealed how Tom had astonished many by telling them the date of his previous visits to Nashville since the first concert engagement of 1861 and how he had "pronounced the name distinctly and without the slightest hesitation of those callers who he had just met at the pre concert visitation." According to that paper's July 17th announcement, Tom's concert at the Vendome was sponsored by the Ladies Hermitage Association.

Tom performed in Huntsville, Alabama, on July 25th, returning to Tennessee for concerts in Chattanooga (August 5th), Cleveland (August 7th), Knoxville (August 10th). Tom was booked for performances at Greenville, Morristown, Bristol, Johnson City, Maryville and the other points in Tennessee, returning to Knoxville at McArthur's Music Hall the afternoon of the 18th and at night playing in Logan's Temple. It was reported that he "distinctly" remembered playing a piano at Staubs Theatre on his first visit to that city in 1877 when he "initiated perfectly an original composition played for him by a Prof. Knoke." With such strenuous scheduling it is obvious that Mrs. Eliza Bethune, like previous "owners" gave little attention to the physical pressure being placed on Tom; it may be for this reason that a writer for the *Chattanooga Times* said: "the poor Negro should be retired as he has already more than earned his liberty." Going next to North Carolina, the *Wilmington Morning Star* on September 24th noted that the "north half of the balcony (first gallery) at the Opera House has been reserved for the first of the colored people at the Blind Tom concert on September 28th." After a month of giving concerts in North Carolina, he was taken to South Carolina. Concerts in

Charleston (October 9th) and Columbus (October 19th) were to crowded houses. According to the *Mobile (Alabama) Daily Register,* his concerts there on November 17th drew larger houses than when he last appeared there. Remaining in Alabama for several more weeks, he ended the year with a December 30th concert in Birmingham at the O'Brien Opera House "to poor business."[17]

Notwithstanding evidence of several months of strenuous concert travels through the south, the November 24, 1891, *Freelance, Fredericksburg, Virginia* paper published an article about "Blind Tom's decline" describing him as then "spending the closing days of his life amid the pathetic scenes of an insane asylum." That this was still being circulated in some areas, the *Musical Courier* in its December 30th issue wrote that "the rumors of Blind Tom's mental decline were contradicted by a New York acquaintance of Mrs. Bethune who said the eccentric Negro was traveling and performing with all his old vigor."

When Tom appeared in Louisville, Kentucky, for a four-concert engagement (January 6-8, 1892) receipts were attached to satisfy a judgment obtained for legal services rendered by an attorney upon the occasion of a former visit.[18] When announcing Tom's concerts at Liederkranz Hall in the *Louisville Courier* on January 2nd, it was stated that: "He is like the Niagara Falls or the Mammoth Cave, one of America's quiet wonders, only they last forever and Blind Tom will not." Although the January 16th *Huntsville Gazette* advertised Tom as giving concerts in Florida soon after, he returned to the east, with an appearance in Cincinnati, Ohio, before his March 1st performance at Newburgh, New York's, Academy of Music, Odell reports that Tom appeared on March 26th as part of a benefit concert at the Brooklyn Tabernacle with several other Black artists among whom was a Miss Tillie Janes, advertised as "The Creole Nightengale."[19] It seemed that this vocalist enjoyed a more local prima donna status in Brooklyn than "Black Patti" whose February 24th White House concert followed her critically acclaimed concert tours the previous years (1890 and 1891) in South America and the West Indies. As a recipient of seventeen gold medals from these concerts, when writing about her White House concerts, a *Washington Post* reporter described her as the "medalist of the age."[20]

On February 28th a reporter for the *Black Washington Bee* said Black Patti had created "a sensation among Washington's best society and won a reputation of which she should feel proud, one who is an honor to the colored race!" Still further were reports of her "standing room only" crowds at several other concerts given in the capital. On April 24, 1892, the *New York Times* advertised an historic GRAND AFRICAN JUBILEE at Madison Square Garden that, besides featuring the "Black Patti" and other "Negro entertainment," featured a cakewalk competition as well. In reviewing the concert, which was titled "The Black Patti and the Cake Walk," a *New York Herald* reporter said:

> There was a study in black and white at the Madison Square Garden last night. About three-fourths of the scene, though, was in white. The big garden had been prepared for a rather unique entertainment in which the "Black Patti," heralded as "the greatest singer of her race," a lot of oddities, musical and otherwise, all colored, and Levy's American Band took part.
>
> About five thousand persons were in the Garden at nine o'clock. The boxes were well filled, as were the arena seats, by people whom one would not often see at a cakewalk. Many of the ladies wore dazzling toilets, and evening dress was general among the men.
>
> The last cake walk at the Garden drew a crowd, but was generally regarded as a "fake." Shrewd people believed, however, that there was money in a "high toned" cake walk, with other "colored" attractions thrown in, and the show last night was the result.
>
> After the band, an alleged Alabama quartet, a double quintet of banjos and a really meritorious "Jubilee Chorus," the audience was regaled with a Southern shuffle executed by three colored damsels. Four Negroes then indulged in a "Battle Royal," or "Hit a Head When You See It." This was a free fight with soft gloves and caused amusement.

Concerning Sissieretta Jones, he wrote:

> Madame Sissieretta Jones walked to the platform.
> Her breast was covered with the medals which
> she had received from earlier performances. She
> was smiling broadly and is of immense propor-
> tions, very black, but with pleasing features. She
> was perfectly self-possessed. She began the
> cavatina from Meyerbeer's opera "Robert le
> Diable." After a few notes, the audience saw that
> she had a remarkably strong voice, which she used
> with discretion. Her effort was loudly applauded,
> as was her first encore, the familiar "Way Down
> upon the Swanee River," which she sang in excel-
> lent taste. Recalled again she sang "The Cows are
> in the Clover" very effectively, her upper notes
> being especially sweet. She received an ovation.

According to the reviewer, "buck dancing," a "buzzard lope
dance," more jubilee singing and Levy's band preceded the post-
intermission numbers by Black Patti, among them being the
"Sempre Libera" from Verdi's "La Traviata," followed by the cake
walk which involved about fifty "very earnest and comical contes-
tants." Interestingly, despite her already-earned international fame,
Sissieretta Jones considered this great jubilee with its mammoth
crowds a turning point in her concert career, with the artist quoted
as saying "I woke up famous after singing in Madison Square Garden
and didn't know it."[21] Given the many tours with Levy's Military
Band including the heavily advertised *Pittsburgh Exposition* of
1892 that fall, it is obvious that her assessment had some validity.

Undoubtedly, for several weeks, Blind Tom and Sissieretta
Jones were among the leading musical attractions in New York.
However, when "Black Patti" made a June 15th appearance on a
benefit concert sponsored by the Society of Sons of New York, for
which she received another medal, the June 14 *Montreal* (Canada)
Daily Star was advertising Tom's concerts at Queen Theatre. Be-
fore leaving for Canada, Tom had performed to good crowds in
Newark, New Jersey, and Troy, New York.[22] He returned to the
States by fall, with the *Clipper* announcing concerts in several
places in New Jersey, among them being Englishtown (September

29th); Point Pleasant (September 30th); Toms River (October 1st); Baneget (October 3rd); and Long Branch (October 5th). Odell reports that Tom's October 21st concert in Flushing, New York, where he "delighted an audience of a hundred hearers," at the Baptist church was repeated at the same place on December 6th before a "moderate sized audience."[23]

While many of Blind Tom's concerts were announced throughout the year in the *Clipper* and other local newspapers, many music journals were continuing to publish earlier press releases concerning his removal from the stage. For example: the December 26, 1891, *Freeman* reported "Blind Tom, the great musical prodigy, is said to be dying in a New York insane asylum and that the last of his unique musical entertainments was given at Music Hall in St. Louis." Following a statement in the February 1892 *Musical Messenger* that Blind Tom was "now an inmate of an asylum for mental treatment," J. Jay Watson, a noted New York music teacher, wrote three detailed eye-witness accounts concerning the pianist in that magazine. In the August issue, he told readers about a test he had put Tom through at his musical conservatory during one of the pianist's early New York engagements when he was under the management of his previous slaveowner. Despite Tom's inability to fully perform to his satisfaction some accompaniments to his own violin performance of Delphin Alard's "Fantasie," Watson admitted that of "all the musical prodigies whom I have yet met (and they are not few) Blind Tom has certainly disappointed me the least"; he admitted that he and those other musical persons present at the examination were "satisfied that Tom's wonderful musical ability consisted in the fact of his being able to catch any piece readily that had a pleasing, simple melody, but strange chord progressions he must hear several times in order to be able to follow them."

In the September issue, J. Jay Watson wrote about his second testing of Blind Tom the following day, which took place at the home of Mr. John Bethune. At that time he was utilizing a musical method to determine "if indeed, Tom was the idiot which the dear public had been led to believe." According to him:

> In order to prove that Tom was possessed of ordinary common sense, I asked him if he knew what key in flats was synonymous to another key in

sharps. He promptly answered, "No." I then played a piece upon the piano in the key of C Major, at the same time informing Tom that by making the signature twelve sharps and playing precisely as I did before, there would be no difference in the music. I then explained to him that the key of D double flat (twelve flats), was synonymous to the keys which I had just used, when played or sung, although appearing different on paper. Tom seemed to comprehend this explanation perfectly, and when told that there was a key formed by the use of flats precisely like each key formed by the use of sharps, and vice versa, I found that he soon had no difficulty whatever in putting this theory into practice upon the piano in any key that I mentioned. This at once decided to all present that Tom was something more than a "poor idiot," as idiots do little reasoning.

Besides offering his own assessment, Watson gave the following by one of Tom's instrumental teachers:

Tom also played some upon the violin, cornet, guitar and flute. Mr. T.G. Withers, the eminent flutist of New York City, who gave Tom flute lessons for some time, and with whom I had a conversation upon his subject under consideration agreed with me, that Tom was far removed from an idiot.

Whenever Tom visited New York City he also studied the piano very diligently with Prof. Poznanski.

In his third paper, published in the October issue, Watson told of having John N. Pattison, a then well-known American pianist, test Tom. Taking place at Watson's music conservatory, Tom was requested to play "Yankee Doodle" with his right hand, "The Star Spangled Banner" with the left, and sing George Root's "Tramp, Tramp, Tramp, the Boys Are Marching," to which:

Tom rolled up his almost sightless eyes, and with
much dignity straightened himself up well upon
the piano stool, performing the allotted task with
apparent ease. I now adopted new tactics by striking a mixture of keys upon the piano to the number of a dozen or more, "hap hazard," holding
them firmly down. I requested Tom to name them.
Wonderful as it may seem, Tom did name each
one of these keys correctly and as fast as his
tongue could articulate.

Watson ended the three-part series with the following testimonial from the celebrated violinist, Ole Bull, saying:

While visiting the celebrated violinist, Ole Bull,
at his home in Norway, I took occasion to question him as to his opinion of Tom's musical powers. Ole Bull, who had heard Tom at various times,
said to me that he thought the boy possessed great
musical feeling, that he was a marvelous freak of
nature, and that no other person living could ac-
complish Tom's peculiar musical feats and imitations. He considered Tom's organ of imitation in
a variety of ways absolutely astounding, especially
those of a car engine, a fiddler, a music box, stump
speeches after the style of great orators, etc. Ole
Bull thought that Tom's wondrous powers of imitation was the only correct hypothesis by which
we can draw conclusions.

> "Admit this as a fact; at once all's clear,
> Which else must prove a solveless riddle
> here."

Tom is among the stark miracles that have jumped
fully tuned upon the earth at odd times ever since
the days of Tubal Cain, and as such is worth
hearing.

Undoubtedly the writer had sent these recollections to the *Messenger* before the pianist performed his New York concerts that fall since his reminiscences gave no indication that he had attended or heard about those concerts.

On April 14, 1892, John McCrone, as attorney for Irene Ackerman, had filed another suit against Mrs. Bethune in the New York State Supreme Court, charging her with failure to pay the "said sum of $3,304.75 so directed by said Order of January, 1891, nor any part thereof."[24] In his opinion, such payment was possible since "said Idiot was and is a person possessed of a wonderful musical ability to earn money as a musician, having commanded in time prior to the appointment of said Committee sums amounting to from $10,000 to $20,000 per year" and following her control, she "commenced to use him uninterruptedly in giving public musical concerts in different places throughout the country, traveling from place to place, retaining the possession of said Idiot and deriving large sums of money as the proceeds and profits of his said abilities and services."[25] McCrone further charged that Mrs. Bethune was "aware of a claim secured by lien upon real estate against the Estate of her former husband, John G. Bethune, in the state of Kentucky for $30,000 applicable to the indebtedness and "could have been collected by her with due diligence." In addition he alleged that:

> said Defendant has been and remained within the State of New York and the jurisdiction of this Court; that her residence in this city which was at No. 7 St. Marks Place was abandoned by her long prior to said January 9th, 1891, and that she has since had no office or place of residence therein and plaintiff charges that her said absence and residence outside the State has been and is with the view and intent to enable her to evade the process and Orders of this Court, and prevent an accounting and to defeat efforts to secure the proper performance by her of her duties as committee.

Because of his accusations, attorney McCrone asked the Court to have Mrs. Bethune "render an account of the particulars of

Tom's musical exhibitions, giving information about sums received and paid out on account of each such exhibition so the Court can determine whether she has faithfully discharged her duties as Committee by the use of the abilities and services of said idiot" and that "judgment be made and for costs."

On November 16, 1892, Mrs. Bethune, through her attorney, Thomas F. Byrne, filed a response "To the Honorable, the Supreme Court, New York County," saying that "beyond wearing apparel valued at $20 and, which have long since been worn out, no property or estate of Tom has come into her possession," and that the "only other matter alleged to belong to Tom is a Judgment against the John G. Bethune Estate which liens none of the Attorneys have taken any step to collect on the ground that they are alleged to be insolvent, and following her own investigation feels it to be a waste of time and money to attempt collection."[26] Responding further, she said:

> That your Committee has furnished the said Idiot with attendance, care, and comfort, and has supplied a piano upon which he delights to play, and your Committee with a view of employing her own time and abilities, and to earn wherewith to continue to furnish the said Idiot with the attendance, care and comfort above referred to, has since he came into her custody given concerts or musical entertainments in connection with others and otherwise, and at such times has generally permitted the said Idiot to appear before audiences and perform upon the piano, and your Committee found the same on occasions remunerative and on other occasions not, but on the whole sufficiently remunerative to induce your Committee to continue so to do, and in furnishing the said Idiot with change of air and places and healthful exercise, greatly conducive to the good health and temper of the Idiot. That your Committee refers to the foregoing, because of the fact that numerous person claiming to have rendered services in connection with the appointment of your Committee, contend that it is the duty of your Committee to make contracts for the exhibition of the

said Idiot for the purpose of creating an estate
wherewith the said claims shall be met. But your
Committee has received no directions from the
Court except that contained in the order appoint-
ing your Committee, concerning the care and custody of the person and property of the Idiot.

By then, Mrs. Bethune, though not using his name, was married to attorney Albrecht J. Lerche, who represented her in the
successful 1887 custody suit against General Bethune. Such information was brought out by attorney Treadwell in the New York
Supreme Court hearing of his April 1892 suit against Lerche for
monies owed for professional services, one being his successful
defense of Mrs. Bethune in the Jack Dempsey, July 21, 1888, salary
dispute. Treadwell, who had shared a law office with Lerche, told
the Court he "appeared at thirty-five hearings before the Refereee
concerning Blind Tom, each taking half a day to an entire day,
appeared at twelve other appointments where hearings were postponed, and prepared many other Affidavits for Appeals in Lerche's
behalf when decisions were rendered against him. When asking
for proof regarding his statements about the Albrecht Lerche-Elisa
Bethune marital status, Treadwell replied: "I was told by the priest
who married them, and he pointed them out to me," and it was
his feeling that "the marriage took place before the June 9, 1890
Judgement against Mrs. Bethune for $3,304 dollars."

During cross-examination, Lerche admitted to being Mrs.
Bethune's husband but said it was not before all the legal suits,
thereby he had "never promised to pay an Attorney for her." As to
the $3,304 judgement, Lerche said "I never agreed to be respon-
sible for that Suit in any manner, that was brought against a Committee, and it was a judgement by default against the idiot." In his
September 13, 1892, response, Lerche denied the allegations, saying "the plaintiff (Treadwell) was fully paid the value of any services rendered and since certain of said services were so care-
lessly and negligently performed as to be worthless, and damaged
him, as defendant, in an amount beyond the value of any services
by him performed." When questioned about his legal status in the
profession, Lerche admitted to being a "Solicitor in the United
States Court and not an ordinary lawyer" which is why he gave
cases to Treadwell. Under further questioning he said he was in
Washington when being admitted to the Bar in Albany, New York,

but had never taken the oath and signed the roll there. However, he had signed his name to cases in the United States Supreme Court in the District of Columbia and practiced law in the state of Kentucky. As a further explanation about his failure to practice law in the state of New York, Lerche acknowledged that he did not practice in those states where he took retainers.

Since Treadwell at that time was practicing in the state of New Jersey, he had appointed Louise B. Lynch to represent him in his claim which he said was "for his services as Lerche's attorney and counselor from December 20, 1888 through January 1, 1892; the amount requested was $1,870 with interest." Undoubtedly, many of the decisions regarding the Blind Tom musical exhibitions and his personal well-being were being influenced by Albrecht Lerche. After five years as Tom's Committee, Mrs. Bethune had obviously strengthened her grasp on his affairs; not only were her money-earning capabilities increased through the return of Tom's musical exhibitions in the southern states that year, but by marrying her attorney she had attained a personal managerial partner with legal expertise.

Notes

1. *New York Clipper* (January 25, 1890).

2. *Rock Island Argus* (February 1, 1890); *Davenport Iowa Times* (February 1, 1890).

3. *American Musician* (April 2, 1890).

4. *New York Clipper* (September 27, October 11, October 18, 1890).

5. See: Supreme Court New York County (December 5, 1890) "In the matter of Thomas Wiggins commonly called Blind Tom, an Idiot" November 27, 1890.

6. Ibid. (January 9, 1891).

7. See: William Alexander Mabry. "Disfranchisement of the Negro in Mississippi," *Journal of Southern History* (1938), 318-333 and Vernon L. Wharton. *The Negro in Mississippi, 1865-1890* (University of North Carolina, 1947), 199-215. Of the 133 delegates, Isiah Montgomery was the only Black. A wealthy conservative planter-businessman who founded the all-Black town of Mount Bayou, Mississippi, he was the only one to list himself as a Republican who met in the historic Mississippi Constitutional Convention of 1890 to rewrite the 1868 Reconstruction Constitution. Shock and indignation followed his accommodation on the suffrage question which he rationalized by implying the literacy and property restrictions would encourage Blacks to obtain knowledge and regain their franchise on their own.

8. James H. Dorman. "Shaping the popular image of Post-Reconstruction American Blacks: the "Coon Song" Phenomenon of the Gilded Age" *American Quarterly* (December, 1988), 450-471.

9. Robert Toll. *On With the Show* (New York: Oxford University Press, 1976), 118.

10. Henry T. Sampson. *Blacks in Blackface: A Source Book on Early Black Musical Shows* (Metuchen, N.J.: Scarecrow Press, Inc., 1980), 6-7.

11. *Cleveland Gazette* (January 24, 1891).

12. *Times Picayne* (March 16, 1891).

13. *Brookhaven Leader* (April 2, 1891).

14. *Nashville American* (July 22, 1891).

15. *New York Clipper* (January 16, 1892).

16. *New York Dramatic News* (January 23, 1892).

17. Odell's *Annals* (vol. 15, pp. 38, 371, 517).

18. See: Willa E. Doughtry. *Sissieretta Jones: A Study of the Negro's Contribution to Nineteenth Century American Concert and Theatrical Life* (Ph.D., Syracuse University, 1968).

19. *New York Clipper* (May 27 and June 10, 1892).

20. Odell's *Annals*, vol. 15, p. 541.

21. See: Irene Ackerman against Elise Bethune, Supreme Court of the State of New York, New York County, April 14, 1892.

22. "In the matter of Thomas Wiggins," Supreme Court, New York County (November 16, 1892).

23. See: New York Supreme Court-General Term-Second Department "Louise B. Lynch against Albrecht J. Lerche," Case on Appeal (January 7, 1893).

24. The bill was originally $1,975, with $105.00 paid, therefore a balance of $1,870 remained. Exhibit A offered evidence of Treadwell's claim and bill of particulars.

25. "In the matter of Thomas Wiggins," Supreme Court, New York County (November 16, 1892).

26. See: New York Supreme Court-General Term-Second Department "Louise B. Lynch against Albrecht J. Lerche," Case on Appeal (January 7, 1893).

Chapter Three

(1893–1894)

ON JANUARY 7, 1893, a judgement was entered against Albrecht Lerche in the New York Supreme Court. Still serving as the representative of L.B. Treadwell was Louise B. Lynch, as plaintiff, who continued her effort to collect $1,870 with interest from Lerche as decided in the Queen County Trial of April 5, 1892. In the Bills of Particulars titled "Case of John A. Dempsy against Elise Bethune," Louise Lynch lists twenty-one services to the then defendant from December 20, 1888, to February 25, 1890. In "The Matter of Thomas Wiggins, an Idiot," she maintains that thirty-five hearings before the referee were among services rendered from March 13, 1889, to April 17, 1891. Other professional services were delivered for him as Executor of a Maragareth Eigl in Surrogate Court, New York County and a taxation case for a Phoebe A. Henderson in the Kings County Supreme Court.[1]

In the September 13, 1892, trial Albrecht Lerche denied the allegations, saying:

> I. L.B. Treadwell, the Plaintiff's alleged assignor, was fully paid the value of any services rendered to defendant, and defendant further alleges that certain said services were so carelessly and negligently performed as to be worthless to the defendant, and damaged this defendant in an amount beyond the value of any services by him performed.

II. He has not sufficient knowledge or information to form a belief as to the allegations contained in the paragraph of said complaint
marked three.

III. The defendant answering the complaint and
by way of counterclaim alleges that the
plaintiff's alleged assignor at the time in the
complaint set forth so negligently and care-
lessly performed certain legal services by him
agreed to be diligently performed, that this
defendant suffered loss and damage to the
amount and for which the defendant demands
judgement in the sum of five hundred dollars.

Still further, he desired the costs of action.

At a Circuit Court and special term hearing before the Supreme Court at the Long Island City, Queen's County Court, January 4, 1893, Justice Charles F. Brown ordered that Lerche's "Motion for a new Trial be denied." The Court records filed on January 7th noted that:

Hon. Charles F. Brown and a jury, and the jury
having found a verdict for said plaintiff, and against
said defendant therein, for one thousand dollars
damages, and the said verdict having been entered
in the minutes of the said Court; not, on motion
of L.B. Treadwell, plaintiff's attorney, it is hereby
adjudged that the said plaintiff do recover of the
said defendant the sum of one thousand dollars
found by said Jury, together with $130.33 for
plaintiff's costs and disbursements, as adjusted in
said action, amounting in all to $1,130.00, and
have execution therefore.

> J.G. Sutphen
> Clerk

Treadwell testified that before bringing suit and hiring Louise
Lynch as his attorney, Albrecht Lerche "frequently promised and

agreed to pay but never did so except to pay the sum of $105" thus assuring the Court that Lerche was "cognizant of all services rendered after Consultation and Advice with him." During Treadwell's cross-examination, Lerche said that the $105 came from the Committee in the "Blind Tom Case" which Treadwell knew, as it represented the equal division of the $210 received and agreed to in their then partner relationship as lawyers. Still further, were some receipts in an envelope signed by Treadwell. Adding that although he had only appeared once before the referee during Blind Tom's case, Treadwell was himself "the attorney responsible for the Case." The proceedings ended with Lerche still maintaining that he was not married to Mrs. Elise Bethune before the many suits regarding "Blind Tom" and "never promised to pay an attorney for his wife, who he married later, so there could be no Contract on that issue."

Following more testimony (January 4th) and the Court rendering a verdict in favor of Treadwell for the sum of $1,000, Lerche's attorney moved for a new trial which was denied. Also denied was the motion that "the Verdict was excessive, and contrary to the weight of evidence."

On February 7th, Treadwell, in a sworn deposition in the Queens County Court, said that Albrecht Lerche "willfully and corruptly committed perjury" in the trial since, despite his denial, "Elise Bethune was already his wife on the 20th day of December, and continued to be up to the 17th day April, 1891, during the pending of two certain Actions in the New York State Supreme Court involving her."[2] In a March 13th affidavit, attorney Lerche brought an action against Treadwell in the New York State Supreme Court to "recover damage in the sum of ten-thousand dollars for malicious prosecution and false imprisonment on February 13th."[3] Saying that Treadwell had "willfully intended to injure his good name and reputation in an appearance before Daniel Noble, Justice of the Peace of Long Island City and without sufficient or probable Cause charged him with perjury with a Warrant issued for his arrest."

Following an examination of the facts on February 27th, wherein the judge declared there was "sufficient and probable Cause to believe him guilty," Lerche said he "was imprisoned in one of the station houses in Long Island for two days wherein there was no provisions for food or proper care until a March 1st proceeding before Justice Pratt of the State Supreme Court. It was that judge who "vacated and set aside the Warrant of the Justice of the Peace since no sufficient or a probable Cause was shown for the Arrest." For this reason, Lerche, in his affidavit, was bringing suit against Treadwell, saying:

> That the said charge of perjury and the arrest thereunder were extensively published in several newspapers among them being *The Brooklyn Free Press, The New York Daily News, The New York Evening Sun, The Brooklyn Citizens*, and several other papers as this deponent verily believes through the procurement of the defendant Leman B. Treadwell.

> That said Leman B. Treadwell, the defendant, herein, is a non-resident of the state of New York, and resides in the city of Rahway, County of Huron, State of New Jersey as appears by said affidavit hereto annexed.

> That while deponent was falsely imprisoned as aforesaid he contracted a severe cold from which time he has been and still is acutely suffering, and for which illness he is, and has been under medical treatment.

> That by reason of the premises this deponent has suffered a great distress of body and mind and has been injured in his good name and reputation and has paid out large sums of money in procuring his release from imprisonment to his damage in the sum of ten thousand dollars ($10,000).

> The deponent prays that the defendant be arrested and dealt with according to law.

On March 14th, Lerche received the following favorable response to his March 8th application to the Supreme Court Queen's

County "Undertaking on Order of Arrest" against Leman B.
Treadwell under the Code of Civil Procedure No. 559:

Ironically, during the same month Mrs. Elise Bethune (his wife)
as "Blind Tom's Committee" was also involved in "An Action for
Accounting" for the $3,304.75 still due Irene Ackerman as Execu-
tor of the last Will and Testament of Daniel P. Holland against the
Blind Tom Estate. Although Court-directed to pay on January 9,
1891, Mrs. Bethune, according to the deposition, had not paid any
part of the monies. Such failure to pay was unacceptable, since,
as the deposition noted, in May 1888, Mrs. Bethune filed an account, saying that "she had not net proceeds of concerts in her
hands amounting to $1,076.69; that the use of the abilities and
services of the idiot in giving musical concerts was reasonably
worth the value of $10,000 a year as a net sum." Given this,
attorney Ackerman, as plaintiff, was asking that Mrs. Bethune, as
defendant:

> State and render an account of her proceedings
> as committee, setting forth the particulars as to
> her use of the idiot in giving musical exhibitions,

and the times and places as to each such exhibition by her, with the sums received and paid out
on account of each such exhibition; that she be
chargeable with the sums which are the reasonable value of the services and abilities of said idiot
in giving musical exhibitions during the time she
has used his said abilities as aforesaid; that she
be held accountable and chargeable with the
amount of the judgement demanded in favor of
the idiot's estate; and that it be determined
whether she had faithfully discharged her duties
as committee by the use by her of the abilities
and services of said idiot as aforesaid, and that
she be directed to pay to plaintiff from the property of the idiot's estate in her hands the amount
of the judgement in favor of the plaintiff, as aforesaid; and that on her failure or neglect to personally attend in this action, it be then found or determined by such an accounting cannot be had.

Because this complaint was not part of the original "Daniel Holland vs. Elise Bethune" 1888 hearing, Justice Edward Patterson
dismissed the complaint. In his written judgement on June 30th,
he maintained that:

In all Cases affecting committees of incompetent
persons, the court being really the custodian of
the property of such persons, and the committee
being merely the hand of the court, a primary
consideration is the comfortable and reasonable
support of the incompetent person; and there is
nothing in this case whatever to show that any
moneys realized by Mrs. Bethune as the committee are more than sufficient to create a fund, the
interest of which would support the idiot and his
mother during their lives; and under well-known
principles it would be improper to direct, in a suit
framed as this is and with merely such allegations
as are now made, the application of any of those
moneys to the payment of any debts whatever of

the incompetent person.

Still further he stated, "since Blind Tom (an idiot) was without property or estate," in his opinion, Mrs. Bethune had:

> merely utilized his services in concerts given by her at her own expense and at her own risk, and his services and his peculiar musical talents have been used. It does not appear that it was altogether for her own emolument, but it may have been for the purpose of creating a fund to sustain him and those dependent upon him, and to afford them a support, which certainly the committee was not bound to give from her own resources simply because she maintained the relation of committee to him.

When filing his June 30th judgement, Judge Patterson ruled that "Mrs. Bethune, as Committee was not and is not required to spend any moneys to attempt the collection of the Nov. 1, 1887 Judgement in the United States Circuit Court for the East District of Virginia Decision of $7,500 against James N. Bethune (Blind Tom's former owner), thereby no accounting from her since being appointed Tom's Committee was required." He felt that: "the exhibition of Blind Tom, when conducted with proper regard to his comfort was not in conflict with the duties required from the committee by law"—one fact being that:

> the said Elise Bethune, at her own expense, furnished a professor of music to play upon a pianoforte and has, at her own expense furnished a pianoforte, that the idiot might hear and reproduce select music on such instrument; and the said Elise Bethune, has at her own expense and risk given concerts at which the said idiot assisted, playing upon the piano musical selections so heard by him.

While dismissing the complaint in Mrs. Bethune's favor, the judge said his decision was "in no way to operate to the prejudice of Irene Ackerman's effort to secure the unsatisfied claim of January 9, 1891 for $3,304.75 against Mrs. Bethune."

Undoubtedly, when rendering his decision on these factors, Judge Peterson had seemingly failed to take into account that the main source of Mrs. Bethune's income was derived from the earnings she received for exhibiting Blind Tom. And despite his own statements about her hiring a "musical professor" for Tom, he continued to describe him as an "Idiot" though being one would be contrary to any notion of having the capabilities of being taught.

Since the March 11th *New York Clipper* reported that "Blind Tom had a slim house" at his March 1st Newbury, New York Academy of Music concert, it might be assumed that these numerous litigations had affected Mrs. Bethune and attorney Lerche's full-time managerial activities. Other competition would have come from the many public and private musical events surrounding the March 4th inauguration of Grover Cleveland as the twenty-first president of the United States. Not only was Cleveland the first Democrat elected president after the Civil War, but he was the only one to serve a second term after having been defeated for re-election at the end of his first term.[4] Some New Yorkers may have even attended the many festivities in the nation's capital where "Black Patti" and Joseph Douglass appeared as major musical attractions on the March 5th "Grand Military Concert" sponsored by the United States Marine Band with Jules Levy, the famous cornetist at the Albaugh Grand Opera House. According to the *Washington Post,* "the boxes and body of the house were divided about equally between the races, while the gallery was filled with colored people." Describing "Black Patti" as "the pet and pride of the colored element," the writer conceded that "even the most arrogant Caucasian was obliged to admit that she sang like an angel, albeit a black one."[5] Joseph Douglass, a violinist, was likewise applauded for his performance of a fantasie of an air from "Il Trovatore," and Ovide Musin's "Mazurka de Concert."

The March 27, 1893, *Brooklyn Daily Eagle* advertised that Blind Tom and twenty other volunteers would give a benefit concert for the Brooklyn Tabernacle church fund the following night. However, according the March 29th issue, although the concert drew a "standing room only enthusiastic crowd" the "only important and disappointing change in the program was the non-arrival of Blind Tom, whose place was filled by Luke Pulley, a colored pianist, who played several selections blindfolded." Since each of the twenty performers were, according to the advertisement, limited to only one number with all proceeds going to the church, Tom's owners might have decided such an appearance was not in their best financial interest.

On May 21st, Tom performed to a fair-sized audience in Newark, New Jersey's, Miners Theatre where his "Imitation of a Railroad Train" excited musical people in the same wonderful manner as in the past.[6] According to the May 11th *New York Dramatic News,* Tom was to start a short tour through the state, then fill an engagement in New York City. The July 1st *Dramatic News* reported that Tom did "fairly well" in his June 3rd and 4th concerts in Troy, New York, followed by successful engagement in Waterbury, New York's, Burton Opera House (June 24th).[7]

From May 1st to October 30th, the country was involved in the historic World's Columbian Exposition at Chicago's Jackson Park, its purpose to celebrate the four-hundredth anniversary of Christopher Columbus's discovery of the New World, of which the United States was only a part. Because of the 150 white classical buildings, it was dubbed the "white city," with thirty buildings erected by states and territorial governments.[8] There were, according to historians, forty-six foreign nations and nearly all American states as official participants with the Duke of Veragua, a lineal descendant of Columbus, in attendance. This exposition became a late-nineteenth-century symbol of American technology with featured displays by General Electric and Standard Oil. Also introduced was the world's first amusement area, the Midway Plaisance. Throughout there was an emphasis on integrating agriculture with industry, the Agriculture Building given equal prominence with Manufacturers. As noted by Justus D. Doennecke "rarely had large masses of machinery been placed in so aesthetic an environment since practically every exhibit hall was surrounded by exotic plants and faced with the bodies of reflecting waters or the wooded island."[9] Besides external sculpture, most buildings were internally decorated by sculpture and murals. Though not fully integrated into the celebrative scheme, music enhanced the fairgoers' experience of the exposition. In addition to the music and festival halls, were the ornately decorated bandstands with temporary musical facilities arranged throughout the exposition from time to time.

Under the musical leadership of Theodore Thomas, the Bureau of Music planned for a continuous scheduling of serious and light concerts.[10] A permanent exhibition orchestra performed symphonic recitals under Thomas' direction, choral presentation were under the direction of William L. Tomlin (Apollo Club choral leader) and popular band music performed at the bandstands located throughout the fairgrounds. Although the twice-weekly symphonic concerts required admission, the daily noontime popular music recitals were free of charge, with the fifty-piece Sousa band favored. Several military bands from different European countries also performed. The *Philadelphia Public Ledger* of March 31, 1893, advertised that German, Swedish and Welsh singing societies were part of the musical events with twelve children's concerts by Sunday school and public school groups and especially organized children's choruses; chamber music and organ recitals were frequently offered with local Chicago musicians employed for various private functions being held throughout the city. With the onslaught of the 1893 recession, and fearing a deficit, fair directors in an effort to save money decided to terminate the six-month contract of the Exposition Orchestra two months before the fair ended since only one-fourth of the fairgoers were attending these classical concerts. On August 12th, Theodore Thomas resigned.[11] A partially reformed orchestra under the direction of Max Bendix presented twenty-nine light music concerts for the remainder of the fair. Ironically, as Sandy Mazzola noted, "although the fair officials disbanded the Exposition Orchestra, they were willing to subsidize more admission-free band concerts as their showcase to the world."[12]

Music was also on the verge of an American-consciousness against the still prevailing dominance of Germanic and Austrian influences. It was in the year of the exposition that Antonin Dvorak, the Bohemian nationalist composer-director of the National Conservatory in New York, composed his *New World Symphony*, a work that incorporated native folk songs. Such was the result of his hearing the singing of Negro spirituals by Harry T. Burleigh, one of the conservatory's Black students, that fascinated Dvorak, leading him to advocate that the melodic and rhythmic characteristic of ex-slave songs should become the foundation for an American school of composition.[13] When writing about this in 1918, Burleigh said:

It was my privilege to sing repeatedly some of the old plantation songs for him at his house, and one in particular, "Swing Low, Sweet Chariot", greatly pleased him, and part of this old "spiritual" will be found in the 2nd theme of the first movement of the Symphony in E minor, first given out by the flute. The similarity is so evident that it doesn't even need to be heard; the eye can see it. Dvorak saturated himself with the spirit of these old tunes and then invented his own themes.

Among the international entertainments at the Midway Plaisance was a Dahomean village with sixty "native warriors," who entertained all day with drumming and chants. In the August 20, 1893, *New York Tribune*, a long article about the "Songs and Dances of the Dahomeans" appeared under the "Folk Music in Chicago" section, where the relationship between their music and dances and those of Black Americans was brought out. Fairgoers could also hear Black polyrhythmic and syncopated improvisational sounds from those many Black itinerant musicians who provided entertainment on the outskirts of the fairgrounds. According to Terri Waldo, "Scott Joplin (later dubbed King of Ragtime) had assembled a small band, consisting of cornet (which he played), clarinet, tuba and baritone horn" for such gatherings and they were also entertained by his piano-playing in the city's sporting district.[14]

This interest in their music did not deter Black leaders or the members of the Afro-American Press Association from protesting the fair's discriminatory practices. Not only were there no Blacks represented on the fair's planning committees and a scarcity of positive racial exhibits, but they also faced discrimination in employment.[15] To offset criticism, Exposition managers announced a "Colored Jubilee Day" for August 25th to celebrate the progress of the Negro. Although Frederick Douglass was appointed as Haitian Commissioner by the Haitian government (dedicating their pavilion January 2, 1893), he and the noted anti-lynching crusader, Ida B. Wells, through the Afro-American press, asked Blacks to "contribute five-thousand dollars toward the printing of the booklet, *The Reason Why the Colored American Is Not in the World's Columbian Exposition*," which some editors did not support, feeling that "the monies requested could be used more effectively for racial uplift." In Douglass' opinion, "The Dahomean village showed Africans in 'barbaric rites' and acting like monkies."[16] He did, however, deliver the principal address at the fair's "Colored Jubilee Day" where he castigated exposition officials about their exclusion of Blacks in a speech titled "The Race Problem in America." Paul Lawrence Dunbar, then a rising young poet, recited his poem "The Colored American" and tenor Sidney Woodward, baritone Harry T. Burleigh and mezzo Desseria Plato sang. The Fisk Jubilee Singers did several Negro spirituals, and Joseph Douglass performed on the violin.

Selections were given from Will Marion Cook's opera "Uncle Tom's Cabin." According to the February 12, 1893, *New York World*, the then nineteen-year-old violinist-composer, following his return from studies in Berlin, had written this work in opposition to the omission of Blacks in the World's Fair since "it occurred to him that there was more eagerness to hear the Negro in music than in any other line." Though advertised to sing the leading role, Sissieretta Jones (Black Patti) failed to appear "owing to some misunderstanding among local managers to the Colored American Day."[17] According to the August 26th *Dramatic News*, she was performing in Saratoga Springs with a noted orchestra. A few days after his participation in the program, Frederick Douglass relinquished his post as Commissioner for Haiti, a position he held for eight months. To show their appreciation for his work in their behalf, Haiti's President Hyppolite sent him a large size photograph of himself be-starred and be-ribboned in presidential attire.[18]

Given the long-held practice of Tom's owner to separate him from the Black community, it is not surprising that he was not among those musical celebrities at the fair's "Colored Jubilee Day." Still further, was the fact that on September 2nd an appeal hearing with Louise B. Lynch, as plaintiff, against Albrecht Lerche was held in the Queen County Supreme Court challenging the January 7th decision concerning monies still owed for services rendered in connection with Blind Tom. On December 1st, the three Justices (Hons. Joseph F. Bernard, Jackson O. Dykman, and Calvin E. Pratt):

ORDERED AND ADJUDGED: that the said judgement and order denying a new trial be and the same is hereby affirmed with costs to said plaintiff and respondent and that the sum of one hundred and fourteen dollars costs as duly taxed herein and that plaintiff have execution therefore.

While the request for a new trial was denied, the decision favored attorney Lynch in her monetary complaint against Lerche.

According to the January 13, 1894, *Dramatic News*, Tom "drew two large and well-pleased audiences in Cumberland, Maryland's Academy of Music on Christmas Day." On December 27th, the following appeared in the *New York World*:

BLIND TOM'S EARNINGS

Mrs. Ackerman Says She Can Show Where They Have Been Invested by Mrs. Bethune.

Mrs. Irene Ackerman of Washington, as executrix of the estate of Daniel P. Holland, made a motion on yesterday before Judge Traux, of the Supreme Court, for an Order requiring Mrs. Elise Bethune of East Twenty-first Street, show cause why she should not be punished for contempt.

The Motion grew out of litigation which began over thirty years ago over the possession of "Blind Tom", or, as he was legally known, Thomas Wiggins. "Blind Tom" was born in slavery. The Bethune family retained Tom in their possession a long time after the Proclamation of Emancipation. He was weak-minded, and they maintained a sort of guardianship over him until 1887 when he was declared insane. Mrs. Elise Bethune, daughter-in-law of John G. Bethune, was then appointed his guardian.

Lawyer Daniel P. Holland of Washington, had been instrumental in freeing Tom from the absolute

control of the Bethune family. Mrs. Irene
Ackerman is the executrix of Holland's will. She
brought Suit against Mrs. Bethune for professional
services. The court ordered that Mrs. Bethune pay
the amount of the fees, $3,340—out of the money
which Tom had earned by his musical services.
The plaintiff alleged yesterday, that, although Mrs.
Bethune swore that she had no property as a result of Tom's work, she had, in fact, made $35,000
by it. The plaintiff further declares that she can
locate the property bought with the money so
earned.

Decision was reserved

According to the *New York Sun*, attorney John McCrone, in
his motion, had maintained that "nothing, not even the Emancipation, had ever freed Tom, and he was held in slavery as strong
then as before the War." He also noted that "Blind Tom, despite
being adjudged a lunatic in the 1887 Court Case, with Mrs. Bethune
made guardian of his estate, has not been too insane to play since
declared a lunatic." Still further, "Tom played on a salary for concerts since she became his Committee and the salary has been
used in his maintenance with her insistence that her failure to
comply with the Order was based on their being no funds of the
Estate to pay the Holland claim." In McCrone's opinion, "the large
tract of land which Mrs. Bethune purchased at Navesink highlands
should be credited to the Blind Tom Estate."

On December 28th, a decision was rendered in Mrs. Elise
Bethune's favor, dismissing the complaint "upon the merits, because the Plaintiff stipulated to take no further proceedings in the
action without costs." On January 4, 1894, the *New York Tribune*
reported under its "bits of legal news" section that: "Judge Traux
had appointed William Woodward Baldwin as referee to find out
whether any one or property belonging to Blind Tom could be
discovered in New York state to pay the several thousand dollars
for legal expenses incurred in those litigations." On January 13th,
a reporter for the Black *Cleveland Gazette* told readers that "Blind
Tom was still alive and the legal contest over him and the thousands made for the Bethunes (White) goes bravely on." It was his
feeling that "Tom's aged mother, Charity Wiggins, living in Geor-

gia, rightfully deserved at least some of his earnings, since she never received a dollar from the Bethunes." Though printing the same article that appeared in the New York papers about the case, unlike the White press, the *Gazette* titled it "Blind Tom Still a Slave" leaving no doubt as to how some Blacks viewed his status.

By January 1894, Tom's exhibitions were becoming more frequent and involved greater travel. For example, the *New York Dramatic News* reported concerts in Tyrone, PA (Jan. 3), Greensburg, PA (Jan. 12) and Urbana, Ohio (Jan. 30). The January 26th *Clipper* reported that Tom was in Pueblo, Colorado, January 18th and the February 4th *Cincinnati Enquirer* reported on his concerts soon after in Baltimore, Maryland, at Ford's Opera House with scheduled concerts in their city February 8-10th. According to the *Baltimore Sun*:

> A Mr. Stoddard, the well-known organist, put Tom's memory to a convincing test. He had met the pianist 17 years ago, and knowing of his wonderful memory, proposed to test it by calling on Tom unannounced. Arriving with a Mr. Ford, he saluted Tom with the expression, "How are you Mr. Stoddard?" The test was acknowledged a complete success.

From the *Cincinnati Press* came good reviews of Tom's four concerts at Pike's Opera House which were similarly repeated several days later during his Indianapolis, Indiana, engagement at the Grand Opera House. According to the February 14th *Indianapolis Journal*, "the audience was not large but appreciative" and his two-hour program, which included "recitations were given with so much expression that the audience felt he had more intelligence than for which he is generally credited." Describing Tom's hands as "enormous bunches of digits that seem to be powerful enough to strangle an ox," the reviewer nevertheless felt "the dexterity with which he manipulated the keyboard was something wonderful to behold." And while a Prof. C.F. Henson, organist at the Meridian Street Methodist Church, following his test of Tom admitted that: "Tom did not execute the pieces exactly as he did it, he ran along the same theme idea, perfectly duplicating several bars near the middle and coming very near finishing the piece to the notes."

Following a concert on May 5th in Beatrice, Nebraska, to "poor" business, Willa Cather, the noted novelist, while a student at Nebraska State University in Lincoln, Nebraska, heard Tom perform and wrote the following unsigned review for the May 18, 1894, *Nebraska State Journal*:[19]

It was a fair audience that gathered at the Lansing last night to listen to Blind Tom. Certainly the man was worth hearing—at least once. Probably there has never been seen on the stage a stranger figure or one more uncanny. He is a human phonograph, a sort of animated memory, with sound producing powers. It was a strange sight to see him walk out on the stage with his own lips—another man's words—introduce himself and talk quietly about his own idiocy. Then, too, he would applaud himself, and apologize, still in the third person, for his lack of courtesy. There was an insanity, a grotesque horribleness about it that was interestingly unpleasant.

With regard to the music, it was wonderful to see what the man could do. It was as if the soul of a Beethoven had slipped into the body of an idiot. In his ears and in his fingers Tom is the peer of some masterful musicians. The movement from the "Sonata Pathetique" he rendered sympathetically, with real feeling and perception, and the Intermezzo from "Cavalleria Rusticana" was graceful and delicately played, that is, as gracefully as the very unsatisfactory piano would permit. It seems as if Tom were enough afflicted by nature without the additional hindrance of that "upright." "The Hungarian Rhapsody No. 2" and Paderewski's "Chant d'Amour" were played with some genius, for certainly that may be called genius which has no basis in intellect.

This was the chief part of the real music. Besides these, Blind Tom played some of his own compo-

sitions and gave imitations of storms, banjos, and
bagpipes. He offered to repeat, by ear, any piece
that anyone in the audience might play. Professor Lichtenstein of the Western Normal came for-
ward and played Gottschalk's "Tremolo," a piece
that apparently was a little too difficult for a successful test. Still Tom did much better than one
would expect.

Tom is really a wonderfully gifted player. He has a
marvelous ear and wonderful delicacy of touch,
but these gifts are shut up in the body of an over-
grown child. One laughs at the man's queer actions, and yet, after all, the sight is not laughable.
It brings us too near to the things that we sane
people do not like to think of.

Though not a performing musician, Willa Cather, from her
early childhood and throughout her college years at the University of Nebraska (1890-94), was part of a lively cultural environment which featured a number of local and traveling theatrical
and musical performances. Lincoln, being a railroad city, became
a convenient stopover for first-rate traveling companies and concert artists on their way to Denver and San Francisco. As a critic-
columnist she developed certain ideas about music which, according to Richard Giannone, became central in her fiction. In his
opinion, her account of Blind Tom's concert reveals "the dualistic
idea of soul that derived from her view of human personality—
belief in the power of music to penetrate the inmost heart of things
and to provide an unfathomable speech to express the best in
man."[20] At the university Willa Cather was closely acquainted with
Dr. Tyndale, the *Journal's* music critic who aided her musical insights by not only taking her to concerts but telling stories about
the artists. Occasionally she attended operas in Chicago. In his
biographical study of the novelist, James Woodress noted that her
music reviews were not "chiefly concerned with value judgement
since her interest in the whole world of art ranged widely in her
reviews."[21] Georg Seibel, another friend from her post-college years
in Pittsburgh, said "she was not interested in music for itself, but
for the personalities connected with it," something evident in her
review of Blind Tom's concert.

Richard Giannone contends that the "Blind d'Arnault," blind musical genius in Cather's most famous novel, *My Antonia* (published 1918), was based on her hearing Blind Tom in Lincoln, and Blind Boone, who she heard several times in her hometown of Red Cloud, Nebraska, the locale of the novel. Despite her making "Blind d'Arnault" a "mulatto" and a letter written to a friend saying her character was a composite of Negro musicians, especially drawn on Blind Boone, her having had Blind d'Arnault be slave-born with his musical talents discovered and early developed by the slave master's daughter was more likely a characterization based on Blind Tom. Still further, the following description of d'Arnault's performance in the novel offers an inescapable similarity to the commonly held characteristics of Blind Tom:

> As a very young child he could repeat, after a fashion, any composition that was played for him. No matter how many wrong notes he struck, he never lost the intention of a passage, he brought the substance of it across by irregular and astonishing means. He wore his teachers out. He could never learn like other people, never acquired any finish. He was always a Negro prodigy who played barbarously and wonderfully. As piano-playing it was perhaps abominable, but as music it was something real, vitalized by a sense of rhythm that was stronger than his other physical senses—that not only filled his dark mind, but worried his body incessantly. To hear him, to watch him, was to see a Negro enjoying himself as only a Negro can. It was as if all the agreeable sensations possible to creatures of flesh and blood were heaped up on those black-and-white keys, and he were gloating over them and trickling them through his yellow fingers.[22]

On May 24th, Tom performed in Omaha's First Congregational Church. According to the *Omaha Bee*, after the concert, ice cream was served as a fund-raiser for the refurbishing of their young women's home. It is doubtful that attorney Lerche accompanied his wife and Tom on this mid-Western tour since he was involved in further litigation with Louise B. Lynch on February 8th and

12th. On April 13th, attorney Leman B. Treadwell, then in the Oklahoma Territory, filed a petition, after being sworn under oath as Louise B. Lynch's attorney in her case against Albrecht J. Lerche that in such capacity he:

> herein desires and intends to appeal from said reversal of this judgement to the court of Appeals of the State of New York within the time provided by law therefore after defendant shall have served him with a copy of said order of judgement of said General Term reversing the aforesaid.

The above was concerning decisions made in January 1893 concerning the sum of $1,133.00 against Lerche, as defendant, which he appealed at a September 1893 hearing. Considering his being in Oklahoma, attorney Treadwell was requesting the "cause may be allowed to go over the term."

When announcing Tom's appearance in Salt Lake City, Utah, the August 11th *Deseret News* reporter said: "so many years have elapsed since Tom was seen in the West that people believed him dead, but his managers announce him very much alive, and offers a forfeit of a thousand dollars to any one who will show he is not the original Blind Tom." Describing his appearance, the August 14th *Deseret Evening News* reporter wrote that:

> the eighteen years which have elapsed since he last appeared in Salt Lake City have visibly aged him, but made no alteration in his marvelous gifts; his wholly head is still jet black, but his face looks much older, and his bulk has materially increased. In intellect he is still the same child as ever. It is almost pathetic to hear him invariably clap his hands over his own performances, and equally so to see him slowly repeat the lessons that have been taught him in making announcements to the audience.

Relating the following humorous incident as an example of Tom's weak intellect, the reporter recounted how:

One of Blind Tom's numbers on the program was
to play a selection in imitation of a banjo and guitar, this by means of a patent attachment applied
to the strings of the piano. Mr. Jenkins, the enter-
prising piano agent, while the curtain was down,
impressed it on Tom to announce to the audience
that the banjo and guitar attachment was only
found on the Everett piano; Tom, in his stammer-
ing announced, "Ladies and gentlemen, Tom will
now give an imitation of a banjo and guitar by
means of an attachment found on *every* piano."
Obviously, Mr. Jenkin's consternation may be
imagined, but Tom went on and played his selection in serene unconsciousness that he had not
fully done his duty.

In this reporter's opinion, Tom's selection of Liszt's "Hungarian Rhapsody" was chiefly remarkable for the fact that it had been
acquired merely by hearing others play it. Though not performed
without fault, that they be "executed at all from memory is the
remarkable thing." The review ended with him telling readers that
"Tom is now under the charge of the courts, a sort of ward in
chancery. The lady who acts as his guardian sat by the doorkeeper;
it is said he has acquired a large sum of money which is profitably
invested for him." Undoubtedly such information was given by
Mrs. Bethune since the issue concerning Tom's monies was well
known.

Since Tom returned to Seattle for concerts the following month
(September 17-18th) it is obvious that those August concerts had
been both musically and monetarily profitable. According to the
September 18th *Seattle Post-Intelligence*: "When Mr. Russell, a
local manager of the Condroy Theatre led him on stage to a
crowded house, the applause made it clear that a large proportion
of the audience recognized in him the only genuine Blind Tom,
his features, walk and peculiarities being unmistakable when he
talked." Because September 16th was a Sunday, Mrs. Bethune,
under Mr. Russell's leadership, took Tom to the convent where he
gave a program for the nuns which included variations on "Nearer
My God to Thee," that "affected all present."[23] A convent student
played one of her original pieces for Tom to reproduce, a feat the

reporter said he had witnessed being done by Tom twenty years earlier.

When he returned to Seattle for concerts on October 4-7th, it was announced that he would present a sacred concert for his last engagement and "to the skeptics who doubt that this is the original Blind Tom an opportunity is offered to make $5,000 which Mrs. Bethune offers to anyone who will produce evidence to the contrary."[24] Regarding his compositional skills, the reporter said that "one of Tom's latest compositions is a polonaise, which for rhythmical time and beauty of harmony excels as his previous efforts and will be played at his concert by special request." On October 8th, he appeared in Tacoma, Washington, where, according to the *Tacoma Ledger* (Oct. 9th) "there was a very large and fashionable audience." On October 12-15th he performed at Arion Hall in Portland, Oregon. Questions concerning this being the "original Blind Tom" allowed Mrs. Bethune another opportunity to create excitement over his concerts as she advertised her willingness to pay $5,000 to anyone "able to bring the slightest evidence that he was not." On October 27th, the *Oregon State Journal* reported another successful concert in Eugene, Oregon.

Tom performed at the Metropolitan Theatre in Sacramento, California, on November 3rd, followed by three more in San Francisco. On November 10th the San Francisco *Chronicle* announced they had been a "tremendous success." Other California concerts took place in Oakland (week of November 21st), Stockton (December 9th) and Santa Barbara (December 17th). He returned to San Diego on December 22nd. Advertising that concert in the December 17th *San Diego Evening News*, the reporter described him as "a profound psychological wonder."

The December 18th *Evening Sun* noted that:

> Unlike the great masters, whose manipulation result from days of unwearied study, his instruction comes from a higher power, and his philosophers are pleased to term genius, which enables him, without a knowledge of either language sing in German, French and English.

From press reports released to the *New York Dramatic News*, these California concerts were a financial success. Following another concert in San Bernadino on January 4th, 1895 (his last in the state), the reviewer described him as "bulky and awkward in figure with the hands of a burden bearer, his touch wonderfully delicate and his technique like that of a conservatory graduate."[25]

Although the winter of 1893-94 and summer following witnessed widespread unemployment, strikes met by violence, and a march on Washington, D.C., by a group of jobless men, known as Coxey's army, seeking relief, it seems to have been one of Mrs. Bethune's most successful periods since becoming Tom's Committee. The "Panic of 1893" began on April 21st of that year when U.S. gold reserves fell below the $100 million mark, considered a safe minimum.[26] Since the April 1893 *Indianapolis Freeman* reported that the Hyer Sisters were leaving the stage because of fewer and fewer successful performances, it is evident that the Depression had some effect on Black performers who had found a lucrative following during the previous decades.[27]

Blind Boone, Sissieretta Jones, Joseph Douglass, Flora Batson and Sidney Woodward were forging ahead in their concert careers. Mme. Marie Selika, who toured Europe from 1887 through 1892, returned to Ohio in 1893, established a music studio, and continued to concertize.[28]

In addition to championing the songs of Blacks, Antonin Dvorak in the April 1894 *Etude* study of the Negro voice was reported as saying:

> It requires not only voice and ear to sing well, but a necessary requisite is the singing temperament and the easily, affected, and susceptible imagination. I have not noticed these qualities so much in the voice of white people as in those of the colored ones. In volume, their voices are superior to those of the whites, and in timbre the equal if not the superior. Colored people have every requisite to make good opera singers. Their fondness of show, vanity, love of color and mimicry makes them natural actors.

Such evaluation probably stemmed from the January 23, 1894, concert he conducted at the National Conservatory where Sissieretta Jones performed "Inflamatus" from Rossini's "Stabat

Mater" and an aria from Meyerbeer's "Robert le Diable." According to Paul Stefan-Gruenfelldt, the chorus was sung by an all-Negro choir from St. Philips Episcopal Church; and with the exception of one White girl who appeared as a piano virtuoso, the student musicians were all Negro musicians.[29] It was also the year that Harry T. Burleigh was selected from sixty White applicants to the position of baritone soloist in the wealthy all-White St. George's Episcopal Church on Stuyvesant Square, a position he held for fifty years.

Besides those individual Blacks who were finding some success in the concert arena, other Black musicians were able to gain ensemble experience in the all-Black cast traveling shows like Nate Salisbury's *South Before the War* which had a cast of about five hundred for the huge plantation scenes. Another was the *Creole Show*, which brought females into the show and replaced the plantation with an urban environment. According to Allen Woll, "in 1893, the ensemble embarked on a lengthy tour from Boston to Chicago (during the World's Fair) and finally to New York City, where it nudged the respectable Broadway theatre zone."[30] While, as Thomas L. Riis said, "the Panic of 1893 roused theatrical owners and agents to attempt to achieve some new, more efficient booking arrangements, the uniqueness of Blind Tom's Exhibitions seemed to offer Mrs. Bethune a rare opportunity for continuing to sell him to managers as a one-person Act having now given successful concerts from New York to California."[31]

Notes

1. Details of the Arguments and Exhibits are part of the New York Supreme Court General Term. Second department Court published transcript "Louise B. Lynch, Plaintiff and Respondent against Albrecht J. Lynch, Defendant and Appellant," pp. 23-67.

2. See: State of New York, Queen County deposition before a Daniel Noble.

3. *Miscellaneous Reports*, Vol. III (Albany: James B. Lyons, reporter) 1893, pp.126-131.

4. Elected in 1884 as the twenty-second president, he was defeated by Benjamin Harrison in 1888 and elected again in 1892. Because of the four years between elections, he is therefore counted twice in the roll of presidents.

5. *Washington Post* (March 6, 1893).

6. Newark, New Jersey *Journal* (May 23, 1893).

7. *New York Dramatic News* (July 1, 1893).

8. For information about this historic event, see: *Memorial of the World's Columbian Exposition* (Chicago: A. L. Stone and Company, 1893); David F. Burg. *Chicago's White City of 1893* (University Press of Kentucky, 1976); Justus D. Doennecke. "Myths, Machines and Markets: The Columbian Exposition of 1893," *Journal of Popular Culture* (Winter, 1972), pp. 535-549; Hubert Howe Bancroft. *Book of the Fair* (New York: Bancroft Company, 1894); Daniel T. Miller. "The Columbian Exposition of 1893 and the American National Character," *Journal of American Culture* (Summer, 1987), pp. 17-21; and Emmett Dedmon. *Fabulous Chicago* (New York: Random House, 1953).

9. Justus D. Doennecke. *Op. Cit.* 541.

10. Sandy R. Mazzola. "Bands and Orchestras at the World Columbian Exposition," *American Music* (Winter, 1986), pp. 407-427.

11. From the outset, Theodore Thomas had been involved with controversy. The first concerned Ignacy Paderewski's May 2nd concert, where he allowed him to perform on a Steinway paino, although the Commission made a rule that no non-exhibiting piano maker's instrument could be used. Steinway & Sons and several other eastern firms had declined to exhibit their pianos because of the rivalry between Chicago and New York for the location of the fair. Since it was against Theodore Thomas' artistic principles to disallow Paderewski to perform on a Steinway, having already engaged him as a known Steinway-playing artist, he sneaked one in under the label of "hardware," causing the press to label him "a small despot" and "pragmatic curmudgeon," among other negative descriptions. See: Arthur Lowesser. *Men Women and Pianos* (New York: Simon & Schusters, 1954).

12. Sandy R. Mazzola. *Op. Cit.* 417.

13. Harry T. Burleigh, (1866-1949), singer-composer, wrote over 300 vocal songs, including arrangements of spirituals, for solo voice and choral ensemble and several for violin and piano. His arrangement of "Deep River" in 1916 was an important contribution to American music as it was set in the style of an art song for solo voices; considered one of the early Black nationalistic composers.

14. Terri Waldo. *This Is Ragtime* (New York: Hawthorne Books, Inc., 1976), p. 50.

15. Elliott Rudwick and August Meir. "Black Man in the 'White City:' Negroes and the Columbian Exposition, 1893," *Phylon* (Winter, 1965), pp. 354-361.

16. A journalist-lecturer and Civil Rights leader, Ida Wells-Barnett's newspaper office was destroyed by a White mob after her editorial denouncing a March 9, 1892, lynching of three friends (accused of rape) appeared in her *Memphis Free Speech,* when she was in Philadel-

phia. In 1895 she published *A Red Record,* a statistical record of three years of lynching and urged Black institutions to join in her anti-lynching crusade. See: David M. Tuckner. "Miss Ida B. Wells and Memphis Lynching," *Phylon* (Summer, 1971), pp. 112-122; Alfredo M. Duster, editor. *Crusade for Justice: Autobiography of Ida B. Wells* (Chicago: University of Chicago Press, 1970) and Dorothy Sterling. *Black Foremothers* (Old Westbury, N.Y.: Feminist Press, 1980), pp. 60-117.

17. "Uncle Tom: An opera written by a colored composer just completed," *Indianapolis World* (February 18, 1893).

18. Benjamin Quarles. *Frederick Douglass* (New York: Atheneum Press, 1968), p. 347.

19. According to a Miss Bullock, a fellow student at the university, the unsigned article was by the writer; also identified as being by her was Joan Crane. *Willa Cather: A Bibliography* (Lincoln: University of Nebraska Press, 1982), p. 261.

20. Richard Giannone. *Music in Willa Cather's Fiction* (Lincoln: University of Nebraska, 1968), p. 9.

21. James Woodress. *Willa Cather: Her Life, Her Art* (New York: Western Publishing Company, 1970), p. 177.

22. Willa Cather. *My Antonia* (Boston: Houghton Mifflin, 1918), pp. 188-189. Also Ella Mae Thornton. "The Vivid Description of Negro Genius is supposed to be based on Blind Tom," *Columbus Magazine* (May 31, 1941), pp. 27-28.

23. *Seattle Post* (September 17, 1894).

24. *Seattle Post Intelligence* (October 5, 1894).

25. *San Bernadino Evening Sun* (January 5, 1895).

26. The Depression did not lift substantially until the poor European crops of 1897 stimulated America's exportation and importation of gold.

27. Eileen Southern. "The Origin and Development of the Black Musical Theater: A Preliminary Report," *Black Music Research Journal* (1981-1982), p. 7.

28. Rosalyn M. Story. *And So I Sing: African-American Divas of Opera and Concert* (New York: Warner Books, 1990).

29. Paul Stefan-Gruenfelldt. *Antonin Dvorak* (N.Y. Dreystone Press, 1941), p. 227.

30. Allen Woll. *Black Musical Theatre: From Coontown to Dreamgirls* (Baton Rouge: LSU Press, 1989), p. 11.

31. Thomas L. Riis. *Just Before Jazz: Black Musical Theatre in New York: 1890 to 1915* (Washington: Smithsonian Institution Press, 1989), p. 17.

Chapter Four

(1895–1899)

ON JANUARY 21, 1895, the *New York Times* reported that General James N. Bethune, Tom's former "owner," who was then 92, was critically ill in Washington, D.C. The reporter described him as "the first newspaper editor in the South to openly advocate secession" and considered "almost the pioneer for free trade in the country." In 1840 General Bethune advocated "free trade and direct taxation." Though he served as attorney general for the state of Georgia, after the Civil War it seems he became more widely known as the "original owner of Blind Tom, the Negro musical prodigy" rather than for his distinguished pre-Civil War political and journalistic career.[1] For example, when the February 14th *Washington Post* announced his death, the headline appeared as:

BLIND TOM BETHUNE

The Death of His Old Master Recalls the Prodigy.

MUSIC WAS HIS MIND'S MISTRESS

An Interesting Recital of How the Marvelous Genius of the Human Contradiction Was Discovered and Given to the World—His Child Life in Georgia and His Subsequent Career Upon the Concert Stage—His Present Whereabouts Unknown.

Despite the fact that Tom had continuously given concerts in New York, New Jersey, Pennsylvania and other eastern states during the previous year, it is interesting that the reporter wrote that: "because of General Bethune's death, public interest will now naturally recur to this phenomenon and the question will arise as to his whereabouts." Even at the time of writing, Tom was concertizing throughout the state of Texas.

The long obituary account offered the former slaveowner family another opportunity to continue their own self-serving account about their role in Tom's musical development. It describes Tom's mother, Charity, as a type of the old-time Southern Negress, tender-hearted and sympathetic, who discovers her child to be "mentally useless with the grief touching." The reporter gives the following statements regarding Tom's training, which undoubtedly came from General Bethune's son, James A. Bethune, who General Bethune was visiting at the time of his death. Using dialect, the reporter wrote that:

> Tom was nearly two years old when Charity made known her trouble to her master. "He kin tawk, Mass' Tom," she moaned, "but he don't say nuffin cept whut you say fust. Den he say it arter you."

> "Bring him to me," said the general. "If I can teach my pinter dog to bring my gloves and whip and fetch a dead bird I can teach a nigger to do as much."

> Charity brought Tom up to the big house from the quarters.

> "Tom, sit down," ordered the general.
> "Tom, sit down," repeated the child, still standing erect.

> His master repeated the words, at the same time taking him by the shoulders and seating him. The next time he said, "Tom, sit down," the boy did so, repeating, however, the words, a habit he kept until he passed out of contemporary sight. This

> object-lesson of Gen. Bethune's was followed im-
> plicitly by Charity, and Tom was taught to make
> his wants known and to follow instructions given
> him solely by the direction of his instincts; trained,
> in a word, like a dog.

Besides this evident non-human characterization of Tom, it shows the Bethunes' unwillingness to acknowledge that Tom displayed intelligence since few, if any other two-year-old, could grasp the language and have the ability to remember statements verbatim. Since dogs are trained while humans learn, such a comparison was baseless.

Continuing the commonly held stories in the press and promotional booklet about Tom in the 1860s as to how the "kind slave owners" were directly involved in developing Tom's musical talents, though still characterizing him as an "idiot," the reporter wrote:

> He was still a baby when he roamed away from his
> parents' cabin one day and strayed up to the for-
> bidden precincts of the big house yard.

> He First Hears the Piano

> One of Gen. Bethune's daughters was playing upon
> a piano, which her father had just given her. The
> child scarcely out of infancy, listened, fascinated
> and thrilled. The sleeping chords within him were
> touched. Trembling and writhing he crawled up
> the steps and into the parlor and crept to the side
> of the player. It was not exactly proper, according
> to high Southern ideas, for a half-naked pickanniny
> to come uninvited into the mansion, and the event
> naturally caused talk. Gen. Bethune was equal to
> the occasion, when he learned of the occurrence.

> "The child is music crazy, poor little thing," he
> said. "Let it enjoy itself. Perhaps it may learn to
> play one day and make its life bearable."

Naturally his daughters objected to such an object as a slave baby in the house, but Gen. Bethune prevailed upon them to let Tom touch the piano keys. Charity dressed him up and he was taken up to the house. His little fingers could hardly bear down the keys, yet his touch brought forth harmony—a faint echo of the air that was being played when he first heard the piano. Gen. Bethune was a man of strong impulse and determination. He made up his mind at once to cultivate the germs he had seen and to ascertain what they would bring forth. He was practicing law in Columbus, Ga., and went into town from his plantation every morning.

Tom Becomes a Performer

He had ample means to carry out any fancy that might seize him, so as it was entirely out of the question for Tom's talents to be nurtured upon the piano at home, he purchased another instrument for the boy, and had it placed in one of his office rooms in Columbus. Every morning Charity would dress Tom up and bundle him in his master's carryall and every day the little fellow would play the piano. Of course, he did not really know one key from another and sheet music to him was like Sanskrit to a Choctaw, but the child was able to play correctly any tune that was played in his hearing. Gen. Bethune would hire wandering musicians to come and play for Tom, and the prodigy would almost go into spasms of delight. Then he would be placed on the piano stool and would repeat everything that he had heard. When Alexander H. Stephens, Robert Toombs, and Lamars and the other great legal giants of Georgia would come to Columbus court it was common to hear one of them say: Come on, let's go down to Jim Bethune's office and hear his nigger boy play the piano.[2]

Obviously, the use of the term "it" throughout is another example of how the Bethunes were unwilling to characterize Tom in human terms. Charging Tom's mother, in part, for their legal loss of Tom in 1887 to Gen. Bethune's former daughter-in-law, the reporter said that:

> Charity, poor, trusting creature that she was, was approached by wily agents of far-seeing managers. Visions of great fortune were held out before her entranced eyes, and the upshot of it, was that she applied to have Gen. Bethune removed as Tom's guardian, and another person appointed in his place. Judge Bond granted her request, and Blind Tom began that wonderful journey through the United States which is so well remembered by the theater-goers of a generation ago . . .
>
> But poor deluded Charity never knew realization of the dreams she had cherished. Those who had Tom in charge threw her aside as worthless baggage and too great an encumbrance to be bothered with, so she crawled home to old Mass' Jim Bethune's, where she was cared for by him and his until she died.

Obviously, the Bethune family was trying to describe themselves as people of compassion and understanding since the court records will show that not only was their recounting full of misinformation, but more important, Charity Wiggins, who was still alive, had returned to Georgia to live with her children; also, Gen. Bethune had not lived in Columbus since 1865.

After the unusually long detailed account about Blind Tom, the *Post* reporter gave some details about General Bethune's career, noting that in spite of his "activity in the affairs of his country, he was only once a candidate for office, and upon that occasion defeated in a Congressional election on account of his extreme views."[3] Since his son, Joseph Robertson, was married to the assistant solicitor of the Treasury, it is obvious that General Bethune had, to some degree, influenced his own children in their decision to enter the legal profession. He had been widowed since

1858 and had never remarried, which given his political importance in Georgia was not unexpected. After a private ceremony at
his son's residence in Washington following his death, the General's
body was taken back to Columbus, Georgia, for interment beside
his wife. The February 14th *Columbus-Enquirer Sun* (where he
was one-time editor), when announcing General Bethune's death,
titled the article "A Very Remarkable Man," recounting how he
had been in Columbus a few months earlier to visit his daughter,
Mrs. M.M. Hansard, and despite his age "was in excellent health,"
and "manifested the liveliest interest in current affairs." After relating information similar to that given about the deceased in the
Washington Post, the obituary article ended with a reminder to
the *Columbus Enquirer Sun* readers that "the Negro pianist, Blind
Tom, was among General Bethune's slaves, together with Tom's
father and mother and numerous brothers and sisters." From such
obituary accounts, it seems evident that Blind Tom's slave-con-
nections with the Bethunes had become more important as an
identifying factor in their lives rather than from their own professional attainments. One can postulate that the Bethunes failure to
keep track of Tom's whereabouts was one way of thwarting Mrs.
Elise Bethune in her effort to collect the court-ordered payment
of $7,000 from the July 31, 1887, Equity Petition Suit in Alexan-
dria, Virginia's, Circuit Court.[4]

It's not certain that Mrs. Elise Bethune knew of her former
father-in-law's death since she was traveling with Tom in the state
of Texas where he gave his first concert on January 10th at the
Quannah Opera House "before a large audience."[5] When announcing Tom's January 18th concert at the Pueblo, Colorado, Grand
Opera House, the January 15th *Pueblo Daily Chieftain* described
him as "a most singular contrast" who was "a helpless idiot with
scarcely sense enough to know when he is hungry, or to feed himself when he is hungry, yet endowed with a musical gift far beyond
the average musician." After asking readers to compare Tom's
musical gifts with "the pupils of Liszt who owe their proficiency to
hours and days of tedious practice supported by an indomitable
resolution to succeed," he said that Tom is "little moved from the
higher order of animal, yet has the so-called divine faculty of music." Obviously the reporter chose to ignore or may never had
been made aware that Tom had many years of study with the finest teachers and that most of his time was spent on the keyboard.

Although the January 16th *Daily Chieftain* reporter wrote that Tom's "range of theme is great whether it be a Beethoven 'Sonata' or a wild African plantation hymn," the published program offers no evidence of his performing the latter. According to the January 19th concert review, since Tom had not been in Pueblo for seventeen years, not surprisingly he had a "large and enthusiastic audience."

In an announcement concerning his two concerts in Colorado Springs the following day, the paper in that city used a review from Tom's Denver appearance which mentioned "the doubt expressed as to this being the original Blind Tom until an older man present gave assurance that it was the "same performance style and physical similarities" he had witnessed from a Blind Tom Exhibition he attended twenty years earlier.[6] According to the January 20th *Colorado Gazette* among the large crowd of women and children, were blind pupils from the deaf and blind school. The reporter added that "Tom is under the care of the Courts and the manager has to report regularly regarding him" and added that Tom "must have made several fortunes during his public life for several owners."

By January 26th Tom had returned to Texas for a concert in Fort Worth where many there had also believed him dead. Mrs. Elise Bethune, in response to this, told the reporter that "such reports were inspired by malice from a man who once had a contract with the old Negro and traveled through the country with him." Though not stated, one might assume that she was referring to General Bethune, whose death would come a few days later.[7] Again, one questions their characterization of Tom as an "idiot" while saying he was capable of making a contract.

It is highly unlikely that many Blacks were among those at Tom's March 1st concert in Austin, Texas, since the *Austin Daily Statesman* announced "a memorial program the same day by the colored people in honor of the late Honorable Frederick Douglass, the great representative of their race on this continent at the Opera House." Douglass, at age 78, had died at his Anacosta Heights, Washington, D.C., home on February 20th. According to the March 4th *San Antonio Daily Express* Tom showed an unbelievable remarkable memory when he demonstrated his ability to recall specifics about past meetings with a Dr. Amos Graves and Capt. Joseph Bennet (both in the audience) during the Civil War, including what hotels the meetings took place—one in Louisville and the other in Nashville. According to the *Chattanooga Press* Tom told the reporter that the people of that city had "nobly supported him and from their applause were sure they appreciated and understood the highest attainments of classical music," then added that he had "traveled all over the world and played to the most critical audiences."[8] That Tom had made such conversational interaction, using the given vocabulary, should have dispelled any of that reporter's own descriptions of Tom as an "idiot." According to the *Dallas News* the hall Tom performed in was so uncomfortably cold that he "wore a mink boa around his neck and seemed to suffer from his hands growing cold on the piano keys."[9] According to the *New York Dramatic News*, Tom's concerts in Galveston on the 27th and 28th were before "small audiences" and though the March 28th *Galveston Daily News* reviewer gave a similar assessment of those in attendance, he was greatly impressed by Tom's performance of the famous Liszt "Cavaleria Rusticana Intermezzo."

The *New York Dramatic News* announced several other Texas concerts: Houston (April 3rd); Huntsville (April 8th) with a grand receipt of $221.50; Marshall (April 12th); Gainsville (April 18th); and Paris, Texas (April 26th). The March 26th *Houston Daily Press* advertised him as "the eighth wonder of the world," being "an idiot as black as Negroes can be produced." According to their March 29th issue, his audience at the Opera House "was of such proportion as is calculated to make the heart of any manager glad. The house was covered from pit to dome with a large number of ladies occupying seats in the gallery and his performance of Gottschalk's 'The Last Hope' caused overwhelming applause."

Notwithstanding inclement weather, the May 6th *Pine Bluff (Arkansas) Daily Commercial* reported a "fair-sized audience," and though describing it as a "most satisfactory performance," suggested that the performance would be "much more pleasing should the management make the announcement." To that reporter "to hear Tom make his own announcements, and applaud himself, exhibited him as a perfect imbecile in every other matter but music." *The Little Rock Arkansas Gazette* announced that "instead of the round-about of his boyhood, Tom would appear in an immaculate dress suit for his appearance in their city the next day."[10] Reviewing two concerts in their city, the May 9th *Mem-*

phis Commercial Appeal was of the feeling that "so varied was the list of his exhibitions that it cannot be said he wearied his listeners." Other concerts in Tennessee were in Huntingdon (May 15); Nashville (May 16, 17); Murfreesboro (May 17); Columbus (May 19); and Chattanooga (May 26th). In addition to his performance in Nashville's Vendome Hall, Tom gave one to what probably was an all-Black audience at the St. John A.M.E. Church. According to the June 22nd *New York Dramatic News,* his June 6th Bristol, Tennessee, concert, the last in the state, was before a "large audience" followed by a similarly financial successful one in Raleigh, North Carolina, on June 13th.

In 1896, Orelia Key Bell, published the following poem in her book of poems:[11]

I

HUSH! hearken! 'tis the tinkling of an elfland tambou-
    rine,
A tintinnanbulary sweep of faerie fingertips.
—Now it soars in silver treble—now it sinks and, diving,
    dips
Down to the very bottom of the deeps of sound, I ween.
        Hear it bound and hasten
        Down its diapason,
Like a mighty current down a deep ravine;
        Upward lightly tripping,
        Now, like children skipping,
Tripping, skipping, slipping o'er a bowling-green.
        'Tis Aeolus sighing hither,
        Flutt'ring softly as a feather
        From the hovering wing of Nox.
        All my senses he entices
        With his oriental spices
As his soft mesmeric fingers wandlike overpass my
        Drinking in his breath harcotic,
        yielding to his touch hypnotic,
I am sinking—I am drifting—I have reached the Lethe
    docks.

II

        Was I sleeping?—
        Some one weeping
    From the cypress hedge is creeping—
'Tis some isolated spirit seeking redress for its wrongs.
Nay! some madman—hear the gnashing
Of his teeth, and see the flashing
        Of his eyes!—some madman, certes, who has
        wrench'd his prison-thongs.

Hist how his uncanny laughter
Echoes from each startled rafter—
Now, as if possess'd of legions from infernal regions, he
Shrieking goes around the gable,
Like the banshee in the fable,
With a weird reiteration on an eldritch ecstasy.

Was I dreaming?
Moonlight streaming
O'er me sets my opal gleaming—
'Tis some mystic incantation from that spell hath set me
free.
All is calm and still and sober
As a moonbeam in October
—As a midnight moonbeam resting on a mid-October
sea.

III

Hurrah! make room for Jumbo!—You gamins! clear the
track there!
There's a cage of mad hyeans—I say! you'd best step
back there!
Thumpty! thumpty, here he comes!—
Humpty Dumpty, with his thumbs
Stuck aside his nose.
—There's a lady on a chariot
With a snake (how can she carry it!)
Wound from head to toes.
Whick-Whack! goes the whip of the ring master.
Round, round go the ponies—faster—faster!
See her whil!—
The circus girl,
Round and round in giddy gyres.
Thro' the ring
Watch her spring!—
A salamander wreathed in fires.
Now the clown
Assists her down.
Does he smile, or does he frown?

Hip! hurrah! stand aback!
Humpty's turn now—clear the track!
Whick-whack! goes the whip of the ring-master—
Round, round goes old Humpty—faster—faster—
See him stumble,
Watch him tumble!—
In the sawdust roll and fumble!
Now he faces his disaster—
Is he proud, or is he humble?
Does he grin, or does he grumble?

Hush! look up, and still your laughter,
Shut your eyes, and hold your breath!—
     There's a woman from the rafter
     (Samson nerve her!
     God preserve her!)
Hangling, dangling by her teeth!

IV

'Tis a burial in mid-ocean
In midwinter. With emotion
Round the corpse the crew are crowding.
Round the corpse that they are shrouding
     In the snowy winding-sheet.
'Tis the priest that they are shrouding
     In the snowy winding-sheet.
This one chants Ave Marias,
That one counts her beads by tears,
Some emblam the silver hairs,
   Others kneel and kiss the feet.
One—perhaps his mother—tries
To pray alound—but drops her eyes,
And lifts her empty arms aloft in voiceless agony.
     —Hush! O hearken! Do I dream?
     Have I cross'd the Jordan stream?
     Seraph voices, mingling soft,
     Bear my ravished spirit aloft—
     Upward, upward to the sky.
I close mine eyes—a sense of
 Heaven steals o'er me.
Silence profound a moment—then a thunder
Of wild applause. And lo! that sable wonder,
Blind Tom, the genius, sits and blinks before me.

According to a lengthy article about "Blind Tom's retirement" in the May 8, 1897, *Indianapolis Freeman* (reprinted from the *New York Sun*), during this and the previous year Mrs. Elise Bethune had "temporarily withdrawn Blind Tom from the amusement world, so that he might recover his health and at the same time familiarize himself with modern musical compositions." The writer noted that since "Tom had been handed over to Mrs. Bethune with no money and no property, or otherwise, out of the hundreds of thousands of dollars which he had earned during the previous quarter of a century, it was necessary to keep him at work a little while longer to provide for his future maintenance." Obviously Mrs. Bethune's statements about Tom's role in being forced to perform as he was "taking care of his mother, who was then in the south and looked to her son for support" was ludicrous although such statements about her having saved enough money to warrant his temporary withdrawal serves as some written evidence that the 1894 and 1895 seasons were profitable for her. In responding to the question "What has become of Blind Tom?" reporters wrote that Tom was then in a "comfortable cottage at the Highlands of Navesink, on the New Jersey side of the lower New York bay . . . passing hours at the piano, playing his old pieces and practicing new ones." His other amusements, according to the reporter, "came from his imitating the small talk of women and other visitors to the Lerche cottage." According to him:

> Tom holds imaginary receptions, at which the weather, new styles in dress and like topics are discussed by the imaginary visitors, as imitated by Tom in a way that is very comical, but he will not do it if he knows there is anyone listening to him.

Postulating further that "he has all the selfishness of a spoiled child, and jealous of any attention paid to anyone else in his presence," the writer wrote that:

> Tom is willing that his mother should be taken care of out of the money he has earned, but he does not wish to have her or his brothers and sisters near him for fear they may annoy him or prevent his being the sole object of the attention of those around him.

Notwithstanding his classification as "child-like selfishness," the writer adds that:

> Blind Tom is extremely moral and religious in his habits and disposition. He never eats without first offering a prayer, and on Sundays will play only church music on the piano. He will have nothing to do with anyone who uses profane or improper language in his presence.

That Tom could distinguish such behavioral traits offers another argument against his being classified as an "imbecile" or "idiot." Also interesting were those statements regarding his having sibling rivalry since Tom was separated from his brothers and sisters throughout his childhood days. The writer also made known that "Tom has to be carefully watched by a male nurse, especially hired for that purpose." Obviously any reference to Tom's "good morals and religious behavior" were not unexpected given the continuous full-time control by others throughout his daily activities from infancy. About his relationship with his mother, readers were told that:

> It was only after the conclusion of Mrs. Lerche's long legal contest that mother and son were together again for the first since Tom's infancy, but after the novelty of their reunion had worn away it was evident that their tastes and temperaments were so utterly at variance that there was little likelihood of their living happily together. Fate had kept them apart too long. Tom's clouded mind could not realize what his mother had suffered during this long separation. Four-score years of life had made her a withered-up, irritable old woman, set in her ways, and not at all "reconciled to the fact that she found the baby for whom she had mourned so many years turned into a prematurely aged man, fixed in his habits and strangely lacking in the natural affection he should have for her." So Charity Wiggins went back to her old home in Georgia to live with her other children, whose ways she understands.

After giving similar statements about Tom's whereabouts in the *Topeka (Kansas) Colored Citizen*, the writer advanced the theory that "it is not probable that Tom will ever appear in public again since his health is feeble and mind has weakened with age."[12] However, Tom was advertised in the *Fall River Massachusetts* paper as appearing at their Music Academy August 27-28th.[13]

On December 5, 1897, Harry-Dele Hallmark wrote a lengthy article titled "A Master of Melody," in the *North American Press,* where he gave a detailed eyewitness account of what he described as "How Old Blind Tom is Spending His Days From the Public Eye." Besides providing readers with a picture of the Lerche's home where Tom was living, he also offered a silhouette representation of the Tom whom he saw a week before this article appeared.

LERCHE'S HOME — WHERE BLIND TOM LIVE

"BLIND TOM" –AS HE IS TODAY–

Saying that after that morning in the Lerche's home he could now "make exclamation points out of all the interrogation points." Hallmark described Tom as "living in the wooded, sea girt acres of the Highlands of Navensink, where one can see the great ships go down to the sea and watch the seasons grow and fade in leaf, bird and blossom of glorious woods." Since the Lerche's had also bought the Neptune Boat Club property at the foot of the hill, they were, according to Hallmark, "able to keep approach inviolate by land or water." Besides allowing the woods about the house to grow into tangle and disorder, the writer described how:

> Ten small dogs were constituted as a staff of mili-
> tia; one especial, venomous, yellow mongrel told

to watch approach by land or water. The butcher, baker and express wagons were ordered to remain where they belonged; when provisions were needed la femme Lerche would come after them. The way messengers were shoveled out of the territory so terrorized the villagers that even persuasion by coin of the realm couldn't reason the butcher into driving me (Hallmark) to the house in his wagon.

After giving some historical details about Tom, Hallmark wrote that the "queer stories brought to the cities by the Highlanders about a crazy Negro who lived in the vicinity that frightened the children into crying and older people into running was poor old harmless Blind Tom and not a weird, senseless apparition that somebody hooded." Among the tales:

At evening time in the lonely woods one would suddenly fling both hands into the air, making weird sounds with his lips, rolling his great eyes around in an appalling manner.

To shriek and run seems to have been all the Highlanders did. The boy who waves a flag at the railroad curve along the shore, tells of this same Negro appearing on the little platform to take the train. Swede and Italian laborers were loafing around when the queer black man suddenly jumps into the air and applauds wildly and bows and cries "Bravo! Bravo!"

Again there the coward muscles of the onlookers turned for flight, and the slogan of the old-time plantation hands that somebody's hooded-seems to be gaining ground in the Highlands of Navesink.

As a way of explanation, Hallmark felt that since Lerche was of French descent and his wife, Elise Bethune, of German descent, with a fair English-speaking ability who sometimes spoke in French to their neighbors, she was considered to be "the evil eye." When added to this was their fear of Tom, a "sightless, imbecile with weird incantations and gestures," one could not, in his opinion, blame the villagers for their growing fear.

Describing how he had left Philadelphia on a rainy and foggy day, changed trains five times, and after the difficulty of "getting anyone to venture to drive him to the Lerche's house," then hearing "creepy tales" by the person who finally consented to guide him and "a raw-boned horse over hill and vale through slippery roads," the reporter was next confronted by the dogs and "a personage in workman's suit of blue homespun, who roared at him when he met him." Though having to talk through the doorway, that person admitted the Negro was "Old Blind Tom." After relating some information about Tom's daily life, Lerche (whom the writer assumed to be the person) said "whether Tom will ever appear again in public is a question since in his opinion the pianist was a fad and the desire for him over." According to Hallmark:

> No one is allowed to speak to the Negro. When the Lerches leave him they bolt every window and door in the house. Another reason why he and they have remained the mystery, par excellence, of Navesink!
>
> Mr. Lerche did not ask me into the house. He told me that Blind Tom was away. He added that his wife was away also. "Doesn't she live here with you?" I asked. "When she is about," he answered.

However, when departing, the guide made known to Hallmark that Tom "had been peeping out of a battered upstairs window throughout his entire conversation with Lerche."

An article by a John A. Beckett in the September 1898 *Ladies Home Journal* offered proof that despite some claims that Tom died in the 1889 Johnstown Flood, he was still alive and well.[14] Titled "Blind Tom As He Is Today," the writer gives a detailed account of the day he spent with the pianist at the Lerche's home that summer. In addition to his description of the Lerche's home as being a "picturesque two-and-a-half story wooden house with a broad veranda," he published the following picture of Tom in the spacious yard with his dog, who he named Paderewski.

In addition was the picture of Tom being taken for his daily drive with Mr. Lerche, another example given by the writer to support his characterization of the pianist as "enjoying an exist-ence more full of comforts and happiness than fall to the lot of most mortals."

According to Beckett, Tom, on the date of his visit, having expected him to be the piano tuner "to correct a faulty A on his concert grand," opened the door himself; however, when discov-ering he was not "with a child-like droop of disappointment shut the door in his face." When he was let into the house by Mr. Lerche (who had invited him), Tom was asked by his guardian to give Beckett information concerning the piano's short-comings as a "pacifying influence," to which Tom said: "The A is wrong" while pressing his finger on the note; "and then this high A is a little out too," as he sounded another, two or three octaves above the first.

Noting how he "put his finger on each note, without any hesitation," Beckett described Blind Tom's speaking as being in a "rich, full voice and with much simple dignity with a respectfulness in his air and pose."

This was followed by Tom's performance of a "brilliant composition" for the writer who characterized his "technique as good and an execution of runs with perfect ease and fluency." Of Tom's physical aspects and piano presence, Beckett wrote:

> Tom's head and face are not wholly unattractive. He has often been described as a repulsive imbecile except during his moments at the piano. This is not so. His head is small but well shaped. His features are of a strong African type, with low forehead, large eyes, nose and mouth and a general heaviness rather than weakness. His skin is not perfectly black. In his appearance, and in his manner of speaking when addressed—and during the whole day he made no remark to any one actually present except when addressed—he shows intelligence and dignity, with quite a pride of his own at times.
>
> While playing, he moves his body very little; his head is at an angle of forty-five degrees, the eyes upturned, the heavy lower lip pendulous, and there is a sense of utter absorption in the music. He has an odd way of bringing this lower lip up and letting it fall at short intervals, as a fish works his mouth while breathing. He uses only one foot in pedaling—his right—and nearly always it was the loud pedal that he pressed. When the passage called for no pedal he stuck the front of his foot under the pedal. This was invariable. After finishing his piece he stood up and his right hand habitually went up to his face.

About other aspects of his playing Beckett wrote:

> Before I left, Tom played other things for me. I asked him if he had ever heard Gottschalk, and

Tom said: "I play 'The Last Hope.'" This is a composition of Gottschalk's which is better known
than any other. He played it at once. Then, with a
purpose, I asked him if he played "The Maiden's
Prayer," a question one would hardly put to an
intelligent pianist today. But I wished to see how
his memory would carry a piece as old as this,
which he could not have played for years, and I
also wanted to see whether he would show any
disdain for this old threadbare thing which it was
the proud ambition of our mothers to play at their
graduation exercises. Without a moment's hesitation he played it.

Concerning Tom's non-musical activities, he told readers that:

One pleasure which has a healthy side to it, and is
in keeping with Blind Tom's cleanliness, is his daily
bath in the Shrewsbury. In warm weather when
the tide is favorable, he dons his bathing suit, walks
down to the shore from the house and ducks and
paddles about and splashes in the water. He can
take a few strokes, but he labors under the pleasing illusion that he is a peerless, long-distance
swimmer. At first he did not take very kindly to
this agreeable diversion, but he has come to be
very fond of his bath, enjoying it hugely.

Readers were also given some further insights into Tom's character and daily activities by Beckett who wrote that:

Tom never drinks, swears, nor shows any vicious
inclinations. He is scrupulously neat, and most
regular and methodical in his habits. He rises at
seven, has breakfast at nine, dinner at half-past
one, and supper at six. He goes to bed a little after
nine. He has an attendant who looks after him at
mealtime, as he has to have his meat cut for him.
He finds his napkin and tucks that in around his
neck himself. He has a good appetite although by

no means is he a heavy eater. He is fond of fruit— watermelons preferred—likes all kinds of pie except mince, and is very fond of sugar. He never drinks coffee. He is sensitive to cold. Sometimes when he feels a strong breeze blowing on him he will say: "Tom's in a draft. He may catch cold and die. Wouldn't that be terrible?" He has this artless fear of death, yet he has composed a funeral march for himself, in which there is one movement so cheerfully bright as to be almost pathetic. This march was played at the funeral of his master, John G. Bethune, who was killed in a railway accident in 1883.

Tom is of a religious turn of mind. He will play only sacred music on Sunday. He says the Lord's Prayer in his room aloud, and is fond of reciting passages from the Holy Scriptures, being especially fond of Saint Paul's Epistles to the Corinthians.

Since several descriptions of Tom's alleged contentment and spirituality are similar to those in the *New York Sun,* one can assume that these were related to both writers by Mr. Lerche as a way of countering the continuous charges concerning the exploitation of Tom; this fact notwithstanding, Beckett, in a closing paragraph, made reference to the "fortunes Tom made for Colonel Bethune, his son, John G. Bethune, and lastly for the widow of John G. Bethune who is now the wife of the lawyer, Albrecht J. Lerche, in whose residence he saw Tom." That some in the Black community maintained interest in Blind Tom might be surmised from the September 10, 1898, issue of the *Baltimore Afro-American Journal* where the editor referred his readers to the Beckett article since it would "set all the rumors about Tom's death aside" and let his "many friends and admirers know that Tom is still living and plays his piano as in days gone by."

Tom's two concerts at the Boston Theatre on February 5, 1899, were advertised as part of a "Farewell Tour."[15] Obviously ticket sales increased since, in the "local mention section" of the February 2nd *Boston Evening Star,* it was revealed that "judging by the big advanced sale, Blind Tom, the musical prodigy, will be greeted by large audiences in the Boston Theatre; the occasion is his farewell appearance on the concert stage here incidental to his farewell tour of the world." Another inducement might have been the announcement that "as a test of his genius for imitation, two of Boston's best known pianists will play several of their own musical compositions which he has never heard and will play after one hearing." According to the February 6, 1899, *Boston Evening Transcript* Tom was "assisted by the Arion Mandolin, Banjo and Guitar Club." Soon after his "Military Waltz" for organ or piano was published by J.W. Jenkins Sons (Kansas City, Missouri) under the pseudonym C.T. Messengale. It was described on the frontispiece as "the popular hit played by the all-white Fort Riley Military Band."[16] Located between Junction City and Manhattan, Kansas, this fort was established in 1852 to protect wagon trains against Indians.[17]

By the end of the nineteenth century the movement for complete disenfranchisement of Blacks had reunited the South; their state constitutional conventions passed laws to guarantee White supremacy. Besides the exclusion of Blacks from Mississippi's political life at their August 1890 convention, delegates to the South Carolina Convention in 1895 effectively disenfranchised most Blacks by requiring payment of all taxes, literacy tests, property worth $300, a poll tax of one dollar and two-year residency—this at a time when most were living in a neo-servitude share-cropping existence. In 1896 Louisiana became the third state to disfranchise Blacks when a new device, the "Grandfather Clause" was written into their constitution.[18] The United States Supreme Court's "Plessy vs. Ferguson" decision of 1896 upheld segregation in its "separate but equal doctrine."[19] In addition to these legally enforced discriminatory practices, almost 500 lynchings of Blacks occurred within a five-year period.[20]

Despite this and evidence of Northern racial prejudice, Black Americans participated in the Spanish American War which was declared against Spain on December 10, 1898. According to Marvin Fletcher, a military historian, "in this era of increasing legal and economic discrimination, many Blacks saw the War as an opportunity to change their down-trodden position."[21] Perry E. Gianakas, when writing about this war and the "double paradox of Black Americans" says:

> On the one hand, there was widespread sympa-
> thy for down-trodden peoples abroad (the Cubans,
> in this instance); but on the other hand, while
> there was sympathy for the down-trodden farm-
> ers, Populists, and workers at home, there was a
> noticeable lack of sympathy for the down-trod-
> den people of color at home, the one sizable group
> perhaps most needful of organized sympathy.[22]

Four Black regiments in the Army compiled an outstanding combat record in and around Santiago, Cuba, during the war. The 9th and 10th Cavalry particularly distinguished themselves along-side Theodore Roosevelt's "Rough Riders" in the charge up San Juan Hill, and the 24th and 25th infantry regiments fought at Siboney and El Caney, Cuba. Roosevelt told of the bravery of Blacks he saw fighting in the Spanish American War and suggested that the "Democrats devote some time to the wrongs of the men on whose breasts may be seen the scars gained as they fought for the flag."[23] Obviously Roosevelt had good reason to be glad that Black troops were present at the Las Guisimos engagement since, as one writer wrote: "When the Rough Riders fell into the 'ambush' the Spaniards had prepared on that occasion, they were saved by Negro troops." In his September 24, 1898, editorial, Edward E. Cooper of the *Colored American* wrote that "the Negro was no longer on trial, because his loyalty as a citizen had been amply demonstrated on the battlefield." Not unexpectedly, the editorial positions of Black journalists were divided in support of what was later referred to as "the White man's burden." While some felt that Blacks had a duty to destroy Spanish tyranny, avenge the 22 Black sailors killed aboard the USS *Maine* (sunk in Havana Harbor on February 15, 1898), a free Cuba, others argued that Blacks should not fight in Cuba until "the Constitutional rights of black citizens at home had been guaranteed."

Ironically, though the last five years of the nineteenth century became the apex in discriminatory laws and customs, it was also a period of unprecedented heralded Black musical achieve-ments. The year 1898 marked a major point in the development of Black theatricals when Bob Cole produced "A Trip to Coontown." According to Henry T. Sampson "this show was the first to make a complete break from the minstrel pattern, being written with a continuity, and having a cast of characters working out the story from beginning to end, the first show written, produced, managed, and staged by Blacks."[24] In that same year Will Marion Cook's "Clorindy, the Origin of the Cakewalk" scored a triumph in the heart of Broadway. John W. Isham's 1896 "Oriental American" demonstrated that Blacks could perform "material hitherto reserved for Whites since the finale included selections from operas." In that same year, Sissieretta Jones was featured in an "operatic kaleidoscope" as part of the "Black Patti's Troubadours Vaudeville troupe" another example of an audience for Black musical entertainment which appealed to all classes and races. On July 4, 1896, the *New York Clipper* reported that "Black Patti, the Troubadour's attractive stage entertainment, which embraced vaudeville comedy and operatic features with her shining in the operatic olio, then was touring Indiana and Ohio to good business." During the Kaleidoscope, Jones, assisted by an ensemble of singers and chorus, performed scenes from *Carmen, Faust, Il Travatore, Rigoletto* and other operas from the popular repertory, replete with costumes and scenery. The October 10, 1896, *Indianapolis Freeman* reported that Mme. Marie Selika, Mme. Sissieretta Jones, and Mme. Flora Batson Bergen were to make a historic appearance together at the Centennial Jubilee in New York's Carnegie Hall on October 12th. Rachel Walker, the 23-year-old mezzo-soprano who was billed as the "Creole Nightingale," had signed a contract with Mr. Hammerstein for a 25-week engagement and at the close of the tour returned to the Paris Conservatory to complete her studies. According to an editorial review in the *New York Dramatic News* about her concert at Hammerstein's Olympic roof garden concert:

> It is seldom that a singer of such real artistic worth as Rachel Walker is heard at a roof garden, but that such merit is appreciated by Olympic patrons is attested by the storms of applause which nightly reward that artist's efforts. Miss Walker possesses a mezzo-soprano voice of rare beauty and flexibility. She sings with the intensity and appreciation of a real artist, and her talents entitle her to high rank on the concert stage, for hers is not merely a finely trained voice without a trace of personality,

but one full of expression and appreciation of the composer's idea. Her first song was evidently a vocal arrangement of a violin solo, familiar to the concert goer, which enabled her to show her technique, but for her remaining songs she wisely dropped the severely classical and gave "The Last Rose of Summer" and "Swanee River" to the unbounded satisfaction of the audience.

Harry Lawrence Freeman, who won recognition as a Black opera composer when his first opera, *Martyr*, was produced in September 1893 at the Denver Colorado Deutsche Theatre, completed his second opera, *Nada*, in 1898 (performed 2 years later by the Cleveland Symphony). Three art songs of Harry T. Burleigh were published by G. Schirmer in 1898. It was also a landmark year for Samuel Coleridge-Taylor, an Anglo-African composer. Appointed violin teacher at Croydon Conservatory the previous year, he became in 1898 the director of their conservatory orchestra, and his *Hiawatha's Wedding Feast,* a cantata for tenor solo, chorus and orchestra (on a text of Henry Wadsworth Longfellow), was performed on November 11th at the Royal College of Music with the internationally famed composer-conductor, Sir Charles Stanford conducting. *The Death of Minnehaha*, the second of this choral trilogy, was performed October 26, 1899, at the North Staffordshire Festival. Both were widely acclaimed in England and the United States. That Coleridge-Taylor's fame was already established in America before this landmark work is evident by the fact that when the noted Black poet, Paul Lawrence Dunbar, visited England in 1896 to give public readings of his poems, he sought the composer out in order to engage him in joint recitals. Coleridge-Taylor used some of Dunbar's poetry from his "Lyrics of Lowly Life" in his art songs, *African Romances*, p. 17. Although none of the poems specifically refer to Africa, Coleridge-Taylor saw in them romance and ethnic identity.[25]

Besides those Black composers who wrote in the European compositional style, there were many who developed a distinctive style of entertainment music that combined elements of European and African music traditions. Scott Joplin's "Maple Leaf Rag" was published by John Stark, in Sedalia, Missouri, summer 1899. As Eileen Southern noted, this piece "brought unprecedented success, commercially and artistically, to both composer and publisher; the piece sold more than a million copies; more important, it established a model for classic ragtime that was imitated by all rag composers interested in serious composition." Although the "Mississippi Rag" by White songwriter-bandleader William H. Krell was published in 1897, it was the drive and charm of Scott Joplin's piece "that ushered in the 'ragtime era,' one of America's first significant popular notated instrumental expressions."[26]

As for Blind Tom, it seems he performed fewer public concerts. There was, however, more press coverage concerning his physical condition and poetic remembrances about his musical genius.

Notes

1. See: Southall, *Blind Tom*, Book I, pp.4-6.
2. *Washington Post* (February 14, 1985).
3. A newspaper editor in Georgia during the 1840s, he became the first Democrat to take a bold stand for free trade, he advocated abolishment of custom house, and he favored supporting government by direct taxation of states. He was politically associated with Alexander H. Stephen, Robert Toombs, the Calquitts and Lamars, all important political figures at the state and national levels during that time.
4. *New York Times* (July 31, 1887).
5. *Quannah (Texas) Tribune* (January 10, 1895).
6. *Colorado Springs Gazette* (January 18, 1895).
7. *Abilene (Texas) Reporter* (February 1, 1895).
8. *Galveston Daily News* (March 25, 1895).
9. *Ibid.* (March 24, 1895).
10. *Little Rock (Arkansas) Gazette* (May 3, 1895).
11. Republished in *Columbus (Georgia) Magazine* (July 31, 1941).
12. *Colored Citizen*, Topeka, Kansas (October 28, 1897).
13. *Fall River Daily Globe* (August 27, 1897).
14. According to Beckett, based on an identification by a woman of the male victim named Thomas Wiggins, an inscription was put on the Pennsylvania tombstone bearing his name.
15. "Blind Tom's Farewell," *Boston Herald* (January 29, 1899).
16. Copyright, February 18, 1899.
17. See: W. F. Pride. *The History of Fort Riley* (Fort Riley, 1926).
18. Louisiana, in order to protect its poor Whites from the stringent educational and economic requirements of 1896, added the "Grandfa-

ther Clause" to its state constitution. Under the clause, if a man's father or grandfather had voted on Jan. 1, 1867, his name would be added to the permanent registration list, regardless of his ability to comply with voting requirements. Since no Blacks could have met these requirements, slaves obviously had no father who voted, it was a way to "legally" disenfranchise them.

19. In this case the U.S. Supreme Court upheld Louisiana's "separate but equal" segregation law. The ruling was a major setback for integration and marks the beginning of Jim Crow laws. Homer Plessy, a light-skinned Black, brought a suit against the railroad in 1892 after being arrested for riding in a White-only coach.

20. Peter Bergman and Mort N. Bergman. *The Chronological History of the Negro in America* (N.Y.: New American Library, 1969).

21. Marvin Fletcher. "The Black Volunteer in the Spanish-American War," *Military Affairs* (April, 1974).

22. Perry E. Gianakas. "The Spanish-American War and the Boble Parados of the Negro American," *Phylon* (Spring, 1965), p. 34-49.

23. Howard K. Beale. *Theodore Roosevelt and the Rise of America to World Power* (Baltimore: Johns Hopkins Press, 1956), pp. 71-72.

24. Henry T. Sampson. *Blacks in Blackface* (Metuchen, New Jersey: Icarician Press, 1980), p. 9.

25. William Tortalano. *Samuel Coleridge-Taylor, Anglo-Black Composer, 1875-1912* (Metuchen, New Jersey: Scarecrow Press, 1977), Chapter 2.

26. Ellen Southern. *Music of Black Americans*, p. 318. See also: Terry Waldo. *This Is Ragtime* (New York, Hawthorn Books, Inc.); Edward A. Berline. *Ragtime: a Musical and Cultural History* (Berkeley: University of California Press, 1980); and John Edward Hasse. *Ragtime: Its History, Composers, and Music* (New York, Schuman Books, 1985).

Chapter Five

(1900-1903)

AS THE TWENTIETH CENTURY BEGAN, White supremacy had triumphed throughout the South. In George Fredrickson's opinion, "Southern negrophobia was enhanced that year when a religious publishing house brought out *The Negro As Beast* by Charles Carroll since it revived the pre-adamite argument describing the Negro as literally an ape."[1] Rayford Logan said it was "perhaps the most scurrilous book—one of the most vicious in America."[2] Christopher Lasch, while studying racial attitudes that surfaced during the United States' efforts to end the Philippine Insurrection noted that "southern Democrats were almost unanimous in condemning imperialism on the grounds that 'Asiatics, like Negroes, were innately inferior to White people and could not be assimilated into American life.' "[3]

Not unexpectedly, racial overtones of "Imperialism" became a prominent campaign issue in that year's presidential campaign. In his platform, William Jennings Bryan, the democratic challenger, "condemned as un-American, the Course pursued in the Philippines by the McKinley Administration."[4] According to George P. Meeks, most of the Black press was strongly anti-imperialist and emphasized the interconnection between the government's domestic and foreign policy in dealing with dark-skinned people. Letters from Black soldiers serving in the Philippines tended to confirm the view that the military struggle there was a "race war."[5] Not surprisingly, several Black soldiers defected and served as officers in Emileo Aguinauldo's guerrilla army which, since February 1899, continued the same crusade for independence against the United States as from Spanish rule.[6] On February 23, 1900, during a debate on measures affecting the Philippines, George H. White, the Black congressman from North Carolina, while stating his desire for the United States to deal fairly with that multicultural island, asked:

> Should not a nation be just to all her citizens, protect them alike in all their rights, on every foot of her soil—in a word show herself capable of governing all within her domain before she undertakes to exercise sovereignty over those in a foreign land . . . or, to be more explicit, should not charity first begin at home?[7]

In the previous month, he had introduced House Bill 6963, the first bill to make lynching of American citizens a federal crime which, unfortunately, died in committee.

Concerns about western imperialisms upon the "darker races" was evident at the historic Pan-African Conference held July 23-25, 1900, in London, England, at Westminster Hall. Dr. W.E.B. DuBois, the then thirty-two-year-old professor of history and sociology at Atlanta University, chaired the committee charged with drafting an "Address to the Nations"; the document stated that:

> the problem of the twentieth century is the problem of the color line, the question as to how far differences of race—which show themselves chiefly in the color of the skin and the texture of the hair—will hereafter be made the basis of denying to over half the world the right of sharing to their utmost ability the opportunities and privileges of modern civilization.[8]

Although DuBois, along with several other militant Blacks, supported the Democratic Party, primarily because of its anti-imperialist stand and what they felt was a sympathetic attitude toward the Philippines, most Blacks criticized them for "demanding self-government for Filipinos while denying it to Negroes in the American South."[9] According to one observer, "the enthusiasm of White southern Democrats for William Jennings Bryan cooled considerably during the closing weeks of the Campaign when it became apparent that he was seeking support of the Negroes in the North." Though doing little campaigning, President McKinley was re-elected with a greater percentage of victory than in 1896 and Theodore Roosevelt was elected Vice President.

Racism notwithstanding, several Black classically trained musicians achieved some historic accomplishments. For example: Harry T. Burleigh secured a second church position with the wealthy Temple Emanuel-El as its first Black choir member.[10] *Hiawatha's Departure*, the third section of Samuel Coleridge-Taylor's oratorical trilogy (for soprano, tenor, baritone soloists, chorus and orchestra), was performed on February 22nd by the Royal Choral Society in London's Royal Albert Hall. It was also the year that Theodore Drury's colored opera company began to produce grand opera with their successful performance of Bizet's "Carmen" at the Lexington Opera House in New York. According to H.S. Fortune, musical editor for the *Colored American Magazine,* it was "characterized by a high degree of suavity, with a total lack of friction or amateurism."[11]

It may be that the "operatic Kaleidoscope" finale of the "Black Patti Troubadours" where scenes with a nucleus of operatic scenes and selections performed in costumes appropriate to their production had helped create an acceptable climate for Blacks to perform grand opera in their own organization. Obviously Sissieretta Jones was still a major figure in concert circles. Following her concert engagement in Colorado Springs, the January 27, 1900, *Denver Colorado Statesman* reported that "Black Patti has come and gone. Society turned out en masse to see her. All the boxes were occupied and handsome dresses were worn by the ladies and full dress suits by the gentlemen. It was a sight not witnessed often." Joseph H. Douglass, besides continuing his successful concert tours,[12] announced the opening of his violin school where he would sponsor public recitals by advanced students.[13]

In October 1900, Tom's mother was interviewed by W.C. Woodall for the *Columbus Enquirer*, in Columbus, GA. A photograph of her standing at the gate of her cottage was published with the article.

According to Woodall, Tom's mother was living with one of her daughters and in good health. The writer found it an interesting fact that "of the many thousands of dollars made through the genius of her blind son, she had received a comparatively small

Blind Tom's mother in front of her cottage

amount." He reported that she had recently received "fifteen dollars from the manager of Blind Tom, which the humble household appreciated." Though saying "she would like to be with Tom, she was glad to be in Columbus among her people." When asked about the names of her twenty children, Tom's mother "counted them slowly off on her finger, but was unable to recall their names," saying "some died in slavery time, and others while she was in New York with Blind Tom."

At the time of the interview several of Tom's siblings were living in Columbus as cooks, washer women and day laborers at 50 cents a day; one of them was a church janitor.[14] Woodall's description of Tom's mother as "typical of the hundreds of good-natured old aunties, who are found everywhere in the south" offers the post-Civil War "mammie" characterization from slavery. At the time of the interview Tom's mother had not seen her son for many years and seemed to "deeply resent the separation." She said "they stole him (Tom) from me. When I was in New York I signed away my rights."[15] Woodall noted how Tom's mother always referred (during the interview) to her famous son as "Thomas" rather than "Tom" or "Blind Tom." While most people considered her son "an idiot" she described him as "smart-very smart" though he always stuttered.

On January 2, 1901, the *Jersey City (NJ) Journal* announced that Blind Tom would perform at the Bergen Reformed Church the next night under the auspices of the Ladies Aid Society. When reviewed in the same paper on January 4, 1901, the writer pronounced him "Just As Much of a Genius As He Ever Was." Noting that it had been "persistently reported that Tom was dead," he was alive and had given an interesting and enjoyable concert where he delighted and surprised a large audience, among whom were many musical critics. The program was described as "diversified and each number given with a touch and expression that evoked hearty applause." On February 8th, the *Newark Evening News* announced that "The One and Great Historical Blind Tom" would appear in two concerts at their Association Hall. While Tom was performing in New Jersey, a Black pianist from Atlanta, Georgia, was being described as "Blind Tom No. 2." He was said to be "the equal of the original Tom and played at President McKinley's church in Washington, D.C. to the delight of a large and cultural congregation."[16] However, the reporter did not say if this other pianist was blind, what he played, or his age, though characterizing him as a musical prodigy.

The April 20, 1891, *Colored American* in its section "among theatrical people" announced that "the real Blind Tom is still alive and was seen in Washington, D.C. the previous month." Readers were told that Tom would be doing concerts in the fall and encouraged "his many friends all over the country to give him a rousing reception as that would be his last tour." Continuing what had become the common practice of telling readers in concert advertisements that Blind Tom was still alive, the *Seattle Republican* on May 10, 1891, noted that he was "still under the protection of Mrs. Bethune, his legal guardian, who would be on the road with Tom again, giving performances as of yore." He said that Mrs. Bethune was "keeping a zealous guard over Blind Tom, who undoubtedly makes considerable money out of his musical abilities." In the reporter's opinion, "no one seemed to be more entitled to it than she, as she was caring for Tom and his relatives." Obviously, such a statement that Mrs. Bethune had been generous with Tom's earnings to his family was in contrast to the claims by Tom's mother in her interview the previous year.

The *Southern Workman*, in May 1901, published a poem about Tom by James D. Corrothers, a Black Methodist minister and an important literary figure, who pastored churches in Red Bank and Hackensack, New Jersey.[17]

BLIND TOM, SINGING

By James D. Corrothers

I

Long, long ago I saw Blind Tom.
The noisy audience became calm,
And a hush fell o'er the whispering din,
When the blind musician was led in.
A moment vacantly he stood,
'Till, moved by some mysterious mood,
The while the inspiration burned,
He, to the harp that waited, turned,
And, seated there at graceful ease,
He swept his hands along the keys,
Awaking sound so soft and clear
That Silence bent with eager ear
Its faintest whisperings to hear.
He clapped his hands like a little child,
And sang in accents low and mild:
    "Dem a gates ajar I'm boun' to see,
    Dem a gates ajar I'm boun' to see,
    Dem a gates ajar I'm boun' to see,
      O, sinner, fare you well."

II

He turned those sightless eyes to God,
His thoughts in fields of fancy trod,
Where songs unsung and notes unheard,
And sweeter sounds than song of bird,
Floating on vapory mists of light,
Descended 'round the poor blind wight,

Plashing like rain drops o'er the keys!
And sobbed in tender symphonies
O'er flowery dells where silver streams
Fell tinkling thro' a land of dreams.
He paused, and in a moment more,
We heard a cataract's loud uproar,
And rumbling thunder rolled afar,
And maddened cannon bellowed war;
The drums beat and the fifers blew
Many an old tune that we knew.
Then all was hushed, and, solemnly
The curtain of eternity
Arose; and down the star-lit blue
Of the vast heavens great angels flew,
In happy band, to drift along
On the blind singer's rapturous song:
        "Dah's room a 'nuff in heben, I know,
        Dah's room a 'nuff in heben, I know,
        Dah's room a 'nuff in heben, I know,
            O, sinner, fare you well."

III

He paused, as if some power before
Commanded him to touch no more
His throbbing ivory plaything. And,
Obedient to that command,
He ceased, and gazed in thankful mood
Toward the Giver of all good.
(O Father, if to all could come
The things revealed to poor Blind Tom,
We, too, would clap our hands in glee,
Rejoiced they wondrous truths to see.
The scales would leave our blinded eyes,
And earth would be a paradise
Where creed and color, tongue and clime
Would melt away like morning rime;
And, like poor Tom, with self unsought,
All should make melody untaught.)
Long, long with upturned face he stood
As gazing on some heavenly flood.

And no man dared to speak a word-
No soul in that vast audience stirred.
For well we knew that where he stood,
The blind musician talked with God;
Nor did we doubt the silent prayer
Was granted as we watched him there;
For even as he turned to go,
We heard him singing sweet and low:
> "A starry crown I'm a-goin' foh to wear,
> A starry crown I'm a-goin' for to wear,
> A starry crown I'm agoin' for to wear-
>> O, sinner, fare you well."

Interestingly, this poem by a Black theologian who had heard the pianist many years earlier, probably offers one of the only examples of Blind Tom singing a religious song in dialect during his concerts.

On July 23, 1901, it was reported in the *North American* that Blind Tom would give a series of concerts in Atlantic City, New Jersey. The first of these would be a benefit concert for their Poor Children's Relief Fund as the announcement shows:

BLIND TOM AT THE PIANO

Famous Colored Musician, Restored to Health, Enlists for Charity

Blind Tom, who has been six times reported by the newspapers as dead, is still very much alive. His manager has arranged a series of concerts, at which the famous colored musician will render the latest repertoire that his strange power of imitation has brought to him. The first of these concerts is to take place at the Royal Palace Hotel Casino, in Atlantic City, the proceeds go to the North American's Poor Children's Relief Fund. The concert is set for Saturday evening next, July 27.

Mr. Pike very generously donated the use of the Casino for the occasion, saying, as he did so, that

> The North American's charity work for the chil-
> dren of the Galieys is so very worthy that he will
> gladly do everything in his power to help it along.

This was followed by biographical information about Tom. However, a statement about Tom being placed "in an asylum" by his former owners in 1882 was not true since he was performing constantly throughout the South that year.[18] The concert reviews focused entirely on Tom's memory of places and times in the past. As the two examples show, those questioning him admitted to trying to trap him—both times unsuccessfully.[19] In the reviewer's opening statement he wrote that "Atlantic City continues to marvel over Blind Tom's wonderful memory which brought informal crowds to gather around his chair to test it personally." He added that "any hesitancy by him belongs to his speech rather than to his memory." Noted was the fact that Tom never failed to give us a civil "Sir" in his replies:

> W.R. Brackville, of Bellefonte, Pa., tried his hand
> next at the mystifying of this mystery, "Tom, were
> you ever at Bellefonte, Pa.?" "Yes, sir." "When?"
> "I was there in 1871, sir," came Tom's reply in
> non-committal tone. The gentleman looked aston-
> ished, and leaning over, whispered to his wife, "Well
> he's wrong for once, for we didn't move there till
> later than that!" But the woman's wit solved the
> trouble. "Well, Tom, were you there more than
> once?" "Yes, ma'am, I was there the second time
> in 1878." "That's it," said Mrs. Brackville, "that
> was just after we went there." "And, Tom, what
> did you do with yourself on Sunday?" Tom's lips
> lost for a moment their immobility. "Well, ma'am,
> I didn't go to church!" "Indeed you didn't, and we
> did our best to make you."

Obviously Tom's failure to attend church in 1878 by choice is debatable given the reality of his being physically and emotionally controlled and dependent on his then former slave master.

A gentleman from Richmond, Va., asked Tom
when he had given a concert there. And Tom answered readily enough: "In 1865, sir." But in his
next question the gentleman made the mistake of
saying: "Now, Tom I'm going to fool you! Where
did you play?" explaining to neighbors that he
probably thought he played in a theatre, whereas
he had played in a church. But Tom was silent as
the grave until his manager said: "Tom, you know
where you played in Richmond; tell the gentleman." And Tom promptly answered: "I played in
the African M.D. Church." "He did, indeed," said
his questioner, "and we were the only two white
people there, I believe."

According to the reviewer, Blind Tom was taken to the *North
American* reading room where he was shown a gramophone; after
listening to the pieces on the machine, he "astonished his manager by performing them in his next concert." Other concerts that
year were in Philadelphia (Oct. 2nd, Witherspoon Hall), Washington, D.C. (Oct. 6th, Columbus Theatre) and Baltimore, Maryland
(October 8th, 9th, 10th, Academy of Music Concert Hall). Reviewing one of the Baltimore concerts, it was noted that "with the
exception of a perceptible touch of frost about his temple and
perhaps, a gain of several pounds in weight, his mannerisms are
the same, his imitative powers still keep and astounding as ever,
and execution still as faultless."[20] It was also the year Mrs. Bethune
had his "Grand March Resurrection" published by Tiller, Sons and
Danna in New York.

On December 7, 1902, the *Atlanta Constitution* reported the
death of Blind Tom's mother. Titled "Mother of Blind Tom Passes
Away: Tales of Her Wonderful Son," the reporter wrote that "many
of the later generation of Negroes attended the funeral, but she
had long outlived the majority of old friends with whom she was
intimate when first the remarkable genius of her son became a
national wonder." The reporter asked the question, "Was Tom's
gift from prenatal Influence?" He provided the following basis for
asking it:

> Blind Tom's birth raises an interesting question
> in psychology, and has been the subject of com-
> ment in lectures of some of the most eminent men
> of science in the country. Shortly before his birth
> there were a number of young ladies at the home
> of his mother's Owners and they were all musi-
> cians. They played on the piano in the evenings
> and frequently had Charity (Tom's mothers name)
> dance for them, a duty that fell lightly on the shoul-
> ders of the Negro, who violently loved not only
> the dancing, but the music. She took advantage
> of every opportunity to hear the piano and seemed
> enchanted with its melodies. She had a good
> memory and learned many of the selections,
> though not able to play herself. This is supposed
> to account largely or wholly for the wonderful tal-
> ent of her son.

According to the December 26, 1902, *Professional World,*
Tom's mother died in Alabama and was buried in Columbus, Georgia; she was 105 years old. About Tom, it was reported that he
"was still living in semi-confinement with the family made rich by
his genius, at Atlantic Highlands, some twenty-five miles outside
of New York City." In addition "during the summer season he may
be seen any pleasant day standing on the veranda of the house
listening to the birds sing, and, then rush to his Grand Piano to
imitate the warble of nature's songsters."

Although Tom seemingly was not doing concerts in 1902, other
classically trained Black musicians were enjoying successful careers. The *Professional World,* a Black paper founded that year
by Rufus Logan for the State of Missouri, kept readers informed
about the "Blind Boone Concert Company." According to an August 22, 1902, article, Boone's musical talents had brought him a
fortune, making him a "large realty owner, owner of a splendid
farm in Johnson County, Missouri and an elegant and sumptu-
ously furnished home in Columbus, Missouri, where he lived with
his wife." There was also information about Boone's "very liberal
spirit." He had "materially assisted churches and other charitable
and worthy organizations."

In September 1902, the *Negro Music Journal*, a "Monthly Magazine Devoted to the Educational Interest of the Negro Race in Music," was published and became another source about Black musicians.[21] Each entry in the *Negro Music Journal* was devoted toward fulfilling the objective stated by its editor, J. Hillary Taylor in the first issue:

> We shall endeavor to get the majority of our people interested in that class of music which will purify their minds, lighten their hearts, touch their souls and be a source of joy to them forever. It is the music of yesterday and today, or in other words, the old masters like Bach, Handel, Mozart and others: The music of today is given us by S. Coleridge-Taylor, Grieg, Chaminade, Saint Saëns, Paderewski . . . these names being only a few of the many great and good composers and musicians the world has given us.

Though there were only fifteen issues (September 1902 through August 1903), they provide an important source of information about the activities of Black classical musicians at the turn of the century.

The weekly *Colored American*, however, remained the major source about Black classical musicians. On April 12, 1902, it reported about Joseph Douglass' New England concert tour which began in Cambridge, Massachusetts, at the St. Paul AME church that March. The October 4, 1902, issue announced his first concert in Washington, D.C. There followed a successful tour with his performance of "the great work of Wieneawski 'Sauvenir de Moscow' executed only by the greatest masters of the violin." The writer expressed the concerns of Joseph Douglass "to be considered among the rank of violin virtuoso solely on his merits rather than a reverence for his deceased immortal grandfather, Frederick Douglass."

The *Colored American* also covered the concert activities of Joseph Douglass' student, Clarence Cameron White. He attended the Oberlin Conservatory of Music from 1896-1901 and while there "in a class of 183, all White except himself, easily led and was chosen class representative, scoring a pronounced triumph by his scholarly rendition of S. Coleridge-Taylor's 'Gypsy Song.' "[22] Although he was on the faculty of Avery College, Allegheny, Pennsylvania, at the age of 22, he left his teaching position to embark upon a concert career. According to the paper, he was already booked for performances in the large cities in Illinois and Ohio. He also played at the White House for President McKinley, after which his fame spread and he received offers to give concerts throughout the country. His concert debut at Boston's Parker Memorial Hall was on January 3, 1902.[23]

Sissieretta Jones (Black Patti) was likewise having a good concert year. On December 2, 1902, I.M. McCorker in the *Indianapolis Freeman* wrote about her concert where she did selections from several grand operas and was said to "rival the interpreters of the 'Intermezzo' from Macagni's *Cavalieria Rusticana.*" *The Colored American* announced on March 29, 1902, that the Theodore Drury Opera Company would be performing Gounod's opera *Faust* at New York's Opera House. The year also saw the organization of the Samuel Coleridge-Taylor Society of Washington, D.C. It came into being at the instigation of Mrs. Andrew F. Hilyer who had met the composer when she was visiting London the previous year. Her aim was to "form a Black choral group that could perform the works of the distinguished Negro composer."[24] Soon after the *Colored American* was reporting that the society was already engaged in rehearsing "Hiawatha" every Tuesday evening at 7:30 P.M. at Lincoln Memorial Temple. On March 29, 1902, the paper reported that the chorus now numbered over 200 voices and that "great pain will be taken by the committee to select only the best voices, so as to produce the most artistic rendition possible."

On December 21, 1903, the Sunday *Brooklyn (NY) Eagle* printed the announcement shown at the top of the following page. According to this article "it was reported by the press of the country that this musical phenomenon had died suddenly in a New Jersey sanitarium from the result of an operation." One prominent New York physician had even published "an interesting analysis of Tom's brain." Tom's return to the concert stage was a result of interest in him by Percy Williams, an important vaudeville manager who built the Brooklyn Orpheum in 1901.[25] It seems

"BLIND TOM," PIANIST, TO BE HEARD IN PUBLIC AGAIN

Brooklyn Soon to Hear the "Black Wizard of the Keyboard."

MANY BELIEVED HE WAS DEAD.

Famous Negro Musician Retired Years Ago and Lives in Picturesque Home in New Jersey.

---

that when hearing that Blind Tom was still alive, manager Williams found his whereabouts and negotiated with Mrs. Bethune to let Tom perform one week in his vaudeville. He listened to him informally and was assured that this older Tom was still able to "electrify the public and retained his remarkable power of mimicry and retentive memory."

The reporter described Tom as "being in a happy frame of mind and very religious. He was said to play only sacred music on Sunday, said the Lord's prayer and was fond of reciting passages from the Scriptures." Despite these positive statements concerning Tom's keyboard skills, his musicianship and deep spirituality, the reporter seemingly felt it necessary to write negatively about him by saying:

> In appearance he is an awkward, uncouth, and
> ungainly looking man, and looks more like an
> overgrown boy. He is a little over 5 feet 7 inches
> in height and weighs 240 pounds. His woolly hair
> is cut close to the head. He has a low forehead,
> flat nose, thick lips and heavy jaw, and is, in fact

a perfect type of Negro. He usually wears a black
Suit and a plain black bow tie.

After repeating the usual biographical information of how he
began his piano playing as a slave child, the reporter says that
"Tom's mother is still alive, aged 85," which leads one to question
whether Mrs. Bethune knew she had died the previous year.

Because of the vaudeville format, Tom was appearing as the
headline attraction with other entertainers, among them R.J. Jose,
the minstrel with a sweet voice and Macart's Dogs and Monkeys.
According to the December 27th *Brooklyn Daily Eagle,* since the
Orpheum opened December 31, 1900, "to celebrate the anniversary, handsome souvenirs will be given to women patrons at the
Thursday evening concert." Not unexpectedly, the return of Blind
Tom brought out skeptics who questioned whether he was the
real one. The following letter was published in the December 27,
1903, *Brooklyn Daily Eagle*:

> To the Editor of the Brooklyn Eagle:
>
> In reading over the article of last Monday's Eagle
> about the appearance of Blind Tom at the
> Orpheum in this city, I have come to the conclu-
> sion that either Percy Williams, who directs the
> destinies of that place of amusement is being im-
> posed upon, or that he is imposing on a too con-
> fiding public. I know for a positive fact that the
> original Blind Tom whose real name was Thomas
> Wiggins, and as such was buried. The Inscription
> on his tombstone in the Johnstown Cemetery will
> prove this.
>
> > Yours very truly,
> > JOHN P. JENKINS
> > 398 Fourth Avenue, Brooklyn

Percy Williams, when shown the letter, responded thus: "I have
offered to give $1,000 to any local charity if it can be proved that
the Blind Tom who is to appear this week at my house is not the
same man who electrified the country with his playing forty years
ago." That offer still holds good, despite all claims to the contrary.

When trying to reach the letter writer, the *Eagle* reporter discovered the address given to be a vacant lot adjoining the Brooklyn baseball club, and no one in the neighborhood knew a Mr. Jenkins.

When reviewing Tom's opening concert for the December 29, 1903, *Brooklyn Eagle*, the reporter began by telling the numerous ways he supposedly died, saying: "Had Blind Tom died as many times and in as many ways as the newspapers have had him die within the last dozen years, the proverbial nine lives of a cat would have been an insufficient supply." The reporter then listed some of them as:

> Tom has been killed in the Johnstown Flood; He has died of consumption, and his brain has been analyzed by an eminent doctor for a Manhattan "newspaper;" once he fell down an elevator, several times he has lost his life in train wrecks, his body being mangled quite beyond recognition, and on one occasion he leaped from the Eads Bridge at St. Louis. On this occasion, an enterprising western paper announced that Tom heard the murmuring waters below and could not resist the temptation to get nearer to the music.

According to the reporter, many at the concert "were fearful that this pianist might be a freak—a 'ringer' to use a race track term." There were many in the audience who well remembered the "Blind Tom" who electrified the country a third of a century ago and instantly recognized him as the real prodigy of the past. At the conclusion of his concert there was hearty applause and it was felt his best piece from a musician's viewpoint was "The Last Hope" by Gottschalk, which "was well-nigh perfect." The review ended with Tom's playing described as "at time seemed to be almost inspired and the melody would flow with all the natural beauty and the delightful cadence of the rippling of a woodland rill; again there would be a clash of harmony and discord—like sweet bells jingling wildly out of tune." Unfortunately the reporter had to add that "he is the same crude, uncouth, phenomenon that he was back in the sixties." In that reviewer's opinion among the other acts at the Orpheum the best feature (after Tom) was an octet of pretty girls called the Vassar Girls who played on various instruments while the Macart's "dogs and monkeys" and the Sander Trio of gymnasts were entertaining.

In addition to Blind Tom's historic return at the Orpheum, New Yorkers were also able to attend the first complete performance of "Parsifal," Wagner's religious opera, outside of his own theater at Bayreuth.[26] That performance at the Metropolitan Opera House became a milestone in musical and dramatic history (whatever its artistic merit) since it proved that despite the objections by Wagner's widow, "Parsifal" could be successfully performed in other opera houses.

Besides the return of Blind Tom, several other historic events among Black musicians occurred that year. In Washington, D.C., pianist Harriet Gibb Marshall founded the Washington Conservatory of Music which offered Black students an opportunity to obtain conservatory training.[27] In addition was the sponsorship of regular concerts and other cultural activities. Besides the faculty and student recitals were guest recitals by national Black artists. The Burleigh Choral Society was also organized that year by a group of Black musicians who devoted themselves to the study of choruses from great oratorias and cantatas.

The Samuel Coleridge-Taylor Society of Washington (organized the previous year) gave its first concert on April 22, 1903, at the Metropolitan AME Church, when the complete cantata "Scenes from the Song of Hiawatha" by Coleridge-Taylor was performed. According to the May 2, 1903, *Colored American,* this initial concert by the society was "enthusiastically greeted by musicians, music lovers, and society people of both races who filled all available space in the Grand Auditorium of the church." It was performed that fall in Baltimore's music hall where "every seat was sold days before the concert and hundreds were compelled to stand."[28] On June 1, 1903, the society's board of managers invited the composer to come to the United States and personally conduct them in his "Hiawatha Trilogy." Although the composer was excited about the opportunity to conduct an all-Black chorus and Black soloists, he had to wait until the following year to accept the invitation because of professional circumstances in London and other European cities.[29]

Robert W. Carter in the August 1903 *Colored American* applauded Theodore Drury for "the success in his arduous task of presenting Grand Opera with Colored performers before critical audiences in the great western Metropolis." His opera company had presented Verdi's "Aida" at the New York Lexington Opera House on May 11th, with Theodore Drury doing the major baritone role. The artistic success was such that they were being urged to repeat it the next year. According to the writer, the integrated audience had opportunity to witness grand opera with "White and colored performers singing and acting together" saying that "such gatherings helped Caucasians to learn that all of the Negro race are not ragtime characters, but that many possess a discriminating and cultivated taste for the fine arts." This statement by Robert Carter reveals the negative attitude shared by many Blacks about the then popular "syncopated dance music" of their race; while ragtime represents a blending of West African and European elements, many educated Blacks knew that its roots were in the "coon songs" and cakewalk, both outgrowths of the minstrel show which had become primarily a commercial showcase of racist humor.[30]

On February 18, 1903, a major Broadway theater hosted for the first time a full-length musical comedy.[31] *In Dahomey* opened with a cast of fifty headed by Bert Williams and George Walker, with lyrics by Paul Lawrence Dunbar and music by Will Marion Cook. The musical was such a success in New York that it was taken to London's Shaftesbury Theater, the first-time British audiences would see a musical with an all-Black cast.[32] It played for seven months in London, which included a royal command performance for King Edward VII at Buckingham Palace. According to Thomas L. Riis, "after such recognition, the attention of London's Society were assured."[33] On May 24, 1903, the Sunday *Weekly Dispatch* in the "Plays and Players" column wrote that:

> The talk of the theatrical town is undoubtedly of the novel entertainment now being offered at the Shaftesbury Theatre in the shape of the Negro musical comedy. Its success has been instantaneous, and night after night not a stall or a box can be secured. Messrs. Williams and Walker have already become a trade mark, and Mr. Will Marion Cook's music is being whistled and sung all over the town, and will this week be published by Messrs. Keith, Prowse, and Co. . . . There is not

one line in the whole entertainment of nasty in-
nuendo or suggestiveness.

A tour of England and Scotland followed the seven-month
London productions before the cast returned to the U.S. in August
1904.

It is evident that 1903 was a good artistic year for Black theatrical and operatic groups. The *Colored American* of December
1903 reported that Joseph Douglass's western concert tour was a
success, one given for the benefit of the Colored Orphan Home,
the Chandler Normal School in Lexington, Kentucky. Blind Boone
was continuing to perform in the Midwest and gave concerts to
packed houses in Canada.[34]

While the Black press continued to highlight the musical suc-
cesses of Black musicians, interestingly little attention was given
to the historic return of Blind Tom in Brooklyn, New York. It may
be that his return as a headliner in vaudeville left many with the
impression that the "Blind Tom of the past" was no longer as capable of performing the classical repertoire and emphasis was being given to his numerous non-musical achievements.

Notes

1. George M. Fredrickson. *The Black Image in the White Mind* (New York: Harper & Row, 1971), p. 277.

2. Rayford Logan. *The Betrayal of the Negro,* p. 354.

3. Chistopher Lasch. "The Anti-Imperalists, the Philippines, and the Inequality of Man," *Journal of Southern History* (August, 1958), p. 319.

4. Philip W. Kennedy. "The Rachial Overtones of Imperialism as a Campaign Issue, 1900" *Mid-America* (July, 1966), pp. 196-205.

5. George P. Marks, III. *The Black Press Views American Imperialism* (New York: Arno Press, 1971), p. 100.

6. Michael C. Robison and Frank N. Shubert. "David Fagen: An Afro-American Retired in the Philippines, 1899-1901," *Pacifica Historical Review* (February, 1975), p. 69.

7. Originally conceived by Henry Sylvester Williams, a Trinidadian law-yer, as a forum to protest against the aggression of White colonizers by organizing a worldwide pressure group composed of members of the African race. See: Clarence G. Contee. "The Emergence of DuBois as an African Nationalist," *Journal of Negro History* (April, 1964), pp.48-63 and W.E.B. DuBois. *An ABC of Color* (New York: International Publishers), pp. 19-23.

8. Philip W. Kennedy, *Op. Cit.* p. 204.

9. William B. Gatewood. *Black Americans and the White Man's Burden, 1898-1903* (Urbana: University of Illinois Press, 1975), p. 238.

10. Anna K. Simpson. *Hard Trials: The Life and Music of Harry T. Burleigh* (Metuchen, New Jersey: Scarecrow Press, 1990), p. 25.

11. "Grand Opera As We See It," *Colored American Magazine* (June, 1900), pp. 78-80. See also, "Negroes in Comic Opera," *Ibid.* (June 9, 1900).

12. "Violinist Douglass," *Ibid.* (April 21, 1900).

13. "Season, 1900-1901: Joseph Douglass; Violin School," *Colored American* (October 6, 1900).

14. "Blind Tom As Seen by His Mother, Charity Wiggins: An Interview in October, 1900," *The Columbus (Georgia) Magazine* (July 31, 1941), p. 32.

15. Ibid.

16. *Colored American* (January 18, 1901).

17. *Southern Workman* (May, 1901).

18. Southall, Book II.

19. *North American* (August 6, 1901).

20. *Baltimore American* (October 9, 1901). The gramophone was invented in 1889 by Emile Berliner; it was a talking machine that used lateral-cut discs rather than the vertical-cut cylinders of Thomas Edison's phonograph.

21. William E. Terry. "The Negro Music Journal: An Appraisal," *Black Perspective in Music* (Fall, 1977), pp. 146-160.

22. "Mr. Clarence White," *Colored American* (January 18, 1902).

23. Vernon Edwards and Michael Mark. "In Retrospect: Clarence Cameron White," *Black Perspective in Music* (Spring, 1981), p. 54.

24. Maud Cuney Hare. *Negro Musicians and Their Music* (Washington, D.C.: Associated Publishers, 1936), p. 244.

25. Percy Williams (1857-1920) was one of the few in the vaudeville profession loved by those he hired. When he died he left his 30-acre estate at East Islip, Long Island, as a home for aged and indigent performers. In 1893 he created the Bergen Beach resort, featuring a dance hall concession and rides and in 1896, built a casino at the resort which alternated vaudeville with musical comedies and stock company productions. In 1897 he took over the Brooklyn Music Hall, then in 1901 built the Orpheum, Brooklyn. The entire P. G. Williams empire was sold to the B.F. Keith Vaudeville circuit in 1912 for five million dollars.

26. *Brooklyn Eagle* (December 20, 1903).

27. Doris E. McGinty. "The Washington Conservatory of Music," *Black Perspective in Music* (Spring, 1979), pp. 59-69. The school remained

in existence until 1960. Harriet Gibbs Marshall was the first Black American to complete the piano course at the Oberlin Conservatory (1889) but she also studied in Boston, Chicago and with Moritz Maszowski in Paris, France. In 1900 she was assistant director of music of the Colored Public Schools in Washington, D.C. She established the school in 1903, serving as its director until 1923, when she accompanied her husband to Haiti for his government position, then resumed the directorship in 1933 until her death in 1941.

28. "Taylor's Hiawatha," *Colored American* (December 5, 1903).

29. A copy of this letter was reprinted in W. C. Berwick Sayer's *Samuel Coleridge-Taylor Musician; His Life and Letters* (London: Augener Ltd.: 1915), pp. 144-145.

30. Alain Locke. *The American Negro and His Music* (Washington, D.C.: Association in Negro Education, 1936) describes the coon songs as slap-stick farce about "razors, chickens, watermelon, ham-bone, flannel shirts and camp meetings." The term "coon" during and after salvery was merely one of a whole variety of designations for the Negro.

31. Thomas L. Riis. *Just Before Jazz: Black Musical Theatre in New York 1890 to 1915* (Washington: Smithsonian Institute Press, 1988), p. 91. To learn more about this musical, its themes and music examples, see Chapter 6.

32. Jeffrey P. Green. "In Dahomey in London in 1903," *Black Perspective in Music* (Spring, 1983), pp. 23-40.

33. Thomas L. Riis. *Op. Cit.* p. 103.

34. "Blind Boone in Canada," *Professional World* (January 23, 1903).

Chapter Six

(1904–1908)

ACCORDING TO THE JANUARY 2, 1904, *New York Clipper,* Tom remained at Brooklyn's Orpheum Theater until that night. Percy Williams (the Manager) announced that "Blind Tom as the feature is a very clever act indeed." On January 10th, Tom performed at New York's Circle Theater. In the January 12, 1904, *New York Herald* review, the reporter wrote that: "Blind Tom makes a Reappearance. Many times reported Dead but the Old Man returns at the Circle Theatre." Continuing the theme, the reporter noted that the manager had "referred to the many reports of Blind Tom's death within the last thirty years; the first printed in an 1871 New York paper that he died of consumption and with the story was a physicians analyses of his brain." Other death reports noted was one saying "Tom had jumped from the St. Louis bridge." Another reported him as being "killed in a railroad accident near Cincinnati." In the audience were many elderly people who remarked about how Tom had aged, and described him as "now very short and clumsy, his face wrinkled and woolly head slightly tinged with white, but he seems to have musically improved."

According to the *New York Tribune's* Sunday edition under "Theatrical Incidents and New Notes" the Blind Tom concerts "resulted in big houses."[1] After making mention of the false reports of Tom's death the writer said: "the black wizard of the keyboard has just emerged from retirement and is said to have lost none of his power."

February 8th-13th, Tom performed in Cleveland, Ohio's, Empire Theater to good reviews.[2] These were followed by four performances in Buffalo, New York, at the Shea Theater. Shea was complimented in the *Buffalo Daily Courier* for "succeeding in securing Blind Tom since the blind wonder is considered the biggest vaudeville attraction, with managers all over the country trying to book him."[3] According to the February 18th *Buffalo Morning Express,* "Blind Tom proved to be the biggest attraction Mr. Shea ever had in his theater. Despite the terribly cold weather the house is crowded at every performance with Blind Tom being the greatest favorite of the entire vaudeville bill." Among the three selections performed was his own "Battle of Manassas."

Tom's next appearances were in Detroit, Michigan's, Temple Theater (March 7-12th). Although the *Detroit Evening News* reviewer wrote that "Tom's playing as well as he did 30 years ago,"[4] the reviewer in the same paper following his first concert was critical of Tom as a musical entertainer, saying:

> Blind Tom, who has been resurrected for a star in vaudeville attraction, and is at the Temple Theater this week, is not what musical critics would pronounce a finished artist. His selections as a rule are simple ones and he plays them without much depth of feeling and his execution is somewhat mechanical. He is a freak and as such is one of the wonders of the time. Old age has somewhat modified the antics he used to cut at the piano when he startled the world 30 or more years ago. His features are heavier but the vacant stare and idiotic grin are there and the old habit of leading the applause is still one of his characteristics. He made his own announcement, speaking impersonally, and remembers the words of his former manager accurately. His mimicry is wonderful, his improvisation marvelous and he is a curiosity well worth hearing, and seeing.[5]

Obviously the reporter shows contradictions in his evaluation, placing most attention on his physical appearance while telling readers the concert was worthy of their attendance.

Despite the constant mention in the press about Tom's age and health concerns, those managing him continued to exploit him physically for their financial gain. This is evident from Blind Tom's appearances at the San Francisco, California, Orpheum Theater from April 4-16th. According to the *San Francisco Chronicle,* Tom was the "head liner" whose "playing of different selections from familiar operas was delicate and accurate."[6] These appearances were followed by performances at the Los Angeles Orpheum from April 18th-30th. As in San Francisco, a one-week engagement had to be extended a second week due to audience demand. When writing about the vaudeville performers in the *Los Angeles Herald,* the writer wrote that: "Blind Tom, the perennial, needs no introduction since, in his opinion it would be somewhat in the nature of an insult to the intelligence of the audience when a tall slender person with a Bowry dialect gave a sketch of his career much as the man outside a circus talks about the snake charmer within." After describing the enjoyment of those in attendance, the reporter said Tom's "heaviest selection" was Liszt's "Fantasia on Rigoletto's Quartet."[7]

The next month found Tom performing at the Orpheum in Kansas City, Missouri. The following review appeared in the May 14th weekly *Kansas City World,* a Black newspaper:

TESTED BLIND TOM'S
WONDERFUL MEMORY

He Played a New Selection After Hearing It Executed at the
Orpheum.

Blind Tom, the negro musical wonder, who has been the drawing card
at the Orpheum this week, was given
a thorough test of his wonderful memory yesterday afternoon. A committee
of newspaper men selected a piece of
music recently placed on the market
and one which Blind Tom had never
heard.

The selection was entitled "The Fra-
ternity Belle." E. C. Lewis first
played the selection, while Tom stood
and listened. Each note seemed to
find a sympathetic chord in Tom's musical body, for the motions of his hands
and face expressed every little change
in the theme as it was being played.

When Mr. Lewis had finished the
blind negro seated himself at the piano
and reproduced the selection. Although
he played in a different key, the melody
and expression were the same in every
detail.

On June 10th, Blind Tom was back in New York performing at the Circle Theatre as a "headliner" with several vaudeville acts among them being Yiddish parodies by Hosey & Lee.[8] When Hazel Harrison, the 18-year-old Afro-American pianist from La Porte, Indiana, climaxed her German tour by an appearance with the Berlin Philharmonic Orchestra on October 22, 1904, the *Musical Courier* reviewer referred to Blind Tom negatively, saying:

> Her playing is really remarkable when one considers that the colored race has thus far done nothing worth mentioning in music. Our best Negro songs are not the product of the black race, but of that white genius, Stephen C. Foster, and a freak like Blind Tom does not count, because he is not a musical nature, but simply a marvelous imitator. Hence, as Miss Harrison can claim to be the first colored person to attract the attention of the musical world as an artistic performer, she has accomplished much to be proud of. It certainly required great courage on her part to face an audience and the critics in this hotbed of music; but the results show that it was worth while. Is Miss Harrison a musical prophet arisen among the colored race, like Booker T. Washington, to show by her example what others can do if they will try; or is it the Caucasian blood in her veins that is doing the work, for she is not a full-blooded negress? At any rate, with the race question becoming more and more a burning issue in the United States, she stands out as an interesting and isolated case.[9]

On this occasion, Miss Harrison performed the Grieg "A Minor" and Chopin "E Minor" concertos under the direction of August Schurrer. While most reviewers were complimentary about her musicianship, the *Musical Courier Reporter* felt compelled to make her race an issue. Returning to America a year later (following studies and other concerts in Berlin), she was hailed in the Black press as the "world's greatest pianist" and continued her pre-European schedule of teaching and commuting to Chicago for lessons with her teacher, Victor Heinze, who had been a student of the famous pianist-composer Ignacy Jan Paderewski.

Another musical historic highlight for Black Americans took place that year when Samuel Coleridge-Taylor made the first of his three visits to America.[10] On November 16, 1904, the *Washington Post* noted his arrival with the description "Noted Composer Here: S. Coleridge-Taylor of Hiawatha Fame." His first concert that night at Washington's Constitution Hall was devoted to his "Hiawatha Trilogy" with the composer conducting. His principal soloists, among whom was Harry T. Burleigh, and chorus were all Black with the United States Marine Band engaged to accompany the singers. The crowded audience was two-thirds Black. His second concert (November 17th) was more miscellaneous and included an important new work: the *Choral Ballad,* which Coleridge-Taylor wrote for the choral society bearing his name. The work consisted of settings for solo voice and chorus based on poems by Henry Wadsworth Longfellow on slavery. After another performance of his Trilogy at the Lyric Theater in Baltimore, and short visits to Chicago, New York and Philadelphia, Coleridge-Taylor sailed for London on December 13, 1904, "amidst a burst of kudos and acclaim usually reserved for the truly distinguished."[11] Following his Baltimore concert an elaborate reception took place in the Lyric Hotel where flags of Great Britain and America were placed. The central incident was the presentation to the composer of a silver loving cup bearing the following inscription:

A TOKEN OF LOVE AND ESTEEM

to Samuel Coleridge-Taylor, of London,
England, in appreciation of his
achievements in the realms of music.
Presented by the S. Coleridge-Taylor
Choral Society of Washington,
D.C., to their distinguished
guest on the occasion of his
first visit to America to
conduct ' Hiawatha '
and 'Songs of Slavery.' November 16,
17 and 18, 1904.
' It is well for us, O brother,
That you come so far to see us.'

A souvenir from his visit to the M. Street High School for Girls in Washington, D.C., was made of cedar from Cedar Hill, the estate of Frederick Douglass, bearing (in gold) the symbol of the school. As a climax he was invited to the White House by President Theodore Roosevelt, who had been recently re-elected to the presidency. According to his friend, W.C. Berwick Sayers, Coleridge-Taylor left Washington "entirely happy for his own people had acclaimed him, the White people too, acknowledged that he was a living prophecy of all the possibilities of his race."[12] Since he was appointed director/conductor of London's prestigious Handel Choral Society prior to his American visit, Booker T. Washington's statement that Coleridge-Taylor "performed a distinct service by demonstrating to the colored people the possibilities of their race" added to the assessment.[13]

Blacks were also making major contributions to America's popular music that year. A big ragtime contest, sponsored by Thomas and "Honest John" Turpin, was held in St. Louis during the time of the Louisiana Purchase Exposition. Black pianists from all over the nation entered which, according to Eileen Southern, was "as much for the thrill of competing with the country's best rag pianists as for the prize."[14] Scott Joplin published four rags that year: *The Cascades, The Sycamore, The Crysantheum* and *The Favorite. The Cascades* is program music to honor The Cascade Garden, the focal point of the fair. It was a spectacular artificial waterfall, fountain, lagoon and rapids extending into the Midway of the park. Rudi Blesh describes it as "a virtuoso piece, it too flows and ripples while building an infectious swing."[15] John Edward Hasse considers Joplin's *Cascades* one of the most significant ragtime pieces published from a listing of 40 (starting in 1897 and ending in 1927).[16] John Stark (Joplin's publisher) wrote in the advertisement: "Hear it, and you can fairly feel the earth wave under your feet. It is as high-class as Chopin and is creating a great sensation among musicians."[17] Although Joplin's home was then in St. Louis, and he was considered the "King of Ragtime," he was offered no official place in the program. While official programs showed a preference for popular compositions by John Philip Sousa, Victor Herbert, and Stephen Foster, Susan Curtis reveals from her research on the fair, none of the official compositions achieved the popularity of Kerry Mills's "Meet Me in St. Louis, Louis" or Joplin's *The Cascades.*[18] Tom Turpin, whose Rosebud

Club was a gathering place for rag pianists from all over the Midwest, published his "St. Louis Rag" the previous year in honor of the St. Louis World's Fair.

Another historic musical event that year was when, on May 23, 1904, *The Southerner*, with music by Will Marion Cook, presented Broadway with its first integrated cast in a musical. Despite the threats of walkouts and violence, the show finished its New York run without incident and traveled to several major northern U.S. cities.[19] William Hart, a White bass, and Abbie Matchell (Cook's wife), a soprano, were cited as the outstanding singers in the musical. As one New York critic said: "For those who like Black and White, this Black and White is allright."[20]

Throughout the year The Blind Boone Company, with Boone as the main drawing card, performed to large and enthusiastic audiences. Returning to his hometown of Columbus, Missouri, on March 4th, one reporter advertised him as "now holding the place in the musical world once held by Blind Tom."[21] According to the March 10, 1904, *Howard County News*, the Blind Boone Concert Company performed that week to the "largest audience which has ever greeted an aggregation of amusement makers in New Franklin." He noted that ". . . it is claimed that Blind Boone never forgets an acquaintance can recognize by the voice and the impression of the hand years after the last meeting." According to the reviewer "while the classic selections were appreciated, the comic and plantation songs were heartily applauded with the imitation of musical instruments, especially the old timer and his fiddle made the hit of the evening." By now the Blind Boone Concert Company was touring regularly from early September until late June with only Sunday off and being financially stable, was able to do frequent benefits for various charitable causes. Obviously Blind Boone's manager's (John Lange) advertising slogans "We travel on our Merit, not Sympathy" and "Merit Wins, Not Sympathy" were to avoid attracting audiences through pity for his blindness or marketing his talents as peculiarities as had been done with Blind Tom.[22]

On Sunday, January 29, 1905, the *New York World* announced a new vaudeville bill for that coming week (January 30-February 5) at Procter's Fifth Avenue Theatre. The dramatic feature was Thomas W. Broadhurst's drama, "The Holy City" with Edwin Arden as Barabas and Ms. Ida Merwin as Mary of Magdalene. The vaudeville section was headed by Mary Byrne-Ivy, an operatic contralto, with no mention that Blind Tom was one of the performers. On that same day the *New York Times* noted under its amusement section that Blind Tom was also on the program. Although no review of the play or vaudeville acts was noted, the *New York Times* criticized the continuance of the house's policy of entr-acte vaudeville between the acts of a religious theme production, saying "in this case it can hardly be commended as an exhibition of good taste."[23] On Sunday, January 5th, the *New York Times* announced that "Blind Tom will appear at Procter's 5th Avenue." Tommy Russell, the original Little Lord Fauntleroy, was appearing in a vaudeville sketch which, according to the review, "did not have a name on the program because in New York the laws do not permit the production of a 'real play' on Sunday."[24] However, the advertisement in the *New York World* noted that Blind Tom was appearing on the vaudeville program at 1:00 p.m. and with a new sketch featuring "The Silver King" by Henry Arthur Jones and Herman Henson.

Tom would return to New York following a one-week engagement in Newark, New Jersey's, Procter Theater (February 6-11th). In a review on February 7th, the *Newark Evening News* gave its main attention to headliner Robert Hillard and the Obestefer Troup, adding that "Blind Tom, the pianist whose present performances are less wonderful than they seemed years ago when he attracted much attention as a curiosity contributed to the program." As the following advertisement shows, Tom's appearance at New York's Keith Theatre March 27-April 2nd, received greater billing:

KEITH'S

14th St., n'r B'way
Subway Express Station.

Continuous Performance 1:00 to 10:45 P. M.
First Appearance in Vaudeville.
The Grand Old Lady of the Stage.

MRS. ANNIE YEAMANS

MR. LOUIS WESLEY
ARCHIE BOYD & CO.
WARD and CURRAN
NORA BAYES
BROTHERS LEIGH

De Anna's Monkeys & Dogs ┆ Chas. K. and
Howard Brothers ┆ Earl & Wilson

EXTRA
ATTRACTION   **BLIND TOM**

The World's Greatest Pianist.
Prices, 25c. & 50c. Reserved Seats, $1.

According to the April 1, 1905, *New York Clipper*, Blind Tom, who made his first appearance as an extra attraction at Keith's Theatre "astonished by his marvelous technique as he did over a quarter of a century ago." Tom had appeared in Albany, New York, before his New York City return "March 6-11th, 1905 where he had a large attendance."[25]

On April 2, 1905, the *Philadelphia Inquirer* announced an appearance by Tom at the Keith Chestnut St. Theatre (April 3-8th). He was advertised as "a special added attraction who would startle his audience when they fully realize the wonderful God-given gift of memory possessed by this old, blind one-time slave." In the April 4th review, under the headline "Novelties at Keith's Yesterday," the reviewer wrote that:

> Blind Tom, the musician, was a revelation to many in the audience. This old darky, who has been before the public for many years, been reported dead many times and his accomplished feats in music rarely equated, rendered several selections in a truly artistic style. And then he played one of his boyhood compositions which had provoked enthusiasm from many who saw him a score of years ago.

In addition, according to the review, "The famous pianist was given an enthusiastic reception, and played in his usual remarkable manner."

On April 11, 1905, the *Providence (Rhode Island) Journal* announced that Blind Tom would be a headliner at their Keith Theatre for a week (April 10-15th). After giving readers biographical information the writer said that Blind Tom's "act was deeply interesting as a demonstration of the talents of a peculiar character who was familiar to the public of a generation ago."

What seemed to have been Blind Tom's last public appearance took place in Boston, Massachusetts, April 17-22nd. According to the announcement in the April 15th *Boston Evening Transcript*, "Notwithstanding his advanced years, he is said to have lost none of his skill and firmness of touch, and he will be heard in three selections at every performance." To help in the ticket sales it was noted that Tom "will appear nowhere else in New England." Tom was the headliner of 17 acts at Boston's Keith Theatre. A lengthy review in the April 18th *Boston Evening Transcript* leaves no doubt that he had ended his public career still celebrated:

Keith's Theatre: Vaudeville

From Blind Tom to Paderewski! What a change has taken place in popular stars on the piano in the last generation! One was especially impressed by that fact last evening in the conspicuous feature in the bill at Keith's, where a large audience heard for the first time the pianist who had been little more than a name in the present generation. In the sixties and seventies the concerts given by Blind Tom were well known as musical entertainments and concert goers knew of his birth as a half-witted slave, of how he accidentally gave an illustration of the musical side of his nature which had never been suspected, and of how his imitative faculties were developed until he could play, note for note, anything which he had ever heard. Of these things, however, the present generation knew comparatively nothing, and it was a complete novelty to see him as a vaudeville feature.

When the curtain went up two men were seen standing, in the centre of the stage, one a Negro with thick body, clumsy hands, unattractive face with sightless eyes. That was Blind Tom. After his companion had made a spread-eagle speech over the attainments of the sightless musician, Tom made his own announcement of selections, in accordance with his custom. The first was a "Delta Kappa Epsilon March," a composition of the style in vogue before the days of Sousa. It abounded in octaves and noise, but was characterless and simply served to show the generation whose music

Tom represented. Immediately upon the
conclusion the Negro jumped to his feet and
clapped his own hands as enthusiastically
as anyone on the other side of the foot-
lights, explaining as he did it that it was
a part of his imitative way, and he trusted
that it gave no offense. In this speech and
in everything else that he said Tom spoke
of himself in the third person, as an out-
sider might have done. Then he sat down
at the piano again and played, "The Last
Hope," by Gottschalk, and concluded his
number with a fantasie on the quartet from
"Rigoletto." In these he clearly showed
that the hands which had seemed clumsy
were wonderfully supple, and that the
fingers could move over arpeggios, scales
and chromatics in a manner that was simply wonderful when one took into consideration the fact that he was sightless and
mentally deficient in many ways. In the
days when he came before the public tran-
scriptions of popular melodies were all the
rage, and these themes with their variations
were the sort of show pieces which established a pianist as the Paderewski of his
day. It is not at all strange that Blind
Tom made a sensation at his time, and his
work still is wonderfully interesting, notwithstanding his advancement in years.
Musically the taste of the public may have
grown beyond him, so that his selections
seemed just a bit archaic, but the playing
and the novelty of seeing the man of whom
so much had been said and whose death
had been falsely chronicled so many times
made his vaudeville engagement a feature
of unusual interest.

The entire bill at Keith's this week is a
good one, and there are no uninteresting
turns. The illusion "Dida," by which two
girls are made to appear one after another
in the midst of a tank of water, was given
as it was at Hammerstein's in New York.
Afterwards it was cleverly burlesqued by
Bedini and Arthur, whose juggling was as
amusing as ever. Mayme Remington had a
most enthusiastic greeting with her picka-
ninnies, who appeared in several grotesque
outfits, including a Buster Brown rig, and
who pleased their listeners so that many a
small coin was tossed to the stage. Charles
Kenna with an imitation of a circus fakir,
Milton and Dolly Nobles and their supporting company in "The Days of '49" and Nora
Bayes in songs, including "Down Where the
Wurzberger Flows," were among the other
well-liked features of the bill.

On Saturday, June 13, 1908, Blind Tom died. As his death certificate shows, his real name was Thomas Wiggins.

Although he died at age 59 of cerebral apoplexy at the home of Mrs. Eliza Bethune Lerche in Hoboken, New Jersey, where he lived for several years, his body was taken to the funeral chapel of Frank E. Campbell Company in New York. This is probably the reason the following death notice was telegraphed throughout the nation from New York:

BLIND TOM IS DEAD

FAMOUS NEGRO MUSICIAN DIES IN NEW JERSEY.

Marvel of Three Generations of Play-goers Who Was Born Near Columbus, Ga., Passes Away in Poverty.

New York, June 14—Blind Tom, the famous negro musician, marvel of three generations of play-goers, died yesterday in Hoboken, N. J., where he was living and had been for years in retirement and subsisting on charity.

Thomas Wiggins is the name given in his burial certificate, but the surname was one which the famous pianist adopted. He was born a slave near Columbus, Ga., about 1860. In early childhood, Tom, who was born entirely blind and more than half idiotic, showed himself remarkably imitative, frequently stealing into the house of his master to reproduce on the piano the pieces he had heard played by others. In 1861 he became so proficient on the instrument that he was taken to New York and exhibited as phenomenon and later was widely heard in the United States and Europe.

That Blind Tom had been important in the musical world for over four decades is evidenced by the fact his death notices were prominently placed in many newspapers at a time when the Republican National Convention was meeting in Chicago (June 16-19). William Howard Taft, the then secretary of war in President Theodore Roosevelt's administration was nominated with James S. Sherman of New York as his running mate.[26] Although all four New York papers carried similar long accounts about Tom's many accomplishments, the *New York World* gave attention to Tom's death. It appeared with the following headline in the *Columbus (GA) Enquirer-Sun*:

BLIND TOM'S STORY
TOLD BY N.Y. WORLD

The *New York World* of Monday, June 15, says of the death of Blind Tom:

"Blind Tom" is dead. And the ending of the childish black pianist, at whose wonderful playing thousands have marvelled ever since our grandmothers were girls, was full of pathos.

Three weeks ago, as he sat before his piano in this home of Mrs. Eliza B. Lerche, the widow of his old master at No. 60 Twelfth Street, Hoboken, singing the old melodies with which he had thrilled great audiences before the Civil War, he suddenly stopped and fell face downward on the floor. Mrs. Lerche, who had cared for him for over twenty years, ran into the room, and helping him up found that his whole upper right side was paralyzed.

But Tom couldn't understand that he was different, and soon went back to his piano. When he found that his right hand could not strike the keys he said, with his voice quivering, "Tom fingers won't play."

Again and again he tried. Finally when he realized it was useless his big blind eyes filled with
tears and he wept like a child. Each day he returned to the piano and started some favorite
piece. Discords came quickly, however, and then,
with tear-moistened cheeks, he would rise and
pace the floor until long into the night. His old
mistress sought to comfort Tom, but he would only
sob out "Tom's fingers wont play no mo."

Last Saturday night Tom went to his piano again
and began softly his old lullaby "Down on the
Swanee River," but his voice broke. Sobbing, he
rose and said: "I'm done, all gone missus."

The next she heard was a faint cry and a thump
near the bathroom door. He had dropped dead
from a second shock.

Dr. Charles Gilchrist of Hudson Street, Hoboken,
was summoned, but he said that his services were
too late.

The old pianist will be buried this afternoon from
Frank E. Campbell's funeral chapel at 241 West
Twenty-Third Street, where his body now lies.[27]

The June 17th *Washington Post* gave some information about
the funeral. According to the reporter:

Only a few persons gathered at the funeral chapel.
Mrs. Eliza Bethune Lerche attended with her two
children. Several white variety performers who
had appeared with Blind Tom at different times
were present. Several of his own race who had
not known him but had heard him play, or, all
events, knew of his reputation, came to see the
body.

Rev. G.W. Downs of the Eighteenth Street Methodist Church, read a brief service and "Nearer My God to Thee" was played on a wheezy little organ. Three modest wreaths lay on the coffin. The funeral party started in two carriages to follow the body to Evergreen Cemetery, where the interment was.

Not unexpectedly the weekly *New York Age* (a Black newspaper) reminded readers of the reality concerning the exploitation of Blind Tom. According to the writer in the July 2nd issue, "in every section of the country the big daily newspapers regarded 'Blind Tom's' death as a great loss, and on their editorial pages expressed themselves accordingly. The few editorials from the Negro press did not express any great sorrow over his death but commented relative to the amount of money he made during life and what, if any, he left at his death." Continuing, the writer wrote that:

It is true that Blind Tom made thousands of dollars during his life whereby others grew rich by his piano playing. But it must be remembered, although "Blind Tom" was a musical wonder, he was born a slave, with no business qualifications nor independence of spirit to combat the commercial world. Then again, he was blind, which made him more dependent.

Being blind even during this day and time, "Blind Tom" would have fared much better financially, for in the first place, he would not have been a slave, and, secondly, he would have attained a higher degree of mental development that would have enabled him to think and act more for himself. Regardless of "Blind Tom's" powers at the piano, we cannot forget that he was born a slave and until after the war was carried about the country as recognized goods and chattel.

Even the liberation of slaves did not mean much freedom to him as it did to hundreds of others.

He was under the management of his former master and later the son of his master, and they made money with him long after the Civil War.

It must not be overlooked that "Blind Tom" was taken by his master when very young and turned over to an instructor; that the prodigy developed a fondness as well as unlimited confidence in his master, which was perfectly natural. After slavery days he did not pine for a change—he was satisfied, as were many slaves who had been given their freedom, but who were well content to stay with their former masters. The independence of spirit that now characterizes the race in many quarters was then absent. Conditions were vastly different to what they are today. Financially, "Blind Tom" was a failure—to himself. But, artistically, he was a success and molded sentiment for his people which is oftimes worth more than money.

It was true that "Blind Tom" was born a slave deformed and black, to use the words of Henry Watterson, editor of the *Louisville-Courier Journal* (who had followed the pianist's career for several decades). But within him was a soul that while living expressed itself by the Heaven-born Maid of Melody and charmed thousands of people during his lifetime—white and black alike, a soul that during life created sentiment for the Negro on earth and one that will live in a world without end.

This lengthy article which appeared under Lester A. Walton's "Music and the Stage" section was important for reminding readers of the historical realities surrounding Tom's life, however, he failed to note that since the slavemaster was a lawyer, he knew how to get legal custody of Tom in 1864, by having an illiterate slave mother sign an Indenture Guardianship agreement. Also, that once Tom's money-earning capacities were evident to the slave family, his contact with his biological family was limited, thereby explaining his post-slavery devotion to the Bethune family.[28]

Two other Black weekly newspapers added their concerns about the "charity" theme to the telegraphed announcement from New York. For example, on June 20th the *Cleveland Gazette* reporter wrote that:

> He (Tom) made the white family that had him all his life nearly a half dozen fortunes. When his poor and aged mother in Georgia attempted through the courts for years to get some of his earnings, she was beaten largely because she was poor and could not keep up the fight. The white people continued to make money out of Tom until he was too old to stand the incessant travel. Then they placed him in retirement and paid his expenses until his death, but with little of the vast fortunes he had made for them. They now announce to the world that "Blind Tom" subsisted on charity. It is a fact that some people have no hearts.

In their June 27, 1908, issue, they continued the theme, saying:

> It is a question which was the more aggravating to those remembering the facts about the daily newspaper dispatch statement saying poor Tom's last days were "spent in charity" (on his own hard owned money), or the statement that "Mrs. Lerche took care of the gray-haired, venerable musician tenderly, pitying his plight and admiring the grit and genius he displayed."

Some White reporters also added the "exploitation theme" in their obituary announcements. Surprisingly the *Baton Rouge, Louisiana Daily* of June 20, 1908, after writing the usual biographical materials, said "While he made a great deal of money, it is regrettable that his last days were those of want and he was forced to depend on charity." The June 19, 1908, *Nashville Globe*, when writing about "The Passing of Blind Tom," said "those middle-aged and older persons who had heard Tom will be saddened by his death, but what will surprise most of those who knew of him is the statement that he was during the last years of his life an object of charity." According to the reporter "a fortune was made out of Tom's concerts and when he last visited the south reportedly was worth upwards of $200,000, but it would seem from the press reports, someone other than the blind musician got the money."

Undoubtedly, the most pertinent statements of the "exploitation theme" came from Dr. John Melby, a great-great-great grandson of Tom's slave owner. In summer 1994, he and his wife (both professors on sabbatical from the University of Illinois) began their genealogical research in Columbus, Georgia. According to him "somehow a brother of James John Gunby got custody of Blind Tom. My grandmother remembered Blind Tom and says that John Gunby exploited him for his own financial gain."[29]

Although Blind Tom had been physically separated from his biological siblings most of his life, they reportedly wanted his funeral in Columbus, Georgia, the place of his birth.[30] According to the June 19, 1908, *Athens (Georgia) Banner*, "his four living siblings: Frank and Dan Wiggins and Emily Carter of Columbus and Antoinette Lingress of Birmingham (where his mother died in 1902) felt bitterly toward the Northern women who took him away from Columbus and managed him." Obviously their anger was misplaced since it was their old slave master who had taken him to Virginia and New York to live soon after the Civil War.

In "A Pictorial Study of Tom's Life" in the *Chicago Defender*, photographer Charles T. Magill shows where the Lerches buried Tom, including statements in the caption critical of the burial.[31]

Even in his death notices, Blind Tom was unable to escape racial stereotypes. The *New York Tribune* in an article titled "Blind Tom: Life Ends" informed readers about his many "eccentricities" then ended with a statement that "Tom had a fondness for watermelons, and could always be induced to play for anyone who offered him a piece of the dainty."[32] The *Indianapolis News* on June 17, 1908, noted that "Tom is a most repulsive animal with an abnormal appetite, his passions are strongly developed, and he has no respect for persons or places." The *Dallas (Texas) Morning News* describes him in the title as "Famous Darky Passes Away."[33] Frank J. Davis in the September 1908 *Human Life* Maga-

The grave of Blind Tom in Evergreen cemetery, Brooklyn, N. Y. To the right of the tombstone, indicated by arrow,
in an ill-kept, unmarked grave overrun with weeds, lie the
remains of the man who during his lifetime made three
different fortunes for white people. The spot is called
Pleasant Hill in the D section, and it was found only after
a careful perusal of the Evergreen cemetery records, and
then a search that required more than two hours. Virtually
this man, whose earnings ran into the hundreds of thousands, had been laid away in but one degree better than a
pauper. The section of Evergreen where lies his body is
the poorest and most forlorn part of the burying ground.
If Blind Tom died "unwept, unhonored and unsung,"
certainly he has been buried in that manner.

zine noted that "Blind Tom never learned to eat like a man . . . he
ate sometimes with his fingers, but most often with his mouth
directly in the dishes, like an animal. He ate his meat first when
he wished, his vegetables first when he desired, or his dessert first
if that seemed best. Even Mrs. Lerche could never get him to regu-
late the order in which he ate his courses."

My search in the Free Public Library of Hoboken (where he
lived the last years of his life and died) revealed only minimal
information about his death. The *Hoboken Observer* of June 15,
1908, told readers that:

> Not long after a report of Blind Tom's death in
> 1894, it was discovered that Mrs. Lerche was keep-
> ing him in seclusion at a small cottage in the
> Navesink Highlands. No one was allowed to see
> him there and he was completely out of sight un-
> til his brief reappearance in 1904.

Obviously the writer was not entirely correct since Tom did perform concerts in Texas, Tennessee and North Carolina during the year 1895; Falls River, Massachusetts in 1897; Boston, Massachusetts in 1899; and Atlantic City, New Jersey, in 1901. The *Paterson New Jersey Press* noted in its death notice that Blind Tom's last appearance in their city was on September 10th, 1903, when he gave a concert at Orpheus Hall. The lack of significant knowledge about Tom in Hoboken may be understood if the following article in the *Albany (New York) Evening Journal* of June 15, 1908, was correct. Saying that Blind Tom was "known only to a few in Hoboken" the writer revealed that:

> Mrs. Lerche, who lives in an apartment house at 60 Twelfth Street, Hoboken, could not be seen. Although she has been living at that address for five years, her name has never been put on the doorplate and she has removed the electric bell from the door of her apartment. Her neighbors in other apartments say she never answers the bell and that all her groceries are left in a basket set for the purpose outside the door of her apartment. Although fifty families live in the same apartment building, the fact that an old Negro who played beautifully upon the piano was living in Mrs. Lerche's apartment on the second floor was known only in humor. Only once had any of the other tenants seen Blind Tom in the past five years and that was only for a few minutes last summer, when they saw Mrs. Lerche lead him to a closed carriage when she was going to her summer home at Navesink Highlands.
>
> On several occasions the janitor has been called into Mrs. Lerche's apartments to do some tinkering, but never did he see the blind musician. He only heard him moving around in a bedroom.
>
> Those of the tenants who live near Mrs. Lerche's apartment say that for the last five years and up to within the last two months they had been ac-

customed to hear at all hours exquisite piano music from the Lerche apartment. Sometimes late at night, the music would suddenly begin and continue for several minutes. Very few of those who live in the apartment building knew that it was Blind Tom, who had been playing until they read of his death in the paper Sunday.

Unfortunately, the reporter failed to give the source of the eyewitness account, but it serves to show that Blind Tom was not considered part of the Hoboken, New Jersey, community by those living in that city.[34] In his "Pictorial Pictures of Blind Tom," Charles T. McGill also published the following photo of the Lerche apartment with a descriptive statement:

—On the first floor right at 60 12th street, Hoboken, N. J., where he lived with his old mistress of slavery days, Mrs. Eliza Lerche, Blind Tom died on June 13, 1908. In this rather unpretentious house he lived in retirement for several years before his death. Literally, he ended his days there, unwept, unhonored and unsung. He was unknown, for it was under the name of Thomas Wiggins

The most controversial statements surrounding Blind Tom's death appeared in the June 17, 1908, *Washington Post* where three people at the funeral parlor challenged it being the "real" Blind Tom. The article was titled:

BLIND TOM: A MYSTERY

Doubt That Man Buried Sunday
Was The Original

DEAD MAN'S WORDS QUOTED

Women Who Appeared With Talented Pianist
Says He Admitted He Was Not The "Real" Tom -
Man Who Met the Original 35 Years Ago Thinks
It Incredible He Should Look So Young.

It was followed by information on the funeral, then about their charges:

Looked Young in Death.

Two negro women, who had known Blind Tom when he played twelve years ago, attended the services. They viewed the body and thought they recognized the same face, although the man looked much younger than they had supposed Blind Tom would look.

"I knew Blind Tom well," said J. T. Miller, who stood with a group of mourners after the services, "and met him first thirty-five years ago. He looks now about the same as he did then. It is incredible that the man I knew, the famous Blind Tom, should look so young. I am an actor, and used frequently to meet Blind Tom on my travels. The man I saw buried here to-day looks only a few years older than the man I used to meet."

The Lerche family, with whom the pianist had lived for so many years, had started for the cemetery before this conversation began, and nobody else present knew enough about the pianist's history

"Not the Real Blind Tom."

"I know the man who was buried to-day," said a woman who spoke with a strong English accent, and refused to give her name. "I have often appeared with him in Hoboken concert halls in the last few years. He called himself Blind Tom, but I do not believe he was the real Blind Tom. He had often spoken to me about the real Blind Tom and told me of many of his peculiarities. He told me Blind Tom was an imbecile, while this man was unusually intelligent. He often spoke of his desire to go to Europe, and told me that the other Blind Tom had been fortunate enough to go there and play before royalty. The man buried to-day was under fifty.

According to the reporter "because the Lerche family had left for the cemetery, before the conversation began, and since others present knew little about Blind Tom's history, none could respond." Obviously the women's claim of having performed several times the last few years in Hoboken had little, if any, validity.

The weekly *Washington Bee* (a Black newspaper) wrote about his spiritual character, noting that Tom "never used Liquors or Tobacco." According to the reporter:

> Old Tom, besides having a remarkable genius in the musical line, also had eccentricities. Many times when would-be interviewers called upon him Tom would mumble incoherently, and then burst forth with: "I will not talk! Go away please!"
>
> At other times the man would be genial, shake hands with him and talk half an hour about music and other subjects. He never smoked, chewed, or drink. He never was heard to swear. Several times when somebody in the room where he was uttered an oath, Tom would jump up, raise his hand, and order the offender out of the house.

Undoubtedly this reporter had given Blind Tom the ability to make choices about his dietary desires and able to distinguish when something said in his presence was in good taste. While questionable, it still points out the difference in the treatment of Tom, the person, between Black and White press accounts—even in those about him in death.[35]

Not unexpectedly, the announcement of Blind Tom's death brought forth persons who were still trying to find reasonable explanations for his many accomplishments given the fact he was classified throughout his life as an "untaught idiot." The June 15, 1908, *San Francisco Bulletin*, besides announcing Tom's death, wrote an editorial on the topic "Does Blind Tom's Case Prove Music Not Akin to Mind?" Among the assertions were:

> Blind Tom was born in slavery, he was illiterate and feeble minded, yet he was a remarkable performer and improviser. For years the Philistines

have flung Blind Tom as proof that music is purely sensual and has not a remote connection with intellectuality. Here, they have said, is a great musician but mentally is incapable. The fact that he composes and plays better than most of the musicians that possess brains, therefore proves a musician does not need brains. Blind Tom can feel, but cannot think. Hence we know that music is not an intellectual art.

Here is of course some measure of truth in the statement that one enjoyment of music is sensual. It is produced by physical instruments acting through sound upon the auditory nerves. But there are varieties of sensuality as there are varieties of intellect. . . .

Blind Tom was an idiot in one aspect. He was deficient in the common faculties which enable a man to get on in ordinary things and which nearly all men possess in some degree. But to compensate for his deficiency in this regard he possessed a wonderful facility withheld from the common herd, a faculty from which he had not only intense and harmless pleasure, but by which he was able to make far more money than the average rational philistines can make with all his common sense.

There is a field in the mind where things are left without being defined. The operation of the mind are more sensual than the operation of the reasoning faculties is sensual. Indeed, what the mind knows and thinks can be traced through the sense in the physical world outside the self-consciousness and, in that respect, ratiocination, too, is sensual.

In their death announcement, the *Hartford (CT) Daily Times* of June 15, 1908, ended with:

There are many curious questions about this strange being, but they relate to the psychology of the case rather than such things as concern the general public, and perhaps the difference between him and many other defective organizations was almost wholly in the greatness of the one talent, and the delight he found in exercising it.

Even sixty years later, a Dr. Charles Cramer, writing about mental prodigies, included Blind Tom in the study. He said that "Tom was examined by leading authorities of his day in the field of music. They found he had true pitch and could improvise quite well, but they were utterly unable to explain his great artistic abilities achieved with no formal training."[36]

Richard Restak included Blind Tom in his "Islands of Genius" article in *Science 82* and Jerry Bergman and Wallace DePue included Blind Tom in their "Musical Idiot Savants" study in the January 1986 *Music Educators Journal.* However, the death notice that expounded the most on the "genetic inferior race" theory was Welborn Victor Jenkins "The Tragedy of a Human Prodigy" for the *Atlanta (GA) Independent* of June 27, 1908. Describing Blind Tom as "ugly, and half idiotic" he admitted he had "The most marvelous and unexplained genius of any human we know of which must be accredited to the gods they are kind." Most of his article dealt with a comparison of talent and genius then followed with his own eyewitness account many years ago when he encountered Blind Tom in Atlantic City, New Jersey. Writing of his inability to explain such a musical genius despite obvious physical limitation, he ended with the following statements:

Yes, I see in him a promise to his people. He was undeniably a Negro. The race with which he was identified still labors under the influence of ages of ignorance. But when the slow process of evolution shall have made out of this uncomely mass a race in which more brain shall have given place to more gray matter, what might we expect from a reincarnation of Blind Tom? It is for once and

always a proof that genius is the native inherit-
ance of all races alike and that the Negro though
benumbed by centuries of ignorance, has yet the
supernatural fires in his heart that will look up
and shine more brightly as the ages go by.

That Blind Tom had been an important personality in the national entertainment world for over fifty years is undeniable since
his death notices were found in all state papers. Even the *Langston,
Oklahoma Western Age* announced it though Oklahoma had only
been admitted as the 46th state on November 16, 1907. Accounts
were also published in the leading musical and entertainment
magazines of that day, among them: *Variety* (June 20, 1908); *New
York Clipper* (June 20, 1908); *New York Dramatic Mirror* (June
20, 1908); *The Metronome* (July, 1908); and *The Etude* (August,
1908).

When writing her historic *Columbus Georgia Centenary*,
Nancy Telfair told readers that "for many years Columbus has
been known far and wide as the home of Blind Tom.[37] It is therefore not surprising for the surviving Bethune daughter to want
Blind Tom's body returned from New York to their city and have
him buried in their family plot."[38] Because at that time there was
an ordinance in Columbus preventing colored people from being
buried in the Linwood Cemetery, an alternative burial ground had
to be located. According to Louise Barfield's *History of Harris
County, Georgia 1827-1961*, a Mr. Oliver Poe allowed Tom's remains to be buried on the Warm Springs Road, not far from where
he was born. In 1954 the Georgia Historical Commission erected
a historical marker to his memory nearby on the highway. It reads:

BLIND TOM

200 feet east is the grave of Thomas Wiggins (1843-
1908). As Blind Tom, he thrilled audiences here
and in Europe with his remarkable musical performances. Born a slave, his native genius let him
reproduce perfectly on the piano any sound he
heard, including classical compositions and songs
of birds. His owners, the Bethune family, discovered his rich gift when they heard exquisite mu-

sic in their home near Columbus and found the little boy at the piano. He reached the zenith of his fame on European tours during when he played before royalty.[39]

When the author spoke on her research findings about Blind Tom at Columbus College in November 1984, she visited the marker. The following picture was taken by Mrs. Mahan of Columbus College:

In 1942 a piano was placed in the social room of the Booker T. Washington Apartments honoring Blind Tom. The piano was described as "a baby Grand of the fine Howard make, and manufactured by the Baldwin Company."[40] Clarence E. Hancock proprietor of the Hancock Music Company, gave a "generous discount on the instrument because of the special cause which it represents." The Black community raised $114.00 and the Columbus Housing Authority added $100.00, the remainder subscribed by the tenants themselves. The Blind Tom memorial piano was proposed by the *Ledger-Enquirer* paper "to honor the memory of the world famous blind Negro musical prodigy who was born and reared near Columbus." Dedicating the piano were W.C. Woodall, local editor and historian, Mrs. Ida Wiggins Jones, a niece of Tom's, and the mayor. The city turned out for the program.

Described by some as the "Eighth Wonder of the World," the late Thomas Greene Bethune, known as "Blind Tom," was truly, as Louise Bing said, "AN ENIGMA OF MUSICAL GENIUS THAT ASTONISHED THE WORLD!"[41]

Notes

1. *New York Tribune* (January 10, 1904).

2. *Cleveland Gazette* (February 13, 1904).

3. *Buffalo Daily Courier* (February 15, 1904).

4. *Detroit Evening News* (March 5, 1904).

5. *Ibid.* (March 8, 1904).

6. *San Francisco Chronicle* (April 9, 1904).

7. *Los Angeles Herald* (April 19, 1904).

8. *New York Times* (June 10, 1904).

9. *Musical Courier* (November 9, 1904), p. 6. See also: Jean E. Cazort and Constance Tibbs Hobson. *Born to Play: The Life and Career of Hazel Harrison* (Westport, Conn: Greenwood Press, 1983) and the Hazel Harrison Collection at the Moorland-Spingarn Research Center at Howard University for letters, photographs, and taped interviews with pupils colleagues, and friends.

10. W.C. Berwick Sayers. *Samuel Coleridge-Taylor, Musician: His Life and Letters* (London: Augener Ltd., 1927). Sayers became a librarian in Croydon in 1904 where he met Coleridge-Taylor, then the most celebrated of the local musicians. The two became friends. Also see: William Tortolano. *Samuel Coleridge-Taylor, Anglo-Black Composer, 1875-1912* (Metuchen, New Jersey: Scarecrow Press, Inc., 1977).

11. Ellsworth Jenifer. "Samuel Coleridge-Taylor in Washington," *Phylon* (Summer, 1967) p. 194.

12. Sayers. *op. cit.* pp. 166-167.

13. Ellsworth Jenifer. *op. cit.* p. 196.

14. Eileen Southern. *Music of Black Americans* (New York: W.W. Norton, 1983), p. 327.

15. Rudi Blesh. *Introduction to Scott Joplin: Collected Piano Works* (New York: New York Public Library, 1972), p. xxviii.

16. John Edward Hasse, ed. *Ragtime: Its History, Composers, and Music* (New York: G. Schirmer, 1985).

17. Edward A. Berlin. *King of Ragtime: Scott Joplin and His Era* (New York: Oxford University Press, 1994), p. 137.

18. Susan Curtis. *Dancing to Black Man's Tune: A Life of Scott Joplin* (Columbia, Missouri: University of Missouri Press, 1994), pp. 133-135.

19. Allen Wall. *Black Musical Theatre From Coontown to Dreamgirls* (Baton Rouge: LSU Press, 1989), p. 211.

20. Thomas L. Riis. *Just Before Jazz: Black Musical Theater in New York, 1890 to 1915* (Washington: Smithsonian Institution Press, 1989), pp. 105-109.

21. *Rising Sun* (Kansas City, Missouri, April 29, 1904).

22. Ann Sears. "John William 'Blind Boone' Pianist, Composer: Merit Not Sympathy Wins," *Black Music Research Journal* (Fall, 1989), p. 232.

23. *New York Times* (January 31, 1905).

24. *Ibid.* (February 5, 1905).

25. *New York Dramatic News.*

26. On Sunday, June 14, 1908 (the day before Tom's funeral), the *New York Times* published a two-page biographical pictorial profile of William Howard Taft. He was regarded by the then President Theodore Roosevelt as his successor. The president urged delegates to support Taft's nomination. With the popularity of President Roosevelt, Taft was able to defeat Williams Jennings Bryan, the Democratic candidate, by an electoral vote of 321 to 162.

27. *Columbus Enquirer Sun* (June 17, 1908).

28. See Southall. Blind Tom, Book I "The Guardianship Trial," pp. 45-69.

29. Sherry Lord. "The Melbys Are Vacationing in a Tree—The Family Tree," *Columbus Ledger* (August 21, 1974).

30. "Blind Tom's Folks Disapointed That His Remains Were Not Interred in Columbus, Georgia," *Athens Banner* (June 19, 1908) and "Columbus Wanted Blind Tom's Body," *Birmingham Age-Herald* (June 16, 1908).

31. Charles T. Magill. "Blind Tom: Unsolved Problem in Music History," *Chicago Defender* (August 19, 1922).

32. *New York Tribune* (June 15, 1908).

33. *Dallas Morning News* (June 15, 1908).

34. The same statements appeared in the *Washington Post* (January 17, 1908).

35. "Blind Tom Dead," *Washington Bee* (June 20, 1908).

36. Charles Cramer. "Remarkable Power of the Mind" *Columbus Sunday Ledger-Examiner* (June 25, 1972).

37. Nancy Telfair. *The Columbus Georgia Centenary* (Columbus Georgia Historical Publishing Company, 1929), pp. 255-256.

38. Doone Smith. "Piano Keys Were His Slave," *Colorado Springs (Colorado) Sunday* (September 29, 1972).

39. Katherine Mahan. *Showboats To Soft Shoe: A Century of Musical Development in Columbus, Georgia from 1828-1928* (Columbus, Georgia: Columbus Office Supply Co., 1968), p. 49.

40. "Blind Tom's Memorial Piano Placed in Booker T. Washington Apartments in Columbus," *The Columbus Magazine* (May 31, 1941).

41. Louise Bing. "On What Kind of Wings Do They Fly," *Sunday Ledger-Enquirer Magazine, Columbus, Georgia,* (July 11, 1965).

Chapter Seven

Conclusion

SINCE THE PUBLICATION of my article "Blind Tom: A Misrepresented and Neglected Composer," *Black Perspective in Music* (May, 1975), biographical sketches of Blind Tom have appeared for the first time in leading musical reference books. Among them are *New Grove Dictionary of Music and Musicians* (1980), *Bakers Biographical Dictionary of Musicians* (1978), *The Piano in Concert,* Vol. 1 (1982), *New Dictionary of American Music* (1986), and the *New American Dictionary of Music* (1991). More important, his "Battle of Manassas" was published in *Piano Music in Nineteenth Century America,* ed. Maurice Henson (1975) and his "Sewing Song" in *American Keyboard Music, 1866-1910,* ed. Sylvia Glickman (1990), offering some evidence that his compositions have gained credibility in the musical mainstream.

Through my use of such primary sources as news clippings of that day and court records, it is shown to be highly debatable that Blind Tom (as Thomas Wiggins) died a pauper as reported in some sources. For example: The court records of 1865 establish that Perry Oliver had made $50,000 exhibiting Tom and had paid a $15,000 fee to the Bethunes for the privilege. Obviously, at the outset, Blind Tom was a prize possession for those who owned him. Since the guardianship agreement permitted Col. Bethune to receive ninety percent of Tom's earnings, and there was nothing to guarantee that he would not expropriate the ten percent due Tom and his parents, it is easy to understand that the Bethunes might have "loved" their slave. Black historian Edward Scobie, discovered that Tom's 1866 London concerts brought over

$100,000 to his managers.[1] Also, in the 1886 court trial, a Mr. Joseph Eubanks, who had traveled with Blind Tom for twelve years as the assistant agent-treasurer to John Bethune, testified that those managing Tom cleared $3,000 a month on him, but Tom never got any of the money. It must be remembered that from his date of birth, those "legally" in charge of Blind Tom were in the legal profession, thereby capable of drawing up self-serving contracts that made possible their collection of large sums from Tom's concert tours without accounting for their profits to the courts or to Tom's parents.

According to my research, there is evidence that Blind Tom's concerts were well-attended. His tours were (until his final years) extensive, with multiple concerts scheduled on holidays. Announcements of his recitals were listed in the "musical section" of the *New York Clipper* (a newspaper devoted to the world of entertainment), not among the amateur, variety, minstrelsy, and circus announcements. This is further evidence of how Tom was regarded by his contemporaries as a serious concert pianist. Of some interest in this regard is a letter dated February 17, 1883, from Donelson Caffery to his mother mentioning that students at the Collegiate Institution in Baton Rouge, Louisiana, had been given a holiday to attend a Blind Tom concert.[2] And the musical citizenry of Los Angeles during the 1890s boasted that "Blind Tom" and Remenyi (the famous violinist) gave concerts in their city.[3]

Another common misconception was that Blind Tom concerts appealed primarily to scientific and musical skeptics rather than to respectable musicians. While it is not unlikely that the publicity concerning Tom's astonishing musical and non-musical demonstrations created an aura of excitement among persons merely seeking entertainment, there is supportive evidence showing that he was considered by many more than a musical curiosity. One New York reporter in 1865 referred to Tom as the "Gottschalk of the Negro race."[4] As might be expected, contemporary journalists made frequent comparisons between Blind Tom and Mozart as well as with Beethoven. The fact that Enrique Andreu, a Cuban musicologist, titled his biographical essay on Blind Tom "Tragedio de un Beethoven Negro" is evidence that the practices of drawing analogies between the blind pianist and others was widespread.[5]

Blind Tom was an inspiration to more than one potential musician of his time. In his *History of American Music*, Louis C. Elson reveals that American composer Edgar Stillman Kelly made his decision to "study music seriously after an accidental hearing of Blind Tom."[6] Rupert Hughes, a composer and student of Kelly's, substantiated Elson's claim, saying that "Kelly's diversion from painting to music resulted from his hearing Blind Tom perform Liszt's transcription of Mendelssohn's "Midsummer Night's Dream."[7] According to Portia Washington Pittman (Booker T. Washington's daughter), it was Blind Tom's performance of a Liszt "Rhapsody" at Tuskegee that inspired her to take up a musical career.[8] Nor was his influence limited to Americans. For example, a singer in her *Memoirs* of 1867 recounted the effect that Tom's playing had on Daniel Auber, the most popular French opera composer of his day.[9] Blind Tom's influence reached beyond the music world into that of literature. Blind D'Arnault, the blind musical genius in Willa Cather's novel *My Antonia,* was supposedly modeled after Blind Tom, whom the novelist had heard perform in Lincoln, Nebraska, while she attended the state university.[10]

In regard to the statements that "Tom was entirely untaught," I have wondered why music historians have failed to give credence to the information contained in two articles published in the *Etude* (the most widely read musical magazine published from 1883-1957) about this subject.[11] Tom's managers always hired the most respected musicians in the places where he performed to give him music lessons. One of these teachers, a resident of Philadelphia, who had studied with Franz Liszt in Europe, stated in 1886 that she agreed to give Tom (whom she said repulsed her) a music lesson for three reasons: 1) because of the $5.00 payment, considered then a considerable fee for music lessons, 2) because of her pedagogical and psychological interests in his talents, and 3) because his managers said that Tom had studied with the great Moscheles himself.[12] A music teacher from Atlanta, Professor W.P. Howard, accompanied the Bethunes as Tom's musical tutor on his 1866 European tour for what was then an exorbitant salary of $200 a month plus travel expenses. Professor Howard was quoted in the April 12, 1866, *New York Clipper* as saying that his "financial affairs having collapsed with the Confederacy, and not caring to starve right off, he became a traveling tutor-manager with the famous Tom." Obviously Tom's lessons during his adolescence were more than a casual occurrence. In my opinion, Tom was no "idiot savant," whose abilities resulted from a "natural talent." His musical achievements were acquired as a result of constant musical instruction and considerable practice over the years. He studied with some of the best teachers in the United States and Europe.

To classify Tom as an "idiot" or "imbecile" is a matter open to question. Obviously IQ test ratings or other acceptable sociological and psychological data cannot be offered on Tom's behalf, but there is still enough evidence available to contradict such a classification. Why, for example, would the Bethunes be so determined to retain the legal custodianship of an "idiot" who would be a physical and economic liability to them? How could one be tagged an idiot who wrote poetry, could sing and give recitations in several languages, play the piano, cornet and flute, as well as compose? Nineteenth-century dictionaries define "Imbecility of mind" as being unable to recollect. This being so, how does one explain Tom's amazing ability to reproduce anything after an alleged single hearing (musical or otherwise)? Finally, there is evidence that Tom passed numerous tests designed to test his knowledge of music theory, such as those given him by George Bristow, "generally recognized as the leading theoretical musician in America during that period."[13] As the Black music historian James Monroe Trotter said in 1878, "Who ever heard of an idiot possessing such memory, such finesse of musical sensibility, such order, such method as he displays?"[14] Undoubtedly, the common conception of Blind Tom as an idiot was due to the fact that he displayed certain childish and animal-like behavior on the stage. It is entirely possible that Tom's managers might have deliberately cultivated such behavior in order to suggest to the audience that Tom's genius derived from occult practices. Why should Tom's managers "rechannel" Tom's reactions into more socially acceptable patterns when the "idiot" classification was so profitable?

Considering that Blind Tom's life encompassed the political years of 14 American presidents (Zachary Taylor through Theodore Roosevelt), his life story offers some insight into the musical, historical, and sociopolitical climate of nineteenth-century America. By providing many examples of reviews of Blind Tom concerts within the context of Anglo and African-American concert life of the period, the reader should realize that it is more than a story of Blind Tom. It is a story of Black Americans living in American society during a period of time. As Dr. T.J. Anderson, a noted composer, says, "We now can move away from the myths and anecdotes of the past and come into a more meaningful relationship with this autodidactic composer" and know that Blind Tom's "contributions and accomplishments in music speak for themselves."[15] Hopefully my research has met my objective to "right the historical wrong" that has deprived Blind Tom, the pianist-composer, of his rightful place in the history of American music.

Notes

1. Edward Scobie. *Black Britannica: A History of Blacks in Britain* (Chicago: Johnson Publishing Company, 1973), p. 125.

2. Among the Donelson Cafferey papers, L.S.U. special collections #70803, obviously from the son (or grandson) of the Hon. Donelson, who was U.S. Senator from Louisiana (1892-1900) and a leading political figure of the Democratic Party during the Reconstruction period.

3. Robert Gray. *The Business Man in the Amusement World* (New York: Broadway Publishing Company, 1910), p. 216.

4. *New York World* (April 21, 1866).

5. Enrique Andreu. "Tragedia de un Beethoven Negro," *Revista Musical Chilena: Instituto de Extensio Musical* (October 25, 1947), p. 24-29.

6. Louis C. Elson. *The History of American Music* (New York: The McMillan Company, 1904), p. 235.

7. Rupert Hughes. *American Composers* (Boston: The Page Company, 1941), p. 59.

8. Roy Hill. *Booker T.'s Child. The Life and Times of Portia Marshall Washington Pittman* (Newark, New Jersey: McDaniel Press, 1974), pp. iv, 28.

9. Renee B. Fisher. *Musical Prodigies: Masters at an Early Age* (New York: Associated Press, 1973), pp. 69-72. See the numerous articles scattered throughout *Dwight's Journal* during those years and also see *The Marvelous Musical Prodigy Blind Tom* (Baltimore: The Sun Book and Job Printers, 1868).

10. Willa Cather. *My Antonia, II* (Boston: Houghton Mifflin, 1918). For some documented proof of this as part of her acknowledged autobiographical aspects and analytical studies about her, see Richard Giannone. *Music in Willa Cather's Fiction* (Lincoln: University of Nebraska Press, 1968), pp. 116-122, and "This Vivid Description of Negro Genius is Supposed to be Blind Tom," *Columbus (Georgia) Magazine* (May 31, 1941), pp. 27-28.

11. Eugene B. Abbott, "The Miraculous Case of Blind Tom," *Etude* (August, 1940), and Amelia Tutein, "The Phenomenon of Blind Tom," *Etude* (February, 1918).

12. Tutein. *Ibid.,* p. 91.

13. See further in regard to George Bristow, Gilbert Chase. *American Music* (New York: McGraw Hill, 1953), pp. 326-330.

14. James Monroe Trotter. *Music and Some Highly Musical People* (Boston: Lee and Shepard Publishers, 1878), p. 144.

15. Introduction to Southall. *The Continuing 'Enslavement' of Blind Tom, the Black Pianist-Composer (1865-1887)* (Minneapolis: Challenge Productions, Inc., 1983).

Bibliography

PRIMARY SOURCES

Given the voluminous citations from primary research materials (newspapers, journals and legal documents), such references, which appear in the chapter notes for the particular year, have not been duplicated in this section. It is unfortunate that due to the destruction of records following the sale of the Steinway and Sons Company from its old office on 14th Street in 1925 (letter to the author from John H. Steinway, Vice-President, March 23, 1976), another major source surrounding the career of Blind Tom as a traveling artist for that piano firm was unavailable to me. However, the close relationship between the Bethune family and the company was noted in my second book, in the year 1884, when John G. Bethune was killed in an accident. Mr. L.F. Harrison of Steinway Hall was involved in the funeral arrangements with the father, Col. James N. Bethune.

BOOKS

Abijian, James de T., comp. *Blacks in Selected Newspapers. Census and Other Sources: An Index to Names and Subjects.* Boston: G.K. Hall, 1977, 3 vols.

Adams, James T. *Album of American History.* New York: Scribner Sons, Inc., 1969.

Ammer, Christine. *Unsung: A History of Women in American Music.* Westport, Conn.: Greenwood Press, 1980.

Anderson, David D. *William Jennings Bryan.* Boston: Twayne, 1981.

Anderson, Jarvis. *This Was Harlem, 1900-1950.* New York: Farrar, Straus & Giroux, 1982.

Annals of Cleveland. *A Digest and Index of Newspaper Record of Events and Opinions.* Cleveland, Ohio: WPA Project 16492, Cleveland Public Library Distribution, 1937.

Bibliography

Appelbaum, Stanley. *The Chicago Worlds Fair of 1893: A Photographic Record.* New York: Dover Publication, 1980.

Aptheker, Herbert, ed. *A Documentary History of the Negro People in the United States.* New York: Citadel Press, 1969.

Armitage, Charles H. *Grover Cleveland as Buffalo Knew Him.* Buffalo: Buffalo Evening News Publisher, 1940.

Ash, Roberta. *Social Movements in America.* Chicago: Markham Publishing, 1972.

Ayers, Isaac W. *Contributions to the Art of Music in America by the Music Industry of Boston, 1640-1936.* New York: H.W. Wilson, 1937.

Bardolph, Richard. *The Negro Vanguard.* New York: Vintage Books, 1959.

Barfield, Louise C. *History of Harris County, Georgia, 1827-1961.* Columbus, GA.: Columbus Office Supply, 1961.

Baroff, Edith. *Music in Europe and the United States.* Englewood Cliffs, N.J.: Prentice Hall, Inc., 1971.

Barr, Alwyn. *Black Texans: A History of Negroes in Texas, 1528-1971.* Austin Jenkins Publishing Company, 1976.

Bartlett, Irving H. *The American Mind in the Mid-Nineteenth Century.* New York: Thomas Y. Crowell, 1967.

Beasley, Deliah L. *The Negro Trail Blazers of California.* Los Angeles: Times-Mirror Printing and Binding House, 1919.

Bell, Orelia Kay. *Book of Poems,* 1895- reprint in Columbus Magazine, July 31, 1941.

Bennett, Mildred R. *The World of Willa Cather.* New York: Dodd, Mead & Co., 1951.

Berger, Raoul. *Government by Judiciary: The Transformation of the Fourteenth Amendment.* Cambridge, Mass.: Harvard University Press, 1977.

Bergman, Peter M., and Morton N. Bergman, comp. *The Chronological History of the Negro in America.* New York: Harper and Row, 1969.

Berlin, Edward A. *Ragtime: A Musical and Cultural History.* Berkeley: University of California Press, 1980.

Berry, Mary Frances. *Black Resistance: White Law: A History of Constitutional Racism in America.* New York: Appleton-Century Crofts, 1971.

Bierly, Paul. *John Philip Sousa: American Phenomenon.* Englewood Cliffs, N.J.: Prentice-Hall, 1973.

Biographical Dictionary of the American Congress, 1774-1971. Washington, D.C. Government Printing Office, 1971.

Birdoff, Harry. *The Worlds Greatest Hit: Uncle Tom's Cabin.* New York: S.F. Vanne, 1947.

Black, Henry C. *Blacks Law Dictionary,* 5th ed. St. Paul, Minn.: West Publishing Company, 1979.

Blaustein, Albert, and Robert Zangrands. *Civil Rights and the Negro.* New York: Trident Press, 1968.

Blesh, Rudi, and Harriet Janis. *They All Played Ragtime.* rev. ed., New York: Oak Publication, 1966.

Blum, Daniel, ed. *A Pictorial History of the American Theatre, 1860-1976.* 4th ed. New York: Crown Publication, 1977.

Boardman, Gerald M. *American Musical Theatre.* New York: Oxford Univ. Press, 1978.

Bogle, Donald C. *Toms, Coons, Mulattos, Mammies and Bucks.* New York: Viking Press, 1973.

Bontemps, Arna W. *Anyplace but Here.* New York: Hill & Wang, 1966.

_____. *Chariot in the Sky: A Story of the Jubilee Singers.* Philadelphia: Winston, 1951.

_____. *100 Years of Negro Freedom.* New York: Dodd, Mead & Co., 1961.

Brawley, Benjamin. *The Negro Genius.* New York: Biblo and Tanner, 1969.

_____. *Social History of the American Negro.* New York: Macmillan Co., 1921.

Brignano, Russell C. *Black Americans in Autobiography.* Durham, North Carolina: Duke University Press, 1974.

Broderick, Francis L. *Reconstruction and the American Negro, 1865-1900.* New York: Macmillan, 1969.

Brooks, Robert Preston. *The University of Georgia under Sixteen Administrations 1755-1955.* Athens: University of Georgia Press, 1956.

Bullock, Henry A. *A History of Negro Education in the South from 1619 to the Present.* Cambridge, Mass.: Harvard University Press, 1967.

Burg, Daniel F. *Chicago: White City of 1893.* Lexington, Ky.: Univ. Press of Kentucky, 1976.

Butler, Addie Louise Joyner. *The Distinctive Black College: Talladega, Tuskegee and Morehouse.* Metuchen, N.J.: Scarecrow Press, 1977.

Butterfield, Roger. *The American Past.* New York: Simon & Schuster, 1976.

Cappon, Lester J. *Virginia Newspapers - 1821-1935: A Bibliography With Historical Introduction and Notes.* New York: D. Appleton-Century Co., 1936.

Carroll, Peter N., and Donald W. Noble. *The Restless Century: A History of the American People.* 2. vol., 2nd ed. Minneapolis, Minn.: Burgess Publishers, 1979.

Carruth, Gorton, and Associates, ed. *The Encyclopedia of American Facts and Dates.* New York: Thomas W. Crowell, 6th ed., 1972.

Cashin, Herschel V. *Under Fire with the Tenth U.S. Cavalry.* New York: F. Tennyson Neely, 1899.

Catalogue of the Trustees, Officers, Alumni and Matriculaters of the University of Georgia at Athens, Ga. From 1785-1906. Athens: E.D. Stone Press, 1906.

Cather, Willa. *My Antonia. Book II.* Boston: Houghton Mifflin, 1918.

Cazort, Jean E., and Constance Tibbs Hobson. *Born to Play: The Life and Career of Hazel Harrison.* Westport, Conn.: Greenwood Press, 1983.

Charters, Ann. *Nobody: The Story of Bert Williams.* New York: Macmillan Co., 1970.

Chase, Gilbert. *American Music from the Pilgrims to the Present.* New York: McGraw Hill, 1955.

Chasins, Abram. *Speaking of Pianists.* New York: Alfred A. Knopf, 1957.

Clement, Haney. *The Ragtime Era.* New York: Tower Publications Inc., 1976.

Clements, John. *Chronology of the United States.* New York: McGraw Hill, 1975.

Coleridge-Taylor, Avril. *The Heritage of Samuel Coleridge-Taylor.* London: Dennis Dobson, 1979.

Cotter, John C. *Negro Music in St. Louis.* M.A. thesis, Washington University, 1960.

Crane, Joan. *Willa Cather: A Bibliography*. Lincoln: Univ. Of Nebraska Press, 1982.

Crunden, Robert M., ed. *Many and One: A Social History of the United States*. Englewood Cliff: Prentice Hall, 1980.

Csida, Joseph, and June Bundy Csida. *American Entertainment: A Unique History of Popular Show Business*. New York: Billboard Books, 1978.

Cunningham, John T. *Newark*. Newark, N.J.: New Jersey Historical Society, 1966.

Curtis, Susan. *Dancing to Black Man's Tone: A Life of Scott Joplin*. Columbia, Mo.: University of Missouri Press, 1994.

Dabney, Wendell P. *Cincinnati's Colored Citizens: Historical, Sociological and Biographical*. Cincinnati: Dabney Publishing Company, 1926.

Dale, Kathleen. *Nineteenth Century Piano Music*. London: Oxford University Press, 1954.

Daniels, Douglas H. *Pioneer Urbanites: A Social and Cultural History of Black San Francisco*. Philadelphia: Temple University Press, 1980.

Dann, Martin E., ed. *The Black Press 1827-1890*. New York: Capricon Books, 1971.

Dannett, Sylvia. *Profiles of Negro Womanhood*. Yonkers, New York: Educational Heritage, 1969.

Darlington, Marwood. *Irish Orpheus: Life of Patrick S. Gilmore, Bandmaster Extraordinaire*. Philadelphia: Oliver-Mann-Keller Co., 1950.

Daughtry, Willa E. *Sissieretta Jones: A Study of the Negro's Contribution to Nineteenth Century America and Theatrical Life*. Ph.D. dissertation, Syracuse Univ. 1968.

Davis, Ronald L. *A History of Music in American Life. Vol. II, The Gilded Years, 1865-1920*. Huntington, N.Y.: Robert Krieger Publishing Co., 1980.

Davison, Sister M. Veronica. *American Musical Periodicals. 1853-1899*. Ph.D. thesis. University of Minnesota, 1973.

Dedmon, Emmett. *My Fabulous Chicago*. New York: Atheneum Press, 1981.

Denisoff, R. Serge, and Richard A. Peterson, eds. *The Sounds of Social Change*. Chicago: Rand McNally, 1972.

Derricotte, Elise P. *Word Pictures of Great Negroes.* Washington, D.C.: Associated Publishers, 1964, 13-21.

DeSanto, Vincent P. *The Shaping of Modern America, 1877-1916.* St. Louis: Forum Press, 1973.

Detweiler, Frederick G. *The Negro Press in the United States.* Chicago: University of Chicago Press, 1922.

Deusen, Glyndon G., and Dexter Perkins. *The United States of America: A History. vol. 2.* New York: Macmillan Co., 1962.

Diamond, Sigmund D. *The Nation Transformed: the Creation of an Industrial Society.* New York: G. Braziller, 1963.

Dorsett, Lyle W. *The Queen City. A History of Denver.* Boulder, Colorado: Pruett Publishing Company, 1976.

Douglass, Frederick. *Life and Times* (Chapter 13). London: Collier Books, 1892.

Drimmer, Melvin, ed. *Black History: A Reappraisal.* Garden City, N.Y.: Doubleday, 1968.

Drummond, John D. *Opera in Perspective.* Minneapolis: Univ. Of Minnesota Press, 1980.

DuBois, W.E.B., and Guy B. Johnson. *Encyclopedia of the Negro.* New York: Phelps-Stokes, 1945.

———. *The Philadelphia Negro.* New York: Schocken Books, Inc., 1899.

———. *The Soul of Black Folk: Essays & Sketches.* Chicago: McClurg, 1903.

Dulles, Foster Rhea. *A History of Recreation. Americans Learn to Play.* New York: Appleton-Century-Crofts, 1940.

Eaton, Quaintance. *The Miracle of the Met: An Informal History of the Metropolitan Opera, 1883-1967.* New York: Meredith Press, 1968.

Edward, Arthur, and Thomas Marracco. *Music in the United States.* Dubuque, Iowa: Wm. C. Brown Company, 1966.

Edwards, P.K. *Strikes in the United States, 1881-1974.* New York: St. Martins, 1981.

Eliot, Elizabeth. *Portrait of a Sport: A History of Steeplechasing.* New York: Longman, Green & Company, 1957.

Ellison, Mary, ed. *The Black Experience: American Blacks Since 1865.* London: B.T. Batsford, 1974.

Elson, Louis C. *The History of American Music.* New York: Macmillan Co., 1904, 1915, & 1925.

Emery, Lynne. *Black Dance in the United States from 1619 to 1970.* Palo Alto, Calif.: National Press Books, 1972.

Emery, Michael and Edwin. *The Press and America.* Englewood Cliffs, N.J.: Prentice-Hall 4th ed., 1978.

Engs, Robert F. *Freedoms First Generation: Black Hampton, Virginia, 1861-1890.* Philadelphia: University of Pennsylvania Press, 1979.

Evans, Sara M. *Born for Liberty: A History of Women in America.* New York: The Free Press, 1989.

Ewen, David. *All the Years of American Popular Music: A Comprehensive History.* Englewood Cliffs, N.J.: Prentice-Hall, 1977.

_____. *Story of the American Musical Theatre.* New York: Chilton & Co., 1961.

Farwell, Arthur. *Music in America.* New York: The National Society of Music, 1915.

Faulkner, Harold U. *Politics, Reform and Expansion, 1890-1900.* New York: Harper, 1953.

_____. *American Politics and Social History,* 6th ed. New York: Appleton-Century-Crofts, 1952.

_____. *The Quest for Social Justice, 1898-1914.* New York: The Macmillan Company, 1931.

Ferguson, James S. *A History of Music in Vicksburg, Mississippi, 1820-1900.* D. Ed. Thesis, University of Michigan, 1970.

Filler, Louis. *Late Nineteenth Century American Liberalism.* Indianapolis: Bobbs-Merrill Co., 1962.

Fisher, Renee R. *Musical Prodigies: Masters at an Early Age.* New York: Associated Press, 1973.

Fletcher, Tom. *100 Years of the Negro in Show Business.* New York: Burdge and Co. Ltd., 1954.

Fostle, D.W. *The Steinway Saga: An American Dynasty.* New York: Harper and Row, 1995.

Franklin, John Hope. *From Slavery to Freedom.* New York: Alfred A. Knopf, 5th ed., 1979.

Frederickson, George M. *The Black Image in the White World.* New York: Harper and Row, 1971.

French, Bryant M. *Mark Twain and the Gilded Age: The Book That Named an Era.* Dallas: Southern Methodist University Press, 1965.

Fuell, Melissa. *Blind Boone: His Early Life and His Achievements.* Kansas City, Mo.: Burton Publishing Co., 1915.

Furness, J. C. *The Americans: A Social History of the United States: 1587-1914.* New York: Putnam & Sons, 1969.

Gammond, Peter. *Scott Joplin and the Ragtime Era.* London: Angus and Robertson Ltd., 1975.

Garrett, Romeo B. *The Presidents and the Negro.* Peoria, Ill.: Bradley Univ., 1982.

Garrity, John A. *The New Commonwealth, 1877-1890.* New York: Harper Row, 1968.

Gaston, Paul M. *The New South Creed: A Study in Southern Mythmaking.* Baton Rouge: L.S.U. Press, 1976.

Gatewood, Willard B. *Black Americans and the White Man's Burden, 1898-1903.* Urbana, Illinois: University of Illinois Press, 1975.

Gelatt, Roland. *The Fabulous Phonograph, 1877-1977.* London: Collier Books, 1977.

Gerig, Reginald R. *Famous Pianists and Their Technique.* New York: Robert B. Luce Inc., 1974.

Giannone, Richard. *Music in Willa Cather's Fiction.* Lincoln, Nebraska: University of Nebraska Press, 1968.

Gilbert, Douglas. *American Vaudeville: Its Life and Times.* New York: Dover Press, 1968.

Gill, Dominic, ed. *The Book of the Piano.* Ithaca, New York: Cornell University Press, 1981.

Gillespie, John. *Five Centuries of Keyboard Music: An Historical Survey of Music for Harpsichord and Piano.* Belmont, California: Wadsworth Publishing Co., 1965.

Ginger, Ray. *Age of Excess: The United States from 1877 to 1914.* New York: Macmillan and Co., 1965.

Goode, Kenneth G. *California's Black Pioneers: A Brief Historical Survey.* Santa Barbara, California: McNally & Lofton Publishers, 1974.

Gould, Louis. *The Presidency of William McKinley.* Lawrence, Kansas: Regent Press of Kansas, 1980.

Graebner, William, and Leonard Richard. *The American Record: Images of the Nation's Past.* New York: Knopf, 1982, 2 vols.

Grau, Robert. *The Business Man in the Amusement World.* New York: Broadway Publishers, 1910.

Gray, John. *Blacks in Classical Music.* New York: Greenwood Press, 1988.

Green, Abel, and Joe Louve. *Showbiz from Vaudeville to Video.* New York: Holt, 1951.

Green, Constance M. *Washington Village and Capital City, 1879-1950.* Princeton, N.J.: Princeton University Press, 1963.

Greene, Robert E. *Black Defenders of America, 1775-1973.* Chicago: Johnson Publishing Company, 1974.

Griffith, Louis T., and John E. Talmadge. *Georgia Journalism, 1763-1950.* Athens: University of Georgia Press, 1951.

Groh, George W. *The Black Migration: The Journey to Urban America.* New York: Wright and Talley, 1972.

Grossman, Lawrence. *The Democratic Party and the Negro: Northern and National Politics.* Urbana, Illinois: University of Illinois Press, 1976.

Grout, Donald. *A History of Western Music,* rev. ed. New York: W.W. Norton, 1973.

Grove's Dictionary of Music and Musicians, ed. Stanley Sadie. London: Macmillan Publishers, 1980.

Hall, James W. *Forging the American Character.* Malabus, Fla.: Krieger Publishers, 1971.

Hamm, Charles. *Music in the New World.* New York: W.W. Norton Co., 1982.

Handy, D. Antoinette. *Black Women in American Bands and Orchestras.* Metuchen, N.J.: Scarecrow Press, 1981; second ed., 1998.

Haney, Clement. *The Ragtime Era.* New York: Belmont Tower Books, 1976.

Bibliography

Hare, Maude Cuney. *Negro Musicians and Their Music.* Washington, D.C.: Associated Press, 1936.

Harlan, Louis R. *Booker T. Washington - The Maker of a Black Leader, 1865-1901.* New York: Oxford University Press, 1972.

Harris, Neil, ed. *The Land of Contrasts, 1880-1901.* New York: George Brazillier, 1970.

_____. *Humbug: The Art of P.T. Barnum.* Boston: Little, Brown & Co., 1973.

Hart, Philip. *Orpheus in the New World: the Symphony Orchestra as an American Cultural Institution: Its Past, Present and Future.* New York: W.W. Norton, 1973.

Hartnell, Phyliss, ed. *The Oxford Companion to the Theatre,* 3rd ed. London: Oxford University Press, 1964.

Haskins, James. *Black Theater in America.* New York: Thomas Crowell, 1982.

Hatch, James. *Black Images on the American Stage. A Bibliography of Plays and Musicals, 1770-1970.* New York: Drama Book Specialists, 1970.

Hayes, Samuel. *American Political History as Social Analysis.* Knoxville: University of Tennessee Press, 1980.

Haynes, George E. *The Negro at Work in New York City.* New York: Longman, Green & Co., 1912.

Healy, David F. *The United States in Cuba, 1898-1902.* Madison: University of Wisconsin Press, 1963.

Henri, Florette. *Black Migration Movement North, 1900-1920. The Road from Myth to Man.* Garden City, N.Y.: Doubleday, 1976.

Hill, Roy L. *Booker T's Child: The Life and Times of Portia Marshall Washington Pittman.* Newark: McDaniel Press, 1974.

Hitchcock, H. Wiley. *Music in the United States. A Historical Introduction.* Englewood Cliffs, N.J.: Prentice-Hall, 1969.

Hoffman, Richard. *Some Musical Recollections of Fifty Years.* New York: Charles Scribners, Sons, 1910.

Hollingsworth, J. Rogers. *America's Expansion in the Late 19th Century.* New York: Holt, Rinehart, & Winston, 1968.

Howard, John Tasker. *Our American Music.* New York: Thomas Crowell, 4th ed., 1964.

Huggins, Nathanial. *Slave and Citizen: The Life of Frederick Douglass.* Boston: Little Brown and Co., 1980.

Hull, A.L. *A Historical Sketch of the University of Georgia.* Atlanta, Georgia: The Foote & Davies Co., 1894.

Hunt, Inez L. *The Story of Blind Tom.* Denver, Co.: School District II for use in classroom instruction, 1972.

Hutton, Lawrence. *Curiosities of the American Stage.* New York: Harper & Brother, 1891.

Inge, M. Thomas. *Concise History of American Popular Culture.* Westport, Conn.: Greenwood Press, 1982.

"In Retrospect: Gussie L. Davis (1868-1897) Tin Pan Alley Tunesmith," *Black Perspective in Music* (Fall, 1978), pp. 188-230.

Isaacs, Edith. *The Negro in the American Theatre.* New York: Theatre Arts.

Jablonski, Edward. *The Encyclopedia of American Music.* Garden City, New York: Doubleday, 1981.

Jasen, David A., and Trebor Jay Tichnor. *Rags and Ragtime: A Musical History.* New York: Seabury Press, 1978.

Jensen, Oliver, ed. *The Nineties.* New York: American Heritage, 1967.

Johnson, Harold Earle. *First Performances in America to 1900: Works with Orchestra.* Detroit: Information Coordinators, 1979.

Johnson, James Weldon. *Black Manhattan.* New York: Atheneum Publishers, 1930.

———. *Along This Way.* New York: Viking Press, 1933.

Jones, Howard M. *The Age of Energy.* New York: Viking Press, 1971.

Katz, William. *The Black West.* Garden City, New York: Doubleday and Co., 1971.

Katz, William L. *Eyewitness: The Negro in American History.* New York: Pitman Publishing Corp., 1968.

Keck, George R., and Sherrill V. Martin. *Feel the Spirit: Studies in 19th Century Afro-American Music.* Westport, Conn.: Greenwood Press, 1988.

Bibliography

Kehler, George, comp. *The Piano in Concert.* 2 vols. Metuchen, N.J.: Scarecrow Press, 1982.

Keller, Morton. *Affairs of State: Public Life in Late Nineteenth Century America.* Cambridge, Mass.: Belknap Press of Harvard University, 1977.

Kingman, Daniel. *American Music: A Panorama.* New York: G. Schirmer, 1979.

Kirby, F.E. *A Short History of Keyboard Music.* New York: The Free Press, 1966.

Kislan, R. *The Musical. A Look at the American Musical Theatre.* Englewood Cliffs, N.J.: Prentice-Hall, 1980.

Klein, Herman. *The Reign of Patti.* New York: the Century Company, 1920.

Klein, Milton M. *New York: the Centennial Year, 1676-1976.* Port Washington, New York: Kennikat Press, 1976.

Kleppner, Paul. *The Third Electoral System, 1853-1892. Parties, Voters, and Political Cultures.* Chapel Hill, N.C.: University of North Carolina, 1979.

Kolodin, Irvin. *Metropolitan Opera, 1883-1966.* New York: W.W. Knopf, 1966.

Kolpatzki, Rose Mary. *The Emergence of a National Cultural Spirit in American Music and Music Activities, 1850-1900.* D.Ed. Thesis, University of Ga., Athens, 1976.

Krock, Arthur, comp. *The Editorials of Henry Watterson.* New York: George H. Doran Company, 1923.

Krohn, Ernst C. *A Century of Missouri Music.* New York: Da Capo Press, 1971.

Krummel, D.W., et al. *Resources of American Music History: A Directory of Source Materials for the Study of Musicians in the United States from the Beginning to World War II.* Urbana: University of Illinois Press, 1981.

Kupferberg, Herbert. *Those Fabulous Philadelphians: The Life and Times of a Great Orchestra.* New York: Charles Scribner, 1969.

Lahee, Hanry C. *Grand Opera in America.* Boston: L.C. Page Co., 1902.

———. *Annals of Music in America.* Boston: Marshall Jones, 1922.

_____. *Famous Pianists of Today and Yesterday*. Boston: L.C. Page, 1901.

Lang, Paul Henry, ed. *One Hundred Years of Music in America*. New York: G. Schirmer, 1961.

Langston, John Mercer. *From the Virginia Plantation to the National Capital*. Hartford, Conn.: American Publishing Company, 1894.

Larkin, Oliver W. *Art and Life in America*. New York: Holt, Rinehart & Winston, 1960.

Laufe, Abe. *Broadway's Greatest Musicals,* rev. ed. New York: Funk and Wagnalls, 1977.

Laurie, Joe. *Vaudeville: From the Honkey Tonks to the Palace*. New York: Rinehart-Holt, 1953.

Lawrence, Vera Brodsky. *The Collected Works of Scott Joplin*. New York: New York Public Library, 1971.

Lears, T.J. Jackson. *No Place of Grace: Antimodernism and the Transformation of American Culture, 1880-1920*. New York: Pantheon, 1981.

Leech, Margaret. *In the Days of McKinley*. New York: Harper & Row, 1959.

Levy, Eugene. *James Weldon Johnson: Black Leader, Black Voice*. Chicago: University of Chicago Press, 1973.

Lewis, David L. *District of Columbia: A Bicentennial History*. New York: W.W. Norton, 1976.

Lewis, Gordon K. *Puerto Rico: Freedom and Power in the Caribbean*. Monthly Review, 1963 reprint, 1975.

Locke, Alain. *The Negro and His Music*. Washington, D.C.: Associated Press, 1936.

Loesser, Arthur. *Men, Women and Piano. A Social History*. New York: Simon & Schuster, 1954.

Logan, Rayford W. *The Betrayal of the Negro from Rutherford B. Hayes to Woodrow Wilson*. New York: Collier Books, 1965.

Longyear, Ray M. *Nineteenth-Century Romanticism in Music*. Englewood Cliffs, N.J.: Prentice-Hall, 1969.

Lortie, Francis N.J. *San Francisco's Black Community, 1870-1890: Dilemma in the Struggle for Equality*. San Francisco: R & E Research Associates, 1973.

Louisiana Black Heritage, ed. Robert R. Macdonald, John R. Kemp and Edward F. Haas. New Orleans: State Museum, 1979.

Lovingood, Penman. *Famous Modern Negro Musicians*. New York: Da Capo Press, 1978 (reprint of 1921 edition).

Low, W. Augustus, ed. *Encyclopedia of Black Americans*. New York: McGraw Hill, 1981.

Lowenberg, Alfred. *Annals of Opera, 1597-1940*. London: J. Calder, 1978.

Lyle, Wilson. *A Dictionary of Pianists*. New York: G. Schirmer, 1985.

Lynch, Hollis P. *The Black Urban Condition: A Documentary History, 1866-1971*. New York: Thomas Y. Crowell, 1973.

Mackay-Smith, Alexander. *The American Foxhound, 1747-1967*. Millwood, Virginia: American Foxhaven Club, 1968.

Mahan, Katherine. *Showboats to Soft Shoe: A Century of Music Development in Columbus, Georgia, 1828-1928*. Columbus, Ga.: Columbus Office Supply, 1968.

Majors, Monroe A. *Noted Negro Women: Their Triumph and Activities*. Chicago: Donahue & Heneberry, 1893.

Marks, George P. *The Black Press Views American Imperialism (1898-1900)*. New York: Arno Press, 1971.

Marston, William, and John H. Feller. *F.F. Proctor: Vaudeville Pioneer*. New York: R.R. Smith, 1943.

The Marvelous Musical Prodigy, Blind Tom, the Negro Boy Pianist. Baltimore: The Sun Books & Job Printers, 1868.

Mason, William. *Memories of Musical Life*. New York: The Century Co., 1902.

Matlow, Myron, ed. *American Popular Entertainment*. Westport, Conn.: Greenwood Press, 1977.

Mattfield, Julius. *Variety Music Cavalcade, 1620-1969*. Englewood Cliffs, N.J.: Prentice-Hall, 1971.

Matthew, Myron. *The Black Crook and Other Nineteenth Century American Plays*. New York: E.P. Dutton, 1961.

Matthews, William S. *A Popular History of the Art of Music from the Earliest Time to the Present*. Chicago: W.S.B. Mather, 1891.

McArthur, Benjamin. *Actors and American Culture, 1880-1920.* Philadelphia: Temple University Press, 1984.

McCloy, Shelby T. *The Negro in France.* Louisville: University of Kentucky Press, 1961.

McCue, George, ed. *Music in American Society, 1776-1976: From Puritan Hymns to Synthesizers.* New Brunswick, N.J.: Transaction Books, 1977.

McFarland, Gerald W. *Mugwumps, Morals and Politics, 1884-1920.* Amherst: University of Massachusetts Press, 1975.

McPherson, James M. *The Abolitionist Legacy: From Reconstruction to the NAACP.* Princeton: Princeton University Press, 1976.

_____. *Blacks in America: Bibliographical Essays.* Garden City, N.Y.: Doubleday, 1977.

McRaven, Henry W. *Nashville "Athens of the South."* Chapel Hill: Scherer & Jervis, 1949.

Meier, August. *Negro Thought in America 1880-1915.* Ann Arbor: University of Michigan Press, 1963.

Mellers, Wilfred. *Music in a New Found Land: Themes and Developments in the Heritage of American Music.* New York: Stonehill Publishing Co., 1975.

Merrill, Horace S. *Bourbon Leader: Grover Cleveland and the Democratic Party.* Boston: Little Brown, 1957.

Miller, Loren. *The Petitioners: The Story of the Supreme Court of the United States and the Negro.* Cleveland: Third Publishing Co., 1966.

Miller, Perry. *American Thought: Civil War to World War I.* New York: Rinehart, 1956.

Millis, Walter. *The Martial Spirit: A Study of Our War With Spain.* New York: Vikings Press, 1965.

Molloy, Robert. *Charleston: A Gracious Heritage.* New York: D. Appleton-Century Co., 1947.

Moody, Richard. *Dramas from the American Theatre: 1762-1909.* New York: World Publishing Co., 1966.

_____. *Americans Take the Stage.* Bloomington, Indiana; Indiana University Press, 1955.

Moreland, Lois. *White Racism and the Law.* Columbus, Ohio: Merrill Publishing Company, 1972.

Morgan, Howard W. *Victorian Culture in America, 1865-1914.* Itaska, Illinois: F.E. Peacock Publishers, 1973.

_____. *The Gilded Age: A Reappraisal.* New York: Syracuse University Press, 1970.

Morison, Samuel E. *The Oxford History of the American People.* New York: Oxford University Press, 1965.

Morris, Lloyd. *Incredible New York: High Life and Low Life of the Last Hundred Years.* New York: Random House, 1951.

Morris, Richard B. *Encyclopedia of American History:* Bicentennial ed. New York: Harper & Row, 1976.

Morrison, Theatrice. *Chautauqua: A Century for Education, Religion and the Arts in America.* Chicago: University of Chicago Press, 1974.

Mott, Frank Luther. *American Journalism: A History of Newspapers in the United States through 150 Years, 1690-1940.* New York: The Macmillan Co., 1941.

Mueller, John H. *The American Symphony Orchestra: A Social History of Musical Taste.* Bloomington, Indiana: Indiana University Press, 1951.

Mussulman, Joseph A. *Music in the Cultural Generations: A Social History of Music in America, 1870-1900.* Evanston, Ill: Northwestern University Press, 1971.

Nevins, Allan. *Grover Cleveland: A Study of Courage.* New York: Dodd, Mead & Co. 1962.

_____. *Notable American Women, 1607-1950: A Biographical Dictionary.* ed. Edward T. James. Cambridge, Mass.: Belknap Press of Harvard Univ. Press, 1971.

Nye, Russell. *The Unembarrassed Muse: The Popular Arts in America.* New York: The Dial Press, 1970.

Oberholtzer, Ellis P. *A History of the United States Since the Civil War.* New York: Macmillan Co., 1922.

Odell, George C.D. *Annals of the New York Stage.* New York: Columbia University Press, 1931.

_____. *On with the Show: The First Century of Show Business in America.* New York: Oxford University Press, 1976.

Osborne, Thomas J., and Fred R. Masblut. *Paths to the Present: Thoughts on the Contemporary Relevance of America's Past.* Malabar, Florida: Krieger Pub. Co., 1974.

Osofsky, Gilbert. *Harlem: the Making of a Ghetto,* 2nd ed. New York: Harper & Row, 1971.

Ostrander, Gilman M. *American Civilization in the First Machine Age, 1890-1940.* New York: Harper & Row, 1970.

Ottley, Roi. *New World A Coming.* Boston: Houghton, Mifflin Company, 1943.

Ottley, Roi, and William Westherby. *Negro in New York: An Informal Social History.* Dobbs Ferry: Oceana Publication, 1967.

Pace, Don M. *The Arts in Jackson, Mississippi: A History of Theatre, Painting, Sculpture, and Music in Mississippi Since 1900.* Oxford, Mississippi: University of Mississippi Press, 1976.

Parker, Elizabeth L., and James Abajian. *A Walking Tour of the Black Presence in San Francisco During the Nineteenth Century.* San Francisco: San Francisco African-American Historical Cultural Society, 1974.

Parrish, William E. *A History of Missouri.* Columbia, Missouri: University of Missouri Press, 1972.

Parsons, Stow. *The Decline of American Gentility.* New York: Columbia University Press, 1973.

Pascal, Jeremy, and Burt Rob. *The Stars and Superstars of Black Music.* Secaucus, N.J.: Chartwell Books, Inc., 1977.

Patterson, Cecil Lloyd. *A Different Drum: The Images of the Negro in Nineteenth Century Song Books.* Ph.D. thesis, University of Pennsylvania, 1961.

Patterson, Lindsay. *The Negro in Music and Art.* New York: Publishers Co., 1967.

Paul, Arnold M., ed. *Black Americans and the Supreme Court Since Emancipation.* 1972.

Peltz, Mary Ellis. *Behind the Gold Curtain: Story of the Metropolitan Opera, 1883-1950.* New York: Farrar, Straus, 1950.

Perkins, Dexter, and Glyndon G. Van Deusen. *The United States of America: A History.* New York: Macmillan Co., 1962.

Bibliography

Phelps-Stokes, Ansom. *Tuskegee Institute: The First Fifty Years.* Tuskegee, Alabama: Tuskegee Institute Press, 1931.

Pitre, Merline. *Frederick Douglass: A Party Loyalist, 1870-1895.* Ph.D. thesis, Temple University, 1976.

Plaski, Henry A., and Warren Maer, II, eds. *The Negro Almanac: A Reference Book on the Afro-American.* New York: Bellwether Co., 1976.

Pleasants, Henry. *The Great Singers From the Dawn of Opera to our Times.* New York: Simon & Schuster, 1966.

Poggi, Jack. *Theater in America: The Impact of Economic Farces, 1870-1967.* Ithaca, New York: Cornell University Press, 1969.

Porte, John F. *Edward MacDowell: A Great American Tone Poet, His Life and Music.* New York: E.P. Dutton, 1922.

Porter, Kenneth W. *The Negro on the American Frontier.* New York: Arno Press, 1970.

Quarles, Benjamin. *Frederick Douglass.* Englewood Cliffs: Prentice-Hall, 1962.

_____. *The Negro in the Making of America.* New York: Collier Press, 1964.

Rabinowitz, Howard N., ed. *Southern Black Leaders of the Reconstruction Era.* Urbana: University of Illinois Press, 1982.

Reblitz, Arthur, and Q. David Bowers. *Treasures of Mechanical Music.* Vestal, New York: The Vestal Press, Ltd., 1981.

Redkey, Edwin S. *Black Exodus: Black Nationalist and Back-to-Africa Movements, 1890-1910.* New Haven, Conn.: Yale University Press, 1969.

Reed, Addison. *The Life and Works of Scott Joplin.* Ph.D. thesis, University of North Carolina, Chapel Hill, 1973.

Richardson, Joe M. *A History of Fisk University, 1865-1946.* Montgomery: University of Alabama Press, 1980.

Riis, Thomas L. *Just Before Jazz: Black Musical Theater in New York: 1890-1915.* Washington, D.C.: Smithsonian Institution Press, 1989.

Ritter, Frederic L. *Music in America.* New York: Charles Scribner & Sons, 1890.

Rivers, Travis. *The Etude Magazine: A Mirror of the Genteel Tradition in American Music.* Ph.D. University of Iowa, Iowa City, 1974.

Roach, Hildred. *Black American Music: Past and Present.* 2nd ed. Malabar, Florida: Krieger Publishing Company, 1992.

Robinson, Wilhemena S. *Historical Afro-American Biographies.* Washington, D.C.: Associated Publishers, 1976.

Roseboom, Eugene H., and Alfred E. Eches, Jr. *A History of Presidential Elections: From George Washington to Jimmy Carter.* New York: Macmillan Publishing Co., 1979.

Ross, Danforth R. *The Genteel Tradition: Its Characteristics and Its Origins.* Ph.D. Thesis, University of Minnesota, 1954.

Rossiter, Frank R. *Charles Ives and His America.* New York: Liveright, 1975.

Rousseve, Charles B. *The Negro in Louisiana: Aspects of History and the Literature.* New Orleans: Xavier University Press, 1937.

Rusco, Elmer R. *Good Time Coming: Black Nevadans in the Nineteenth Century.* Westport, Connecticut: Greenwood Press, 1975.

Russell, Theodore C. *Theodore Thomas: His Role in the Development of Musical Culture in the U.S., 1835-1905.* Ph.D. University of Minnesota, 1964.

Sampson, Henry T. *Blacks in Blackface: A Source Book on Early Black Musical Shows.* Metuchen, N.J.: Scarecrow Press, 1980.

Samuels, Charles and Louise. *Once Upon a Stage: The Merry World of Vaudeville.* New York: Dodd, Mead Co., 1974.

———. *Only One New York.* New York: Simon & Schuster, 1965.

Savage, W. Sherman. *Blacks in the West.* Westport, Conn.: Greenwood Press, 1976.

Sayers, W.C. Berwick. *Samuel Coleridge-Taylor, Musician: His Life and Letters,* 2nd ed. London: Augener, 1927.

Schafer, William, and Johannes Riedel. *The Art of Ragtime: Form and Meaning of an Original Black American Art.* Baton Rouge: Louisiana State University Press, 1978.

Scheiner, Seth M. *Negro Mecca; A History of the Negro in New York City, 1865-1920.* New York: New York University Press, 1965.

Schlesinger, Arthur. *The Rise of the City, 1878-1898.* New York: The Macmillan Co., 1933.

_____. *Political and Social Growth of the American People.* New York: Macmillan, 1941.

Schonberg, Harold C. *The Great Pianists.* New York: Simon & Schuster, 1963.

Schwartz, J.W. *Bands of America.* Garden City, N.Y.: Doubleday, 1957.

Scobie, Edward. *Black Britannia: A History of Blacks in Britain.* Chicago: Johnson Publishing Co., Inc., 1972.

Scruggs, Lawson A. *Women of Distinction: Remarkable in Works and Invincible Character.* Raleigh, N.C.: L.A., Scruggs, 1893.

Seltsam, Willie H., comp. *Metropolitan Opera House Annals: A Chronicle of Artist and Performance.* New York: H.W. Wilson, Co., 1947.

Shanet, Howard. *Philharmonic: A History of the New York Orchestra.* Garden City, N.Y.: Doubleday & Co., 1975.

Shaw, Arnold. *Black Popular Music in America.* New York; Schirmer Books, 1986.

Sherman, John K. *Music and Theater in Minnesota History.* Minneapolis: University of Minnesota Press, 1958.

Sherman, Richard B. *The Republican Party and Black Americans: From McKinley to Herbert Hoover, 1896-1933.* Charlottesville; University of Virginia Press, 1973.

Simond, Ike. *Old Slacks Reminiscence and a Pocket History of the Colored Profession from 1865-1891.* Bowling Green, Ohio: Bowling Green University Popular Press, 1974.

Simpson, Anne Key. *Hard Trials: The Life and Music of Harry T. Burleigh.* Metuchen, N.J.: Scarecrow Press, 1990.

Simpson, John E. *Georgia History: A Bibliography.* Metuchen, N.J.: Scarecrow Press, 1976.

Sloan, Irving J., ed. *Blacks in Americas: A Chronology and Fact Book.* 4th rev. ed. Dobbs Ferry, N.Y.: Oceana Press, 1976.

Smith, Bill. *The Vaudevillians.* New York: Macmillan Press, 1976.

Smith, Cecil. *Musical Comedy in America.* New York: Theater Arts Books, 1950.

Smith, Dwight L. *Afro-American History: A Bibliography.* Santa Barbara, California: American Bibliographical Center, Clio Press, 1974.

Smith, Henry N. *Popular Culture and Industrialism, 1865-1890.* New York: New York University Press, 1967.

Smith, Samuel. *The Negro in Congress, 1870-1901.* New York: Kennikat Press, 1940.

Smythe, Mabel M., ed. *The Black American Reference Book.* Englewood Cliffs, N.J.: Prentice-Hall Inc., 1976.

Sobel, Bernard. *A Pictorial History of Vaudeville.* New York: G.P. Putnam & Sons, 1961.

Sousa, John Philip. *Marching Along: An Autobiography.* Boston: Hale Cushman & Flint, 1928.

Southall, Geneva H. *Blind Tom, The Post Civil-War Enslavement of a Black Musical Genius.* Book I. Minneapolis: Challenge Books, 1979.

_____. *The Continuing Enslavement of Blind Tom, the Black Pianist-Composer (1865-1887).* Book II. Minneapolis: Challenge Books, 1983.

_____. *John Field's Piano Concertos: A Historical and Analytical Study.* Ph.D. thesis, University of Iowa, Iowa City, Iowa, 1966.

Southern, Eileen. *Music of Black Americans.* New York: W.W. Norton, 2nd ed., 1983.

_____. *Readings in Black American Music.* New York: W.W. Norton, 2nd ed., 1983.

_____. *Biographical Dictionary of Afro-American and African Musicians.* Westport, Conn.: Greenwood Press, 1982.

Spaeth, Sigmund. *A History of Popular Music in America.* London: Phoenix House, 1948.

Spillane, Daniel. *History of the American Pianoforte.* New York: Da Capo Press, 1969, reprint of 1890 edition.

Spradling, Mary M. *In Black and White: A Guide to Magazine Articles, Newspaper Articles, and Books Concerning More than 15,000 Black Individuals and Groups.* 3rd ed., Detroit: Gale Research Co., 1980. 2 vols.

Sproat, John G. *The Best Men: Liberal Republicans in the Gilded Age.* New York: Oxford University Press, 1968.

Starke, Catherine J. *Black Portraiture in American Fiction.* New York: Basic Books, 1972.

Stearns, Marshall, and Jean Stearns. *Jazz Dance: The Story of American Vernacular Dance.* New York: Oxford University Press, 1968.

Stevens, Katherine B. *Theatrical Entertainment in Jackson, Mississippi, 1890-1910.* M.A. Thesis, University of Mississippi, 1951.

Story, Rosalyn M. *And So I Sing: African American Divas of Opera and Concert.* New York: Warner Brothers, 1990.

Stowe, Lyman Beecher. *Booker T. Washington: Builder of a Civilization.* Garden City, New York: Doubleday Press, 1918.

Stratman, Carl J. *American Theatrical Periodicals, 1798-1967: A Bibliographical Guide.* Durham, N.C.: Duke University Press, 1970.

Takoki, Ronald T. *Iron Cages: Race and Culture in 19th Century America.* New York: Alfred A. Knopf, 1979.

Telfair, Nancy. *A History of Columbus, Georgia, 1828-1928.* Columbus, Ga.: The Historical Publishing Company, 1929.

Thomas, Theodore. *A Musical Autobiography.* 2 vols. ed. by George P. Upton. Chicago: A.C. McClurg & Co., 1905.

Thornbough, Emma Lou. *T. Thomas Fortune: Militant Journalist.* Chicago: University of Chicago Press, 1972.

Tirro, Frank. *Jazz: A History.* New York: W.W. Norton, 1977.

Toll, Robert C. *Blacking Up: the Minstrel Show in 19th Century America.* New York: Oxford University Press, 1974.

Tompkins, Eugene, and Quincy Kilby. *The History of the Boston Theatre, 1854-1901.* Boston: Houghton, Mifflin Co., 1908.

Tomsich, John. *A Genteel Endeavor. American Culture and Politics in the Gilded Age.* Stanford, California: Stanford University Press, 1971.

Toole-Stott, R. *Circus and Allied Arts: A World Bibliography from 1500-1970.* 4 vols. Derby, England, 1958-71.

Toppin, Edgar. *Negro in the United States, Reconstruction to World War I.* Garden City, New York: Doubleday, 1967.

Tortolano, William. *Samuel Coleridge-Taylor: Anglo-Black Composer, 1875-1912.* Metuchen, N.J.: Scarecrow Press, 1977.

Trask, David F. *The War with Spain in 1898.* New York: Macmillan Publishers, 1981.

Treffert, Daryle. *Extraordinary People "Redefining the Idiot Savant."* New York: Harper & Row, 1988.

Trotter, James Monroe. *Music and Some Highly Musical People.* Boston: Lee & Shephard, 1878.

Twombly, Robert. *Blacks in White America since 1865.* New York: David McKay, 1971.

Ullman, Victor. *Martin R. Delaney: The Beginnings of Black Nationalism.* Boston: Beacon Press, 1971.

Upton, George P. *Musical Memories, 1850-1900.* Chicago: A.C. McClurg, 1908.

Vernado, Alban F. *A History of Theatrical Activity in Baton Rouge, Louisiana, 1819-1900.* MA Thesis, Louisiana State University, 1947.

Vexler, Robert I. *Grover Cleveland, 1837-1908. Chronology, Documents, Bibliographical Aids.* Dobbs Ferry, N.Y.: Oceana Publications, 1968.

Wagaknecht, Edward. *American Profile, 1900-1909.* Amherst: Univ. of Massachusetts Press, 1982.

Waldo, Terry. *This Is Ragtime.* New York: Hawthorn Books, Inc., 1976.

Wallace, Irving. *The Fabulous Showman: The Life and Times of P.T. Barnum.* New York: Alfred A. Knopf, 1959.

Wardlow, Ralph. *Negro Suffrage in Georgia, 1867-1930.* MA Thesis, University of Georgia, 1932.

Weimann, Jeanne M. *The Fair Women.* Chicago: Academy of Chicago, 1981.

Wells, L. Jeanette. *A History of the Music Festival at Chautauqua Institution, 1874-1957.* Washington, D.C.: The Catholic Univ. of America Press, 1958.

Wharton, Vernon. *The Negro in Mississippi, 1865-1900.* Chapel Hill: North Carolina University Press, 1947.

White, Gerald T. *The United States and the Problem of Recovery after 1893.* University, Alabama: University of Alabama Press, 1982.

White, John. *Black Leadership in America: From Booker T. Washington to Jesse Jackson.* New York: Longman, Grays Ltd., 1991.

White, William C. *A History of Military Music in America.* New York: The Exposition Press, 1944.

Wiebe, Robert H. *The Search for Order: 1877-1920*. New York: Hill and Wang, 1967.

_____. *The Segmented Society: An Introduction to the Meaning of America*. New York: Oxford University Press, 1975.

Willard, George O. *History of the Providence Stage, 1762-1891*. Providence: Rhode Island News Company, 1891.

Williams, Gilbert A. *The A.M.E. Christian Recorder: A Forum for the Social Ideas of Black Americans, 1854-1902*. Ph.D. Thesis, University of Illinois, 1979.

Williams, R. Hal. *Years of Decision: American Politics in the 1890's*. New York: Wiley Publishing Company, 1978.

Wilson, Douglas L., ed. *The Genteel Tradition: Nine Essays by George Santayana*. Cambridge, Mass.: Harvard University Press, 1967.

Wilson, Garff B. *Three Hundred Years of American Drama and Theatre*. Englewood Cliffs, N.J.: Prentice Hall, 1973.

Wolf, Donna. *The Caribbean People of Color and the Cuban Independence Movement*. Ph.D. Thesis, University of Pittsburgh, 1973.

Woll, Allen. *Black Musical Theatre: From Coontown to Dreamgirls*. Baton Rouge: LSU Press, 1989.

Wolseley, Roland E. *The Black Press, USA*. Ames, Iowa; Iowa State University Press, 1971.

Wood, James Playsted. *Magazines in the United States*. 2nd ed. New York: Ronald Press Company, 1971.

Woodress, James. *Willa Cather: Her Life, Her Art*. New York: Western Publishing Co., 1970.

Woodward, C. Van. *Origins of the New South, 1877-1913*. Baton Rouge: Louisiana State University Press, 1971.

Wooten, Denham Lee. *Annals of the Stage in Little Rock, Arkansas, 1834-1890*. MA Thesis, Columbia University, 1937.

Work, Monroe N. *A Bibliography of the Negro in Africa and America*. New York: Octagon Books, 1928.

Worsley, Etta Blanche. *Columbus on the Chattahoochee*. Columbus, Georgia: Columbus Office Supply, 1951.

Wynes, Charles E. *Race-Relations in Virginia, 1870-1902*. Charlottesville, Va.: University of Virginia Press, 1961.

———. *The Negro in the South Since 1865*. University of Alabama Press, 1966.

Zeff, Larzer. *The Americans in the 1890's: Life and Times of a Lost Generation*. New York: Viking Press, 1968.

Zuck, Barbara A. *A History of Musical Americanism*. Ann Arbor, Michigan: UMI Research Press, 1980.

ARTICLES

Abbott, Eugene. "The Miraculous Case of Blind Tom," *Etude* (August, 1940), pp. 517-564.

"American Negro Newspapers, 1827-1914," *Business History Review* (Winter, 1966), pp. 467-490.

Anderson, Florence A. "Blind Tom's Music," *Cincinnati Enquirer* (July 26, 1865).

Andreu, Enrique. "Tragedia de un Beethoven Negro," *Revista Musical Chilena; Instituto de Extensio Musical* (October, November, 1947), pp. 24-29.

Baldwin, Brooke. "The Cakewalk: A Study in Stereotypical Reality," *Journal of Social History* (Winter, 1981), pp. 205-218.

Becket, John A. "Blind Tom as He Is Today," *Ladies Home Journal* (Sept. 1898), pp. 13-14.

Bennett, W. Lance, and William Haltom. "Issues, Voter Choice, and Critical Elections," *Social Science History* (November, 1980).

Bell, Frank C. "The Life and Times of John R. Lynch: A Case Study, 1847-1939," *Journal of Mississippi History* (February, 1976).

Bing, Louise. "On What Kind of Wings Do They Fly?" *Sunday-Ledger Enquirer Magazine* (July 11, 1965).

"Blind Tom." *Dictionary of Georgia Biography*, ed. Kenneth Coleman and Charles Stephen Gurr. Vol. I. Athens: University of Georgia Press, 1983.

"Blind Tom As Seen by His Mother, Charity Wiggins," *The Sunny South* (October, 1900).

Brown, Ray B. "Shakespeare in American Vaudeville and Negro Minstrelsy," *American Quarterly* (Fall, 1960), pp. 374-391.

Bruce, John E. "A History of Negro Musicians," *Southern Workman* (October, 1916), pp. 569-573.

Burke, James M. "Music at the Louisiana Purchase Exposition of 1904," *Sonneck Society Newsletter* (Fall, 1982), p. 64.

Carper, N. Gordon. "Slavery Revisited: Peonage in the South," *Phylon* (Fall, 1976), pp. 85-99.

Chieck, William F. "A Negro Runs for Congress: John Mercer Langston and the Virginia Campaign of 1888," *Journal of Negro History* (January, 1967), pp. 14-34.

Clapharm, John. "Dvorak's Musical Directorship in New York," *Music & Letters* (January 1967), pp. 40-51.

Cole, Aaron. "The True Story of Blind Tom," *Daily Mail, Freetown, Sierra Leone* (June 29,1955).

Contee, Clarence G. "The Emergence of DuBois as an African Nationalist," *Journal of Negro History* (April, 1969), pp. 48-63.

Cossell, Frank A. "The Columbus Exposition of 1893 and U.S. Diplomacy in Latin America," *Mid-America* (January, 1985), pp. 109-124.

Crannell, Carlyn G. "Public Taste and 'High Art' in Atlanta, 1870-1900," *Atlanta Historical Journal* (Winter, 1980), pp. 51-74.

Davis, J. Frank. "Blind Tom," *Human Life* (September, 1908).

De Santes, Vincent P. "The Republican Party and the Southern Negro, 1877-1897," *Journal of Negro History* (April, 1966), pp. 71-87.

Doenecke, Justus D. "Myths, Machines and Markets: the Columbian Exposition of 1893," *Journal of Popular Culture* (Winter, 1972), pp. 535-549.

Dorman, James H. "Shaping the Popular Image of Post-Reconstruction American Blacks: the 'Coon Song" Phenomenon of the Gilded Age," *American Quarterly* (December, 1988), pp. 450-471.

Draegert, Eva. "Cultural History of Indianapolis: Music, 1875-1890," *Indiana Magazine History* (September, 1957), pp. 265-304.

Edwards, Vernon H., and Michael L. Mark. "In Retrospect: Clarence Cameron White," *Black Perspective in Music* (Spring, 1981), pp. 51-72.

Fisher, James A. "The Political Development of the Black Community in California, 1850-1950," *California Historical Quarterly* (September, 1971), pp. 256-266.

Fite, Gilbert C. "William Jennings Bryan and the Campaign of 1896: Some Views and Problems," *Nebraska History* (September, 1966), pp. 247-264.

Floyd, Samuel A., and Marsha J. Reisser. "Social Dance Music of Black Composers in the Nineteenth Century and the Emergence of Classical Ragtime," *Black Perspective in Music* (Fall, 1980), pp. 161-194.

Frangeamore, Catherine, and Pam Durham. "Not Just Whislin' Dixie: Atlanta's Music 1837-1977," *Atlanta Historical Bulletin* (September, 1977), pp. 15-36.

"Frank Johnson of Philadelphia and His Promenade Concerts," *Black Perspective in Music* (Spring, 1977), pp. 3-29.

Gatewood, Willard B. "Black Americans and the Quest for Empire, 1898-1903," *Journal of Southern History* (November, 1972), pp. 545-566.

"General James N. Bethune, Owner of Blind Tom Was Outstanding Personality in Columbus," *Columbus Magazine* (May 31, 1941).

Gianakaw, Perry E. "The Spanish American War and the Double Paradox of the Negro American," *Phylon* (Spring, 1965), pp. 34-49.

Giannone, Richard. "Music in My Antonia," *Prairie Schooner* (Winter, 1964-65), pp. 346-361.

Green, Jeffrey P. "In Dahomey in London in 1903," *Black Perspective in Music* (Spring, 1983), pp. 23-40.

Grunfeld, Frederick. "Anton Dvorak in the New World," *Hi/Fi Stereo Review* (December, 1965), pp. 63-68.

Harlan, Louis R. "Booker T. Washington and the 'Voice of the Negro,' 1904-17," *Journal of Southern History* (1979), pp. 45-62.

Harrah, Mudge. "Wayne B. Allen: Blind Boone's Last Manager," *The Ragtimer* (September/December, 1969).

Harrington, Fred H. "The Anti-Imperialist Movement of the United States, 1898-1900," *Mississippi Valley Review* (September, 1935), pp. 211-230.

Hawkins, H.C. "Trends in Black Migration from 1863-1960," *Phylon* (June, 1973), pp. 140-152.

Heath, Robert L. "A Time for Silence: Booker T. Washington in Atlanta," *Quarterly Journal of Speech* (December, 1978), pp. 385-399.

Higgens, Renalda. "100 Years Later: Tuskegee," *Crisis* (July, 1981), pp. 268-273.

Hill, Lawrence J. *A History of Variety. Vaudeville in Minneapolis, Minnesota: From its Beginning to 1900.* Ph.D. thesis, 1979.

Bibliography

Hill, Roy. "Conversation With . . . Fannie Douglass, Reminiscences of Yesteryear," Black Perspective in Music (Spring, 1974), pp. 54-62.

"In Retrospect: Black Prima Donnas of the Nineteenth Century," *Black Perspective in Music* (Spring, 1980), pp. 95-106.

Jenifer, Ellsworth. "Samuel Coleridge-Taylor in Washington," *Phylon* (Summer, 1967), pp. 185-196.

Johnson, Abby Auther, and Ronald M. Johnson, "Away from Accommodation: Radical Editors and Protest Journalism, 1900-1910," *Journal of Negro History* (October, 1977), pp. 325-338.

Juhn, Kurt. "Black Beethoven," *Negro Digest* (June, 1945), pp. 33-38.

Kelly, Robert. "Presbyterianism, Jacksonianism, and Grover Cleveland," *American Quarterly* (Winter, 1966), pp. 615-636.

Kennedy, Philip W. "The Racial Overtones of Imperialism as a Campaign Issue, 1900," *Mid-America* (July, 1966), pp. 196-205.

King, Anita. "Blind Tom, a Child Out of Time," *Essence* (August, 1973).

Kirk, John M. "Jose Narti and the United States: A Further Interpretation," *Journal of Latin American Studies* (1977), pp. 275-290.

Larson, Charles R. "The Novels of Paul Lawrence Dunbar," *Phylon* (Fall, 1968), pp. 257-271.

Lasch, Christopher. 'The Anti-Imperialists, the Philippines and the Inequality of Man," *Journal of Southern History* (August, 1958), pp. 319-331.

Lemons, J. Stanley. "Black Stereotypes as Reflected in Popular Culture," *American Quarterly* (Spring, 1977), pp. 102-116.

LeRoy, James A. "Race Prejudice in the Philippines," *Atlantic Monthly* (July, 1902), pp. 100-112.

Lewis, Elsie M. "The Political Mind of the Negro, 1865-1900," *Journal of Southern History* (May, 1955), pp. 189-202.

Liebenguth, Jane Anne. "Music at the Louisiana Purchase Exposition," *Missouri Historical Society Bulletin* (1979), pp. 27-34.

Lord, Sherry. "The Melbys Are Vacationing in a Tree - the Family Tree," *Columbus Ledger* (August 21, 1974).

Lotz, Rainer. "Arabella Fields, the Black Nightingale," *Black Perspective in Music* (Spring, 1980), pp. 5-19.

Mabry, William A. "Disfranchisement of the Negro in Mississippi," *Journal of Southern History* (1938), pp. 318-333.

Magill, Charles T. "Blind Tom, Unresolved Problem in Musical History," *Chicago Defender* (August 19, 1922).

Mansfield, H.W. "Vivid Recollections of Blind Tom by Henry Watterson, noted Kentucky editor," *The Columbus Magazine* (July 31, 1941), p. 31.

Mazzola, Sandy R. "Bands and Orchestras at the World's Columbian Exposition," *American Music* (Winter, 1986), pp. 407-424.

McGinty, Doris. "The Washington Conservatory of Music and School of Expression," *Black Perspective in Music* (Spring, 1979), pp. 59-71.

McKinley, Ann. "Music for the Dedication Ceremonies of the World's Columbus Exposition in Chicago, 1892," *American Music* (Spring, 1985), pp. 42-51.

Meir, August, and Elliot Rudwick. "The Boycott Movement Against Jim Crow Stations in the South, 1900-1906," *Journal of American History* (March, 1969), pp. 756-775.

Merriam, Allen H. "Racism in the Expansionist Controversy of 1898-1900," *Phylon* (vol. 39/4), pp. 369-380.

Miller, Daniel T. "The Columbian Exposition of 1893 and the American National Character," *Journal of American Culture* (Summer, 1987), pp. 17-21.

Mooney, Hughson F. "Songs, Singing and Society, 1890-1954," *American Quarterly* (Fall, 1954), pp. 221-232.

Nixon, Louise E. "Blind Tom: The Incredible Imitator," *Music Journal* (October, 1971), pp. 40 and 61.

Olsen, Dale A. "Public Concerts in Early America," *Music Educators Journal* (May, 1979), pp. 49-59.

Pride, Armistead S. "The Negro Newspapers: Voice of a Minority," *Midwest Journal* (Winter, 1950-1951), pp. 91-98.

Puttkommer, Charles W., and Ruth Worthy. "William Monroe Trotter, 1872-1934," *Journal of Negro History* (October, 1958), pp. 298-316.

Rabinowitz, Howard N. "From Exclusion to Segregation: Southern Race Relations, 1865-1890," *Journal of American History* (1976), pp. 328-350.

Reed, Addison W. "Scott Joplin, Pioneer," *Black Perspective in Music* (Part I, Spring, 1975 and Part II, Fall, 1975), pp. 45-52 and 269-277.

Restak, Richard. "Islands of Genius," *Science 82* (May, 1982), pp. 62-67.

Riegel, Stephen. "The Persistent Career of Jim Crow, Lower Federal Courts and the 'Separate but Equal' Doctrine, 1865-1896," *American Journal of Legal History* (Vol. 28, 1984), pp. 17-40.

Riis, Thomas. "Bob Cole: His Life and His Legacy to Black Musical Theater," *Black Perspective in Music* (Fall, 1985), pp. 135-150.

Robinson, Michael C., and Frank N. Schubert. "David Fagen: An Afro-American Rebel in the Philippines, 1899-1901," *Pacific Historical Review* (February, 1975), pp. 68-83.

Robinson, Norbonne T.N., II "Blind Tom, Musical Prodigy," *Georgia Historical Society Quarterly* (1969).

Rosenfeld, Albert. "Cultural Village that Blossoms Every Summer: Chautauqua in Its Second Century," *Smithsonian* (1981), pp. 80-90.

Rowland, Ray. "Unique Piano Artistry Was Lost with the Death of Blind Boone," *Kansas City (Mo.) Times* (February, 1950).

Rubin, Emanuel. "Jeannette Meyers Thurber and the National Conservatory of Music," *American Music* (Fall, 1990), pp. 294-325.

Rudwick, Elliott. "The Niagara Movement," *Journal of Negro History* (July, 1957), pp. 177-200.

Rudwick, Elliott, and August Meir. "Black Man in the White City: Negroes and the Columbian Exposition, 1893," *Phylon* (Winter, 1965), pp. 354-361.

Saerchinger, Cezar. "Musical Landmarks in New York," *The Musical Quarterly* (January, 1920), pp. 69-90 and 227-256.

Scheiner, Seth M. "The New York City Negro and the Tenement," *New York History* (October, 1961), pp. 304-315.

Schockley, Ann Allen. "Pauline Elizabeth Hopkins, A Biographical Excursion into Obscurity," *Phylon* (Vol. I, 1972), pp. 22-26.

Schlup, Leonard. "Grover Cleveland and his 1892 Running Mate," *Studies in History and Society* (1977), pp. 60-74.

Sears, Ann. "John William 'Blind' Boone: Pianist-composer: Merit, Not Sympathy Wins," *Black Music Research Journal* (Fall, 1989), pp. 225-247.

Smith, Donne. "Piano Keys Were His Slave," *Colorado Springs, Colorado Sun* (Sept. 29, 1972).

Smith, William H. "William Jennings Bryan and the Social Gospel," *Journal of American History* (June, 1966), pp. 41-60.

Southall, Geneva. "Blind Tom: A Misrepresented and Neglected Pianist-Composer," *Black Perspective in Music* (May, 1975), pp. 141-159.

Southern, Eileen, and Josephine Wright, comps. "On Concert Artist 'T.G. Bethune' and 'Sissieretta Jones'," *Black Perspective in Music* (July, 1976), pp. 177-201.

Stearns, Marshall, and Jean Stearns. "Williams and Walker and the Beginning of Vernacular Dance on Broadway," *Keystone Folklore Quarterly* (Spring, 1966), pp. 3-11.

Stoddard, Tom. "Blind Tom - Slave Genius," *Storyville* (No. 2, 1970), pp. 134-138.

"Strange Case of Blind Tom," *Music Journal* (November, 1957), p. 16.

Terry, William E. "The Negro Music Journal: An Appraisal," *Black Perspective in Music* (Fall, 1977), pp. 146-160.

Thornbrough, Emma Lou. "The National Afro-American League, 1887-1908," *Journal of Southern History* (vol. 27, 1960), pp. 494-512.

Thornton, Ella M. "The Mystery of Blind Tom," *Georgia Review* (1961), pp. 394-400.

Thurman, A. Odell. "The Negro in California Before 1890," *Pacific Historian* (Summer, 1976), pp. 171-188.

Toll, Robert C. "Behind the Blackface Minstrel Men Are Minstrel Myths," *American Heritage* (April/May, 1978), pp. 93-105.

Tucker, David M. "Miss Ida B. Wells and Memphis Lynching," *Phylon* (Summer, 1971), pp. 112-122.

Turner, Darwin. "Paul Lawrence Dunbar: the Rejected Symbol," *Journal of Negro History* (January, 1967), pp. 1-13.

Turner, James. "Understanding the Populists," *Journal of American History* (September, 1980), pp. 354-373.

Tutein, Anna Amelia. "The Phenomenon of Blind Tom," *Etude* (February, 1918).

Ulle, Robert F. "Popular Music in Nineteenth Century Philadelphia," *Pennsylvania Folklife* (Winter, 1975/76).

Watts, Rolanda G. "Spelman College: Keeper of the Flame," *Essence* (August, 1981), pp. 12-14.

Woodall, W.C. "Blind Tom, Our Most Famous Personage," *Columbus Magazine* (July 31, 1941).

Young, Percy M. "Samuel Coleridge-Taylor, 1875-1912," *Musical Times* (August, 1975), pp. 703-705.

Index